AF659241

Reader's Guide

to

WILLIAM MAKEPEACE THACKERAY

Reader's Guide to WILLIAM MAKEPEACE THACKERAY

Dr. Matt Bacak

CENTRUM PRESS
NEW DELHI-110002 (INDIA)

CENTRUM PRESS
H.O.: 4360/4, Ansari Road, Daryaganj,
New Delhi-110 002 (India)
Ph.: 23278000, 23261597

B.O.: No. 1015, Ist Main Road, BSK IIIrd Stage
IIIrd Phase, IIIrd Block,
Bangalore - 560 085 (India)
Tel.: 080-41723429
Visit us at: www.centrumpress.com

Reader's Guide to William Makepeace Thackeray

© Reserved

First Edition, 2009

ISBN 978-93-80106-66-3

PRINTED IN INDIA

Printed at Salasar Imaging Systems, Delhi-110035 (India)

Contents

Preface

William Makepeace Thackeray was an English novelist of the 19th century. He was famous for his satirical works, particularly *Vanity Fair*, a panoramic portrait of English society. Both his parents were of Anglo-Indian descent, and his father, Richmond Thackeray, was appointed to a lucrative position as Collector of a district near Calcutta soon after William's birth. Richmond Thackeray died of a fever in 1815, and his son was sent home to England at five years old to be educated, stopping at St. Helena on the way and having a servant point out to him the prisoner Napoleon, who "eats three sheep every day, and all the little children he can lay hands on!"

Thackeray was given the "education of a gentleman" at private boarding schools, including six years at Charterhouse, and the canings and other abuses he suffered in these institutions became the basis for remembrances in essays, such as *The Roundabout Papers*, as well as episodes in novels (*Vanity Fair* and *The Newcomes*, again, offer important examples). He was not a standout as a student, but he went on to Cambridge, where he entered Trinity College in 1819. Thanks to such amusements, his own inability to excel at mathematics, the poor preparation he had received at Charterhouse, and a penchant for gambling and trips to the Continent, Thackeray left the university without a degree after two years.

After leaving Cambridge, Thackeray traveled on the Continent, spending a winter at Weimar, which included an introduction to the aged Goethe. Thackeray's next attempt at finding an occupation led him to the Inns of Court, where he tried briefly to study law and gathered instead more of the atmosphere of "gentlemanly idleness" (Ray 1.149) that was to find its way into *Pendennis*.

Author

Chapter 1

Introduction

William Makepeace Thackeray was born at Calcutta, India, on July 18, 1811, the son and grandson of officers of the East India Company. His father died when William was six, and the following year the future novelist was sent to England to be educated. After some years at private schools, he entered the Charterhouse in 1822, and remained till 1828.

Neither there nor at Cambridge, where he was a member of Trinity College for a year and a half, did he distinguish himself as a scholar; nor he finally left the university because he felt he was wasting his time, and determined to finish his education by travel. During a stay of several months at Weimar he met Goethe, and years afterwards used his reminiscences of the Grand Ducal Court there in his description of Pumpernickel in "Vanity Fair." On his return to England he took up the study of law, and though he was later called to the bar he never practised.

English journalist, novelist, famous for his novel VANITY FAIR (1847-48), a tale of two middle-class London families. Most of Thackeray's major novels were published as monthly serials. Thackeray studied in a satirical and moralistic light upper- and middle-class English life - he was once seen as the equal of his contemporary Dickens, or even as his superior. "This I set as a positive truth. A woman with fair opportunities, and without a positive hump, may marry whom she likes."

William Makepeace Thackeray was born in Calcutta, India, as the only son of Richmond Thackeray, a Collector in the East Indian Company's service. After his father died he was sent to home to England. He was educated at

Charterhouse and at Trinity College, Cambridge. Thackeray abandoned his studies without taking a degree, having lost some of his inheritance of twenty thousand pounds through gambling. In the beginning of the 1830s he visited Germany, where he met Goethe.

During 1831-33 Thackeray studied law at the Middle Temple, London, but had little enthusiasm to continue his studies. In 1833 he brought with a large heritage the National Standard, but lost his fortune a year later in the Indian bank failures and other bad investments. According to an anecdote, Thackeray offered to undertake the task of illustrating Dickens's Pickwick Papers in 1836, but the author himself found Thackeray's drawings unsuitable.

After art studies in Paris, Thackeray returned in 1837 to London and started his career as a hard working journalist. Often he used absurd pen names such as George Savage Fitz-Boodle, Michael Angelo Titmarsh, Théophile Wagstaff, and C.J. Yellowplush, Esq. In 1836 he married a poor Irish girl, Isabella Shawe; they had three daughters.

Their first child, Anne Thackeray Ritchie (1837-1919), became a writer - her impressionistic texts impressed Virginia Woolf, who drew a portrait of her in Night and Day (1919) as 'Mrs Hilbery'. Ritchie (1837-1919) published several novels, and contributed to an 1898-99 edition of her father's works. A prominent intellectual figure of her time and well-acquainted with a number of the great names of British literature, she also wrote memoirs of her contemporaries, including Tennyson (1809-1892) and Ruskin (1819-1900).

Thackeray began to contribute regularly to Fraser's Magazine, Morning Chronicle, New Monthly Magazine and The Times. His writings attracted first attention in Punch, where he satirized English snobbery. These sketches reappeared in 1848 as The book of Snobs, in which he stated that "he who meanly admires mean things is a Snob." In 1840 Isabella Thackeray suffered a mental breakdown, from which she never recovered, through she survived Thackeray by thirty years.

The author was forced to send his children to France to

his mother. The children returned to England in 1846 to live with him. Already in his first novel, catherine (1839), originally written for fraser's magazine, thackeray broke with the literary conventions of his day: "The characters of the tale are immoral, and no doubt of it; but the writer humbly hopes the end is not so. The public was, in our notion, dosed and poisoned by the prevailing style of literary practice, and it was necessary to administer some medicine that would produce a wholesome nausea, and afterwards bring about a more healthy habit."

In the luck of barry lyndon (1844), thackeray portrayed an adventurer, opportunist, and gambler, who serves in the seven years war, first under the english flag and then in the prussian army, gains wealth, and eventually is punished for his imperfections. "Suppose in a game of life - and it is but a twopenny game after all - you are equally eager of winning," thackeray wrote much later in 'autour de mon chapeau' (1863). "Shall you be ashamed of your ambition, or glory in it?"

In vanity fair, set at the time of the napoleonic wars, thackeray created one of the most fascinating immoral female characters, becky sharp, who manages to avoid the fate of barry lyndon: "I think i could be a good woman if i had five thousand a year." (From vanity fair) the book brought thackeray prosperity and made him an established author and popular lecturer in Europe and in the United States.

Vanity Fair was sub-titled 'A Novel without a Hero'. "Everybody in Vanity Fair must have remarked how well those live who are comfortably and thoroughly in debt; how they deny themselves nothing; how jolly and easy they are in their minds." The vast satirical panorama of a materialistic society centers on Becky Sharp and Amelia Sedley, good-natured but 'silly'.

They are two boarding-school friends, whose destinies are contrasted. Clever and ambitious Becky is born into poverty as the daughter of a penniless artist. Her plans to marry Amelia's brother Joseph fail. She marries Rowdon Crawley, but he is disinherited. Becky manages to live at the height of fashion through the patronage of Lord Steyne. When her husband discovers the truth, he departs to become the governor of Coventry Island. Becky is ostracized and she moves to the Continent. In the meantime Amelia's stockbroker father is ruined. Amelia is loved by William Dobbin but she marries George Osborne - he dies in the battle of Waterloo.

Amelia's son is left into the care of his grandfather, who dies and leaves him a fortune. Amelia travels in the Continent with his brother and they meet Becky. Dobbin has returned from India and disapproves Amelia's kindness to Becky. Older and disillusioned, Dobbin and Amelia can marry. Becky regains her hold over Joseph, who dies in suspicious circumstances.

Becky's husband Rowdon dies, and Becky ends the novel in the guise of a pious widow. Thackeray's increasing love for jane brookfield, the wife of an old cambridge friend, led to a rupture in their friendship. The history of henry esmond, esq., appeared in three volumes in 1852, and reflected the melancholic period in the life of the author. By the end of his career, thackeray's disillusionment with contemporary culture seems to have deepened. In the adventures of philip (1862) the protagonist, philip, is out of place in a world that does not accommodate his vision of masculinity.

Thackeray said that he couldn't start a novel until he knew every aspect of his characters. He called victorian times "if not the most moral, certainly the most squeamish." Once, as an editor, he rejected an elizabeth barrett browning poem because it employed the word harlot.

Thackeray became in 1860 the first editor of the cornhill magazine, for which he wrote his raundabout papers, love the widower, the adventures of philip and the unfinished denis duval. Less successful thackeray was with his attempt to stand for parliament. His contacts with friendly rival charles dickens ended in a quarrel, but their daughters continued to be friends. Thackeray died suddenly on christams eve 1863. Just before his death he he had reconciled with dickens.

HUMORIST, WRITER AND MORALIST

Until the publication of Vanity Fair, Thackeray was known as a humorous writer; he wrote regularly for Punch. Thackeray regarded humor as doing more than making readers laugh, "the best humour is that which contains most humanity, that which is flavoured throughout with tenderness and kindness." He was compelled to write the truth about what he saw and how he understood what he saw:

To describe it otherwise than it seems to me would be falsehood in that calling in which it has pleased heaven to place me; treason to that conscience which says that men are weak; that truth must be told; that faults must be owned; that pardon must be prayed for; and that love reigns supreme over all.

There may be wishful thinking in his statement that as the writer "finds, and speaks, and feels the truth best, we regard him, esteem him sometimes love him." In order to tell the truth, the novelist must "convey as strongly as possible the sentiment of reality." Language should identify exactly, not elevate or exaggerate; for instance, a poker was just that a poker, not a great red-hot instrument and a coat was only a coat, not an embroidered tunic.

He disliked Dickens's highly emotional outbursts and vivid personification of objects; Thackeray protested that the very trees in Dickens's novels "squint, shiver, leer, grin and smoke pipes." A realist, Thackeray consistently deflated the heroic and the sentimental in life and in literature.

Thackeray saw the writer as serving a necessary function to raise the consciousness of his readers. Concerned, he asked his mother in a letter, "Who is conscious?" He came to see himself as a Satirical-Moralist, with a responsibility both to amuse and to teach, "A few years ago I should have sneered at the idea of setting up as a teacher at all... but I have got to believe in the business, and in my other things since then.

And our profession seems to me as serious as the Parson's own." He aimed not only to expose the false values and practices of society and its institutions and to portray the selfish, callous behaviour of individuals, but also to affirm the value of truth, justice, and kindness. This double aim is reflected in his description of himself as satiric and kind: "under the mask satirical there walks about a sentimental gentleman who means not unkindly to any mortal person."

Though Thackeray set his novel a generation earlier, Thackeray was really writing about his own society (he even used contemporary clothing in his illustrations for the novel). Thackeray saw how capitalism and imperialism with their emphasis on wealth, material goods, and ostentation had corrupted society and how the inherited social order and institutions, including the aristocracy, the church, the military, and the foreign service, regarded only family, rank, power, and appearance.

These values morally crippled and emotionally bankrupted every social class from servants through the middle classes to the aristocracy. High and low, individuals were selfish and incapable of loving.

Well aware of himself as flawed, he identified with the self-centered and foolish characters he portrayed in Vanity Fair; his object in writing the novel was to indicate, in cheerful terms, that we are for the most part an abominably foolish and selfish people "desperately wicked" and all eager after vanities....I want to leave everybody dissatisfied and unhappy at the end of the story we ought all to be with our own and all other stories.

Good God don't I see (in that maybe cracked and warped looking glass in which I am always looking) my own weaknesses wickednesses lusts follies shortcomings?.... We must lift up our voices about these and howl to a congregation of fools: so much as least has been my endeavour.

His identification with the fools and the sinners of Vanity Fair could not be stated more clearly. The image of the cracked-mirror provided the basis of the drawing for the frontispiece when the serialized novel came out in book form in 1848. What were some of his flaws? By temperament, he inclined to be self-indulgent, liked to eat and drink well, and until he lost his money gambled enthusiastically; today, we would probably say he had a gambling problem. The Bohemian lifestyle and Bohemians had a strong attraction for Thackeray, as he acknowledged:

I like Becky in that book. Sometimes I think I have myself some of her tastes. I like what are called Bohemians and fellows of that sort. I have seen all sorts of society dukes, duchesses, lords, and ladies, authors and actors and painters and taken altogether I think I like painters the best, and Bohemians generally.

As you read the novel, think about whether Thackeray's identification with the characters and perhaps the life of Vanity Fair affects the novel. Does he show a compassion for the follies he describes and for the characters who commit those follies? Is there a sense of connection with them, or does Thackeray adopt a superior stance and look down on them, judging them harshly? Or is Thackeray ambivalent? Is Vanity Fair, as A.E. Dyson says, "one of the world's most devious novels, devious in its characterization, its irony, its explicit moralising, its exuberance, its tone. Few novels demand more continuing alertness from the reader, or offer more intellectual and moral stimulation in return"?

Thackeray's father had left him a considerable fortune, most of which had disappeared by the time he was twenty-three, part lost in an unsuccessful newspaper, part in unfortunate investments, and part through gambling. Finding that he had to earn his bread, he resolved to study art, and in 1834 went to Paris for this purpose.

Two years later he was appointed Paris correspondent of a short-lived paper, "The Constitutionalist," and on the strength of this he married Isabella Shawe, the daughter of an Irish officer. After four years of happy married life, Mrs. Thackeray's mind gave way, and though she lived till 1894 she never recovered. For a number of years he had to struggle to keep his head above water, writing for newspaper and periodicals and doing a good deal of illustrating.

Though he never acquired great technical skill as a draughtsman, he had a gift of turning out amusing sketches, and for ten years he was on the staff of "Punch" as both artist and author. It was in that publication, with "The Snobs of England," that he first achieved popularity, his earlier novels, "Catherine" and "Barry Lyndon," having failed to hit the popular taste. In January, 1847, "Vanity Fair" began to appear in monthly numbers, and by the time it was concluded in the

July of the following year he was generally awarded a place in the first rank of English novelists. Dickens was then at the height of his fame, and, though the two men appreciated each other's work, their admirers were fond of debating their comparative merits a form of criticism which, though futile enough in the case of talents so dissimilar, has not yet entirely gone out of fashion.

"Pendennis," the most autobiographical of Thackeray's novels, came out in 1848 50, and still farther strengthened his reputation. In 1851 he took up lecturing, beginning with the series on the English Humorists of the Eighteenth Century, which he delivered first in London. These were in a sense a by-product of "Esmond," published in 1852, in the autumn of which year he carried them across the Atlantic. He lectured at Boston, New York, Philadelphia, Baltimore, Richmond, Charleston, and Savannah, was received with great hospitality, made many friends, and went home the next spring the richer by some $10,000.

A second tour in America, with "The Four Georges," followed in 1855, and was also successful. Meantime he had completed "The Newcomes," and while in Rome with his daughters for the Christmas season of 1853, he wrote and illustrated for some children the amusing burlesque of "The Rose and the Ring." Thackeray was now one of the notable figures of English society and was financially at ease. In 1857 he stood for Parliament for the city of Oxford, but missed election by a narrow margin. Apparently little downcast, he returned to his literary work and issued "The Virginians," 1857 59.

It is commonly felt that with this book the quality of his work begins to fall off, and none of his subsequent novels achieved great success. In 1860 he undertook the editorship of the newly founded "Cornhill Magazine," and to it he contributed his delightful essays, "The Roundabout Papers." But his health, which for years had been far from good, unfitted him for the labour of editorship, and he resigned in 1862. On the morning of December 24, 1863, he was found dead.

The death of Thackeray was keenly felt through a wide

circle both in England and abroad. His striking figure he was six feet, three inches in height, with a massive head had become familiar not only through his appearances on the platform but through the caricatures of himself that he had whimsically introduced into many of his drawings in "Punch" and elsewhere; and he was held in affectionate reverence by thousands who had never seen him. Though he first made his reputation as a satirist, he was a man without malice and of extraordinarily tender sensibilities.

He had had to struggle hard to gain a footing in letters, and suffered more than his share of domestic sorrow; but he was generously helpful to others, even when he could little afford it, and found his greatest delight in brightening the lives of children. He used to be blamed for cynicism, but it has long been clear that it was the keenness of his appreciation of the loftier possibilities of human nature that lay at the root of his sadness that these possibilities are so seldom realized.

Though he achieved brilliant success in the fields of the burlesque and the essay, it is, of course, on his work as a novelist that his great reputation is chiefly based. But when the attempt is made to rank his novels among themselves, great diversity of opinion appears. Some specialists would give first place to the comparatively little read "Barry Lyndon"; more favor "The Newcomes."

His style nowhere reaches greater perfection than in the astonishing reproduction of the diction of Queen Anne's reign in "Esmond." Yet, all in all, it is safe to say that he never surpassed his first great success, "Vanity Fair." Here we find at their height his distinguishing qualities: his power of conveying the spirit and atmosphere of an epoch, of delineating a throng of people and making them all living men and women, of conceiving great dramatic situations and presenting these so as to display character with the utmost vividness, of stripping away the veils that hide our motives not only from others but from ourselves.

It is doubtful if any English novel possesses a heroine more completely vitalized than Becky Sharp, a creature so amazingly real that critics are occasionally to be found taking sides with her against her creator. And in his description of such figures, in his painting of their backgrounds, and in his characteristically intimate discussion with his readers of their faults and follies, he wields an English style unsurpassed for clarity, ease, and grace, capable of lofty eloquence, extreme tenderness, and fiery scorn, but always appropriate and always sincere.

Among the professional Victorian writers who made a living, or even a fortune, from writing without the aid of outside sources of income, there were a fair number who were incompetent businessmen. Of those who made a fortune, Thackeray probably has the reputation of being the least businesslike.

He is known as a lucky, careless genius, a lazy giant with great powers and equal weaknesses. Although he squandered a considerable part of his £17,000 inheritance through a weakness for gambling and in two ill-fated investments in periodicals, the Constitutional and the National Standard, the loss that threw him absolutely upon the resources of his pen appears to have been a bank failure in India - no fault of his own.

Having struggled back to fiscal competence from his initial ruin, he invested £500 in the railroad mania in which he lost again in the general collapse of 1845. The success of Vanity Fair made his life easier but did not restore his lost fortunes. His lecture tours in America netted approximately £5,000, which Thackeray invested in American railroads and sold out during the Civil War for only £3,895 (Letters 3: 275. Nevertheless, he left his daughters an estate nearly equaling the £ 10,000 apiece that he repeatedly said was his goal.

Explaining the differences between Thackeray and Dickens as professional writers, Anthony Trollope - certainly one of the most business-manlike of authors - wrote:

The one was steadfast, industrious, full of purpose, never doubting of himself always putting his best foot foremost and standing firmly on it when he got there; with no inward trepidation, with no moments in which he was half inclined to think that this race was not for his winning, this goal not to be reached by his struggles. The sympathy of friends was good to him, but he could have done without it. The good opinion which he had of himself was never shaken by adverse criticism; and the criticism on the other side, by which it was exalted, came from the enumeration of the number of copies sold. He was a firm reliant man, very little prone to change, who, when he had discovered the nature of his own talent, knew how to do the very best with it. It may almost be said that Thackeray was the very opposite of this.

Unsteadfast, idle, changeable of purpose, aware of his intellect but not trusting it, no man ever failed more generally than he to put his best foot foremost. Full as his works are of pathos, full of humour, full of love and charity, tending, as they always do, to truth and honour and manly worth and womanly modesty, excelling, as they seem to me to do, most other written precepts that I know, they always seem to lack something that might have been there.

There is a touch of vagueness which indicates that his pen was not firm while he was using it. He seems to me to have been dreaming ever of some high flight, and then to have told himself, with a half-broken heart, that it was beyond his power to soar up into those bright regions. I can fancy as the sheets went from him every day he told himself, in regard to every sheet, that it was a failure. Dickens was quite sure of his sheets.

It is not quite clear if Trollope was aware of the potential double meaning of that last assertion, but Thackeray was. In any case, this passage is the sort of realistic fiction for which Trollope is justly famous. But though it is misleading, if not an outright falsehood, Trollope's Thackeray has stuck in the popular mind.

The image Trollope evoked corresponds generally with the one promoted by Thackeray himself in such things as his vignette drawing of a printer's devil waiting at the door to carry his manuscripts to a presumably impatient printer and by stories like the one James T. Fields told of Thackeray coming to one of his own dinner parties well over an hour late with ink on his fingers announcing the completion of the last sheet of The Virginians.

It is indisputable that Thackeray produced much of his work under the pressure of deadlines. That need not mean he was lazy. John Sutherland has argued that Thackeray may even have written better under pressure than at leisure. Thackeray spoke often in his letters of living, eating, drinking his novels to the exclusion almost of his own daily life.

He relished the creative pressure induced by deadlines, though he also knew the pace would wear him out. It has been altogether too easy to overplay Thackeray in the role of procrastinator, the would-be gentleman of leisure, and to lose sight of the facts concerning Thackeray the businessman and professional writer, This part of the picture can be filled out from two other sources: his comments in his fiction on the craft of writing and the facts of his relations with his publishers revealed in letters, contracts and publishers' account books.

A key episode in establishing the image of Thackeray's view of his profession, its rank, rights, and responsibilities, took place in 1850. Thackeray brought the wrath of John Forster upon his head when, in Pendennis, he had George Warrington remark to Pen on their way home from a dreary publisher's party, "And now that you have seen the men of letters, tell me, was I far wrong in saying there are thousands of people in this town, who don't write books, who are, to the full, as clever and intellectual as people who do?"

Thackeray went on in the voice of his narrator, "And it may be whispered to those uninitiated people who are anxious to know the habits and make the acquaintance of men of letters, that there are no race of people who talk about books, or perhaps, who read books, so little as literary men".

Forster's objection, printed in the Examiner for 5 January 1850, was directed against Thackeray for disparaging literary men as a whole by presenting the Shandons, Waggs, and Bunions of the party as representative of all literary men and women. Forster attributed Thackeray's "attack" to a desire to curry favor with the nonliterary classes. In defending himself, Thackeray gave one view of the professional writer. He claimed never to have "been ashamed of his profession, or (except for its dulness) of any single line from his pen."

He considered the charge that he was currying favor among the nonliterary classes absurd, since in his experience people honored writers, and he would gain nothing through the supposed stratagem of which he was accused. Finally, he defended his portrait of the literary world on the grounds that it was true.

Why, he asked, "are these things not to be described... it such exist, or have existed, they are as good subjects for comedy as men of other callings". Forster would not let the subject alone, showing himself totally unmoved by Thackeray's explanations, He distinguished between identifying humbug in a profession and identifying humbug with a profession.

Here the public debate lapsed into silence without a winner. It is quite likely that Forster was predisposed to pick a fight with Thackeray over this issue because of a long-standing and fundamental difference between them, friends though they had been, concerning the status of professional writers and their role and in society. Forster and Dickens, as has been suggested by Craig Howes, represented the author in a romantic light, as a dignified, inspired artist. The author's role, according to this view, was that of inspirer and castigator - as social conscience for the betterment of society.

Michael Lund has cited various nineteenth-century versions of this view suggesting that authorship is not work like other trades or professions but rather a gift or inspired avocation. Thackeray, on the other hand, had long been speaking and writing from a different perspective, emphasizing the trade relations, admitting the work involved, and making fun of pretentious writing and pretentious writers.

Thus, the controversy over the dignity of literature boils down to one side trying to uphold an ideal and a social responsibility (which they see as doing good) and the other side trying to be honest and unpretentious (which they see as being true). The object of fiction for the one is to change society; for the other, to understand it. There is no resolution for such a controversy.

Privately, in a letter to his friend Abraham Heyward,

Thackeray admitted, however: "The words in Pendennis are untenable be hanged to them: but they were meant to apply to a particular class of literary men, my class who are the most ignorant men under the Sun, myself included I mean.

But I wrote so carelessly that it appears as if I would speak of all, and even if it were true I ought never to have written what I did". Yet this apology expresses regret for having written carelessly, not for having thought the thought. Thackeray did not change his mind about writers; rather, he was sorry to have stirred up this particularly fruitless controversy.

In the novel Pendennis goes on to become a successful novelist, serving first a sort of apprenticeship writing reviews. He later becomes the author of Thackeray's The Newcomes, in which he gives the following description of the profession of authorship:

The drawbacks and penalties attendant upon our profession are taken into full account, as we well know, by literary men, and their friends. Our poverty, hardships, and disappointments are set forth with great emphasis, and often with too great truth by those who speak of us; but there are advantages belonging to our trade which are passed over, I think by some of those who exercise it, and for which, in striking the balance of our accounts, we are not always duly thankful. We have no patron, so to speak - we sit in ante-chamber no more, waiting the present of a few guineas from my lord; in return for a fulsome dedication.

We sell our wares to the book purveyor, between whom and us there is no greater obligation than between him and his paper-maker or printer. In the great towns in our country, immense stores of books are provided for us, with librarians to class them, kind attendants to wait upon us, and comfortable appliances to study. We require scarce any capital wherewith to exercise our trade. "at other so called learned profession is equally fortunate?

A doctor, for example, after carefully and expensively educating himself, must invest in house and furniture, horses, carriage, and men-servants, before the public patient will think of calling him in. I am told that such gentlemen have to coax and wheedle dowagers, to humour hypochondriacs, to practise a score of little subsidiary arts in order to make that of healing profitable. How many many hundreds of pounds has a barrister to sink upon his stock in trade before his returns are available?

There are the costly charges of university education - the costly chambers in the Inn of court -certain expenses all to be defrayed before the possible client makes his appearance, and the chance of fame or competency arrives. The prizes are great, to be sure, in the law, but what a prodigious sum the lottery ticket costs! If a man of letters cannot win, neither does he risk so much. Let us speak of our trade as we find it, and not be too eager in calling out for public compassion.

This description of the author's life and work emphasizes one aspect at the expense of others. Pendennis, as the narrator of The Newcomes, has constantly to remind himself not to think in inflated terms about authorship. This litany of the trade relations and modest requirements reveals that authorship is open to one and all who care to risk the chance of publication. Elsewhere, Thackeray emphasized other requirements, most notably the need to develop, through extensive reading, a sense of history.

The comparison with the professions of medicine and law both elevate and deflate the picture being presented. It is not so difficult nor so lucrative as those relatively bourgeois professions; but if it is like a trade involving paper sellers, printers, and booksellers, it yet also has freedoms and responsibilities unlike those trades which made it nonetheless a profession. Among those responsibilities Thackeray included the moral one of avoiding inflated language and slipshod moral implications - the two main butts of his humorous attacks in Novels by Eminent Hands.

Like Thackeray's celebrated redefinitions of snob and gentleman, his view of the professional writer as tradesman is a double one reconciling in itself traditionally opposing views. just as a middle-class or poor gentleman seemed a contradiction in Regency terms, so too the poet as tradesman seemed contradictory in romantic terms. Both Dickens and Forster remonstrated with Thackeray for his failure to hold high enough the dignity of the profession - their arguments smacking of conventional notions of the smudge of trade. There is a tawdry irony in the notion of Dickens and Forster, both with tradesman connections in their backgrounds, and particularly Forster, who besides writing was a paid employee of a publisher, objecting to Thackeray's portraits of writers as tradesmen.

But Thackeray's view cuts through the pomposity and cant about the dignity of literature to the heart of the ideals of his profession - to love and truth, upholding the ideals without losing sight of the mundane business facts of authors writing for money, relying on and being relied upon in turn by publishers in much the same way that the printers and the paper sellers rely on one another in the business transactions that make books and periodicals.

To admit that the author is one in a line of necessary manufacturers and purveyors of literature that includes the publisher, printer, stationer, and bookstall vendor is to pursue truth where there seems to be nothing to gain except the miserable satisfaction of knowing it. In fact, however, that view is subversive to establishment conventions - a fact that goes a long way toward explaining the disagreement between Forster and Thackeray. Of course, this truth is not the whole truth any more than is that other much better known image Thackeray created of the novelist as the preacher in cap and bells That is to say, Thackeray was not just an exposer of sham, nor was he just a satirist.

Thackeray's double view of the word trade as it applied, without shame, to his own profession, is reminiscent of his similar treatment of trade in Vanity Fair where poor Dobbin in school is the butt of all the jokes because his father, a grocer, pays his bill in goods. Dobbin gains respect by beating Cuff in a fight, but the narrator notes that the lordly little George Osborne's grandfather was a tradesman too. Dobbin's father becomes a respected alderman albeit none too refined a man, and Dobbin is unquestionably the real gentleman of the book.

If authorship and publishing have the taint of trade, they also can have the honour of trade. And where there is honour, there is the risk of dishonor. The ideals of the profession could be traduced not only by inflated rhetoric but by dishonest shows of learning or of sentiment.

In an early review Thackeray complained of writers who sugared their instructions in manners and morals and academic subjects by putting them into fiction, but at the same time he firmly believed in the novelist's responsibility, even in the guise of a clown's cap and bells, to instruct - not with moral platitudes, of course, but with the lessons inherent in what he thought was unvarnished truth.

To the editor of Punch, Mark Lemon, he wrote on concluding the "Snobs of England": "A few years ago I should have sneered at the idea of setting up as a teacher at all, and perhaps at this pompous and pious way of talking about a few papers of jokes in Punch - but I have got to believe in the business, and in many other things since then. And our Profession seems to me to be as serious as the Parson's own".

One need not agree with Trollope that the vagueness or ambivalence in Thackeray's work reveals lack of commitment or conviction or strength. What some of his contemporaries thought of as a feigned "want of earnestness," an "undervaluing of his art," a carelessness about details, plain ineptitude, or tired repetitions in narrative structures may better be understood as the deliberate manifestations of a cast of mind that rejected, or at least suspected, the values represented by earnestness and narrative order. Thackeray's narrative technique undermines surface realism and the sense of certitude and stable values implied by authorial omniscience.

I think it likely that Thackeray deliberately undermined such values because he did not believe in them, because he thought the danger lay in overvaluing art. Thackeray saw more clearly than most of his contemporaries the problems of trying to create or capture "reality" in "fiction," and he knew more clearly than many a historian of his day that the coherence created by the orderly arrangement of historical data, commonly taken for "truth" in "history," is an illusion. Jack Rawlins has recognized and described in some detail Thackeray's habit of undercutting the fictional realities he had created, but Rawlins seems not to have understood the implication of the narrative strategy, deploring Thackeray's refusal to adopt the novelist's responsibility to impose a moral order beneficial to society." In this regard Rawlins agreed with Forster.

From time to time scholars, noting the "lapses" in Thackeray's "artistic values," explain them as carelessness or as the inevitable, though lamentable, results of a hectic mode of production - John Sutherland, in Victorian Authors and Publishers, and N. N. Feltes, in Modes of Production of Victorian Novels, have turned this argument on its head as a means of praising Henry Esmond, which was produced under circumstances different from those attending any other Thackeray work; it is the only novel Thackeray finished before it was published. However, the very same kinds of disruptions of realism occur throughout that book, as a multitude of readers have noted, particularly Elaine Scarry.

John Sutherland has remarked that "the mode of production confirmed in Thackeray a kind of narrative opportunism. One always feels that he has reserved the right to switch the course of his narrative whenever and however it suits him. He alludes jokingly to the arbitrariness of his power over plot in the preface: 'Perhaps the lovers of "excitement" may care to know that this book began with a very precise plan, which was entirely put aside.

Ladies and gentlemen, you were to have been treated and the writer's and publisher's pocket benefited, by the recital of the most active horrors.... Nay, up to nine o'clock this very morning, my poor friend, Colonel Altamont, was doomed to execution, and the author only relented when his victim was actually at the window."

Sutherland opined that this was "high-spirited nonsense" and the "element of truth" about Thackeray's work was the lamentable one of "narrative opportunism." That particular interpretation is apparent only to persons committed to the tradition of English fiction adhering to Jamesian inevitability, to Trollope's insistence on the novelist's right (and need?) to be able to adjust the beginning to the end, to a Joycean refining of the author out of existence.

But it is not "nonsense," high-spirited or otherwise, to anyone willing to face the possibility that these "lapses" (they seem rather too frequent and to come in too strategic locations to be lapses) are, if not deliberate, at least characteristic gestures reflecting a point of view about history, fiction, and reality that is controlled by a value system rejecting the Jamesian striving for realism precisely because realism is a contrived illusion.

The particular example of "opportunism" in question is from Pendennis. It illustrates the carefully planned contrivance of this illusion, for the "communicating leads" and window box that make Altamont's escape possible were first planted, so to speak, 330 pages earlier) and had already been used by Colonel Strong to escape a bailiff.

No reader finding Altamont cornered in the same apartments could be surprised by the escape. To accuse Thackeray of opportunism - that is, to take seriously his remark about relenting at the last moment - is both to underestimate the control he had over his materials and to misunderstand his deliberate exposure of the illusion of reality in order to make his point.

For Thackeray, fiction was fun, and the illusion of reality was fascinating. All his sympathies were on Dobbin's side, for example, when on a school half-holiday the boy sits under a tree, carried away by a book into the world of the Arabian Nights. But he continually insisted that that world was not real; reality obtrudes for the reader of Thackeray's fiction in the form of his "lapses" just as surely as it did for Dobbin when the altercation between Cuff and George Osborne broke in on his fictive Arabian world.

Thackeray addresses the reader, laughs in his sleeve, imagines Jones yawning over the number, and "reserves the right to switch the course of his narrative whenever and however it suits him" because, much as he likes creating the illusion of reality, he likes more reminding his readers that in actuality he, Thackeray, is telling the reader, sitting in a chair, a story.

That is realism with a significant philosophical point: that the author, like the reader, is subject to human limitations of knowledge and judgment. Authors may have a keen view of human foibles but are no better at prescribing for the world than any other reader, Thackeray refused to set himself up to be the hero as man of letters. And for all that, paradoxically, there is more of truth in his sheets than in the pages of many a self-proclaimed regenerator of the age.

Thackeray's realism is one that his contemporaries and, it seems, many later generations of Thackeray's readers have been unprepared to see or accept. Thackeray must have known that, for he introduced his disruptions of fictive realism gently; they can be dismissed as "lapses" or the eccentricities of genius. Perhaps it has been too easy for readers to miss the implications.

Thackeray's sardonic view of aristocratic airs, his tracing of meanness and snobbery from top to bottom of the social scale, his "failure" to produce a moral framework within which the indeterminacies can come to moral closure have variously been explained as gentlemanly detachment, as declining to be the moral enthusiast, or as a weakness of spirit or lack of moral fibre.

Among Thackeray's most enthusiastic fans, these matters have been, at worst, irritations to be ignored. Thackeray] was, to my mind, deliberate and committed in this fundamental point from his early writings throughout his life. But he was not prepared to make the point at the expense of his livelihood or the fortune he intended to make and leave for his daughters.

He was very much aware of the commercial exigencies of novel writing, and it was not his aim to disrupt profits by focusing attention on his private beliefs and values. But there was good and ample reason for him to introduce into his fiction those elements that so irritated John Forster and Charles Dickens and that apparently disappointed Trollope and John Sutherland.

In such passages as the one in Philip where Thackeray discussed the amount of money the paragraph he was writing would earn him or the closing of Vanity Fair where the emphasis falls so heavily on the show and contrivance that his puppets "really are," he reminded his readers that the illusion of realism is created in the reality of storytelling.

The neat wrapping up of loose ends where villains are punished and heroes vindicated and rewarded, Thackeray knew, is an illusion. Reality is ambiguous and indeterminate. The true realist does not know enough to pass out poetic justice justly. So Thackeray reminds his readers constantly and truthfully that the puppet show is not real. He forces an ultimate realism upon his readers by denying the possibility of honest satisfaction in fictive endings.

To him, the truth about the world included the truth about writing fiction for a living, Thackeray's methods expose the sham realism in which the author pretends to know not only what his characters think and do but by what moral standards characters should he measured.

Thackeray's tentativeness, his apparently cynical view of good, and his supposedly infirm or sentimental stance on evil resulted, I believe, from honesty, humility, and simple acknowledgment of the true limits of authorial knowledge. Henry Dodd Worthington's description of his father in James Gould Cozzens's Morning Noon and Night suggests something of what I am trying to identify in Thackeray's character.

Then there was that manner of his. You could not say it was shy, but you felt some lack of self-assertion, by most people associated with weakness, infirmity of purpose....What these were plain signs of I can now see. They were signs of deep and thorough skepticism, That I then didn't see it wasn't, I think, just boyish imperceptiveness, I would guess that few people saw it, that few people ever thought of him as skeptical. What people expect from a skeptic is skepticism in its commoner loud, assertive form of scorning, challenging, contemptuously rejecting.

This kind of skepticism will often be superficial,

professings of men who basically are cynics, men of shallow thinking and loose feeling. My father's kind of skepticism made no show. It worked as a sort of silent patient withholding of judgment, almost as though his mild steady distrust of all appearances or supposed certainties went so far that when he felt serious doubts about anything those very doubts had to he held open to doubt.

To many of his contemporaries, Trollope and Carlyle particularly, Thackeray was a weak man, indecisive, lacking positive force. I believe they mistook his distrust of certainty. The other extreme response to Thackeray, typified by Charlotte Brontë's remarks in the dedication of the second edition of Jane Eyre, calling Thackeray "the first regenerator of the day" who resembled Henry Fielding "as an eagle doth a vulture," is a corrective that goes too far.

Reacting to Thackeray's bold cutting through the cant and hypocrisy of the upper middle class, Brontë and other admirers tended to see in him a prophet whose attack on conventional values established art alternative foundation of values enshrining duty, loyalty, humility, and social responsibility. When upon meeting him Brontë discovered that Thackeray was no Carlyle, her disappointment arose from a misunderstanding not far removed from Trollope's. Alike, they failed to recognize and admire the profound honesty of Thackeray's aversion to overconfident assertions of values. Intense assertion of values was a common Victorian stance, but it was not Thackeray's.

Thackeray's respect for the "uncertainty principle," the humility with which he declined to be sure, is, of course, not peculiar to him, though it was a rare enough position in Victorian England. The position has had its influential manifestations, notably following periods of rigid or excessive authoritarianism. It played roles in the decline of the Spanish Inquisition and the rejection of Puritan rigidity following the excess of the Salem witch trials.

But it can be seen also in the tremendous variety of human foibles tolerated without authorial condemnation in Shakespeare and in the attitudes revealed in Fielding's Tom

Jones, Sterne's Tristram Shandy, and Keats's Odes all hesitating to judge too finely or too finally and, consequently, all creating problems for earnest moralists. In Thackeray's case it is particularly necessary to distinguish, also, between a mere dislike of rigidity or discipline (which he indeed had) and a deeply felt suspicion of certitude (which I think he also had). The former results from an irritable or sensitive personality, the latter from a philosophical position.

In his own day Thackeray's satiric view of the romantic ideals of his profession made him appear weak, ambivalent, his own worst enemy. And that view, with a hefty boost from Trollope, has carried over into the image of Thackeray as an undisciplined craftsman, leading more than one critic to characterize him as a "careless putter forth" or hasty or even lazy improviser [the phrase comes from George Saintsbury's Introduction to Pendennis, in which he also calls Thackeray a shrewd reviser]. And this unflattering view extends to the image of Thackeray the businessman or, as he implied with characteristic deflation, tradesman.

The word tradesman in Victorian England denoted, as it still to some extent does, an outlook and a rank in life that were incompatible with imagination and beauty, which were central to the concept of artist, poet, or even novelist. One equates tradesman in Victorian England with Mr. Pumblechook in Great Expectations and Mr. Polly in H. G. Wells's History of Mr. Polly or, on a higher economic though not sensibility scale, Mr. Freeman in John Fowles's French Lieutenant's Woman, whose industrial and commercial sensibilities are impervious to art.

But Thackeray was a practical man who had learned, from more than one penniless crisis, the reality of writing for money. That reality was a fact to be honestly acknowledged. If authorship had certain high ideals, it included, on the other hand, the mundane practical details of the trade of writing. By using the loaded word trade for the artist, Thackeray undercut both the social snobbery and the mystical trappings of artist, which some writers cultivated.

The social snobbery probably was an unconscious

outgrowth, rather than a desired aim, of earlier proponents of the mystical view. The Victorian version of that view derived at least in part from the notions of poet or artist promulgated by Wordsworth in the preface to Lyrical Ballads, where the poet's sensibilities above the common run of men is claimed, and by Shelley's "Defence of Poesie," where the poet's position as an unacknowledged legislator of the world is proclaimed.

But perhaps the strongest impetus to view the writer's calling in a special light with special capabilities and privileges was Thomas Carlyle's portrayal of the "Man of Letters" in On Heroes, Hero Worship, and the Heroic in History. Thackeray's early send-ups of Dr. Lardner and Sir Edward Bulwer Lytton as pompous snobs playing off their roles as artists in social settings is an indication of his suspicion of the role. As a practicing writer, he turned to the trade rather than the calling in order to deflate the aggrandized view.

Thackeray became, in fact, an able and a reliable businessman who expected publishers and illustrators to fulfill their commitments with equal promptness. To his publishers, Bradbury and Evans, Thackeray wrote in May 1854 to complain of Richard Doyle, the illustrator Thackeray himself had chosen for The Newcomes: "However much I may regard Doyle as a friend it is clear that as men of business we cannot allow our property to suffer by his continual procrastination. The original agreement with Doyle, made between Bradbury myself and him was that the blocks and plates for the ensuing month should always be supplied by Doyle on the 15th of the month current.

I have now written to him, to say that I shall hold him to his agreement and that if by the 15 June the plates and blocks of No 10 of the Newcomes are not in your hands I shall employ another designer". It would have been the height of arrogance and insensitivity for Trollope's Thackeray to require promptness and commitment from another man holding Doyle to standards too rigid for himself. But Trollope's Thackeray was a fiction.

The real Thackeray was a reliable professional masked by a public image. The popular concept of a harried Thackeray dashing off the last lines of the monthly number for the printer just in the nick of time is a romantic misunderstanding of serial publication.

In thirty years of professional writing, Thackeray failed to meet only three deadlines that seriously affected a publisher. Only one of these commitments lay within his power to fulfill. The October 1844 installment of Barry Lyndon was delayed one month for lack of copy, and even then there were mitigating circumstances. He mailed off the October installment on 23 September from Smyrna while on his Eastern tour (recounted in From Cornhill to Grand Cairo), and it arrived too late in London for the October number of the magazine.

He finished the book on 3 November [Ray, Adversity, p. 343; Letters 2: 154-54, 156]. In September 1848 he become so ill he had to suspend the writing and publishing of the monthly numbers of Pendennis for three months, and in August 1859 he was too ill to write a complete final double number for The Virginians, providing instead a one-part number 23 and a one-part final number in September.

Thackeray's sense of the business requirements of authorship was hard won. Though he had earned his livelihood by journalism for ten years when he began Vanity Fair, he was in 1846 still very much a petitioner appealing to the largess of the proprietors of Punch and other publishers, and he was dependent on their valuation of the goods he brought for sale.

But by 1854 the author of The Newcomes saw himself as coproprietor with the publisher, The change is dramatic, and the composition, production, and financial success of Vanity Fair mark the watershed of Thackeray's career as a businessman, transforming him from the investor/ gambler, the writer waiting upon publishers with his goods, into the propertied tradesman who built himself a debt-free mansion at 2 Palace Green, Kensington.

Five chapters of Vanity Fair were written by early spring 1846. Thackeray announced to his mother that serial publication would begin on 1 May, and in March or April the first five chapters were set in type18. Production problems immediately became apparent: when the corrected galleys were paged, it was discovered that the fourth chapter reached page 28 and the fifth chapter extended to the middle of Page 35 Serial publication, however, required exactly thirty-two pages, no more and no less.

The first of May passed with no publication. The type for chapters 1-5 was knocked down and redistributed to the typecases, while Thackeray eked out his living with "The Snobs of England" and "Novels by Eminent Hands" contributions to Punch lasting beyond the publication of the revised initial number of Vanity Fair in January 1847.

What Thackeray learned during the eight-month delay in the publication of Vanity Fair can only be surmised from the regularity of his serial numbers from 1 January 1847 to the end of his life (except in the fall of 1848 and August 1859 when illness, not lassitude, prevented the professional fulfillment of his commitments to the public).

The process he worked out was fairly simple but has only recently been understood by scholars. Except when he wrote The Newcomes, a few numbers of Philip, and Denis Duval, Thackeray never completed a monthly installment before the month it was due at the print shop. Hs contract for Vanity Fair written and signed, curiously enough, on 25 January 1847 as the second installment was being printed specifies that he was to submit copy by the fifteenth of each month.

According to his letters, however, often on about the twenty-fifth of the month he would write that he had "just ended his number." Such statements, along with his frequent self-accusations of procrastination and the picture of the sleeping printer's devil waiting at the door, combine to give the superficial and false impression of a writer who could not meet his contracted deadlines. In fact, the process was a smooth, if hectic, coordination of writing, typesetting, proofreading, correcting, and printing responsibilities.

The reason Thackeray "ended" his numbers on the twenty-fifth or so is that serial publication does not lend itself to the submission of a finished manuscript on the fifteenth.

The first time Thackeray tried that, his installment would have occupied either twenty-eight or thirty-five pages had it been published. Instead, he would submit about three-quarters of an installment to the printer probably by the twentieth or earlier to be set in type.

With as many as five compositors working on a single installment (their names are an the manuscripts), typesetting twenty to thirty pages could be completed in a day or less. The printer's devil would then carry proofs to Thackeray, who corrected them and measured them with a string corresponding in length to a page of the printed book. Arriving at a fairly accurate estimate of the amount of text still required to fill the number, he would revise and augment or cut as necessary.

A printer's boy or the mails would then return the corrected and augmented proof to the printshop. Second proofs with page headings and page numbers embedded would be ready in another day or so, making it possible for Thackeray to read proofs and make final adjustments in length by the twenty-fifth or twenty-sixth of the month. The printers and binders then usually had about five days to get an installment ready for distribution by the last day of the month.

This coordination of production effort lends itself to the concept of writing as a trade. The artist's fancy is not free; the grinding schedule of production curtailed the craftsman's time and forced his energies in ways which Thackeray is on record as both appreciating and lamenting.

The conditions of serial novel writing were not very different from newspaper journalism or the scheduled inches of letterpress Thackeray was responsible for in Punch. Novel writers of Thackeray's standing today may have a fellowship or an advance front the publisher and a full year or eighteen months to write the novel. Not so Thackeray. Yet the pressure was invigorating; he lived, talked, ate, slept his fiction up until deadline time.

Thackeray's enthusiasm for the invigorating aspect of the engines of journalism shows in George Warrington's praises of it in Pendennis:

There she is the great engine - she never sleeps. She has her ambassadors in every quarter of the world - her couriers upon every road. Her officers march along with armies, and her envoys walk into statesmen's cabinets. They are ubiquitous. Yonder journal has an agent, at this minute, giving bribes at Madrid; and another inspecting the price of potatoes in Covent Garden. Look! here comes the Foreign Express galloping ire.

They will be able to give news to Downing Street tomorrow: funds will rise or fall, fortunes be made or lost; Lord B. will get up, and, holding the paper in his hand, and seeing the noble marquis in his place, will make a great speech; and - and Mr. Doolan will be called away from his supper at the Back Kitchen; for he is foreign sub-editor, and sees the mail on the newspaper sheet before he goes to his own.

The mock-heroic tone of the adjective "ubiquitous, " of the exclamation "Look!", and of the juxtaposition of bribes in Madrid with the price of potatoes in Covent Garden introduces a faint distrust of the enthusiasm but does not belie the excitement Warrington feels for the press. The positive part of the passage echoes the spirit of historic significance that prompted the 1832 pressmen's parades in London, complete with a working press carried in a cart producing ink-wet pamphlets on freedom of the press for the crowd.

But Warrington's detachment, echoing Thackeray's own balances the sentiment with the dash and the pun on Mr. Doolan's mundane diurnal oscillation between the printed sheets and his bed sheets. The double view suggests that the situation is too complex to be captured by one feeling or one attitude. That same sleepless engine is also the inexorable, insatiable engine which fed on the writer and caused the haste and the drain of energy which sapped the health of more men than just Thackeray.

Thackeray's sense of the economic realities of publishing was acute-won at the price of two failed literary magazines and years of journalistic hand-to-mouth work. His image of Pegasus drawing a wagon and his unaristocratic equation of the literary profession with the trades are of a piece with his mockery of inflated self-importance in any calling in life. These self-deprecatory remarks cannot be taken to mean more than they do - that literary men must work hard, must meet their deadlines, must accept the consequences of the responses of publishers as merchandisers and readers as the market for art: they must write what will be published and purchased. Thackeray's remarks on his profession do not mean that he held it in low regard or that he had no sense of the dignity of literature.

For Thackeray the dignity of the profession lay in the integrity of presenting the world he knew as he saw it - including the business of authorship. In a letter to John Forster he indicated what humbug he thought lay at the root of attempts to assert the dignity of literature by any other means: "I don't believe in the Guild of Literature I dont believe to the Theatrical Scheme; I think i s against the dignity of our profession, but you are honest and clever men and free to your opinion (thank you for nothing say you) well, believe that mine's loyally entertained too. " Thackeray was saying that the artist cannot with honesty or true dignity hide behind cant about a high calling.

Thackeray's position is neither starry-eyed or simpleminded. He knew the plight of many literary men who could be said to want the dignity of a bare living; his purse was frequently open to them. With similar honesty he acknowledged the ambiguity of good and evil, a view which more positive men took to reveal weakness. Nor is his position uncomplicatedly open and without subtlety of its own.

A chapter of Thackeray's life remains to be written by someone who can see beyond or beneath the surface and untangle the remark in John Chapman's diary for 14 June 1851: "I find that his religious views are perfectly free, but he does not mean to lessen his popularity by fully avowing them, he said he had debated the question with himself whether he was called upon to martyrise himself for the sake of his views and concluded in the negative.

His chief object seems to be the making of money. He will go to America for that purpose. He impresses me as much abler than the lecture I heard, but I fear his success is spoiling him." Thackeray's net worth when he died unexpectedly on 23 December 1863, at age fifty-three, attests for our material age his business success. His house was sold for £10,000. His furniture and personal effects sold for £2,000; his wine for £400. His copyrights brought his daughters £5,000. A total of about £18,000 - one thousand more than his father had left him.

It is difficult to understand in modern terms the meaning of £18,000 or of an annual income O £2,000 to £4,000, which Thackeray was making in the last six or seven years of his life, An exchange rate does not help much because buying power changes as goods and services go up or come down.

According to an article on the Royal Literary Fund in the Smithsonian Magazine (May 1985), London postmen made £50 a year in 1839. Of Anthony Trollope, John Sutherland has said, "With a bit of scrimping £250 was a tolerable annual salary23." Another source claims that £250 was the minimum required to be a gentleman. By such meaningless standards the man who wrote a chapter of Vanity Fair called "How to Live on Nothing a Year" was twelve times a gentleman.

How Thackeray became a writer has been the subject of many books and articles, but recounting the story (with some new material) emphasizes the connections between his experiences as writer and the point of view about the writer's trade presented in the preceding chapter.

It illustrates how a romantic youth developed into a young dilettante; how, without a "useful" education, Thackeray was thrown rather summarily upon the resources of his pen to survive and to support a young and trouble-ridden family; how years of hackwork and dogged determination won for him a combination of pride in his journalistic achievements and a humility or at least unpretentiousness about art; and how, when the laurels of fame and fortune finally became his, he found the dignity of literature in the economic and social rewards for hard labour rather than in the mantle of the hero as man of letters.

His contributions as a schoolboy at the Charterhouse to the Carthusian, as a teenager in 1828-29 to the Western

Luminary, and as a college student in 1829-30 to the Snob and Gownsman (literary newspapers conducted by students at Cambridge) have been described in detail by Harold Strong Gulliver, an account still worth reading, though corrections as well as new material can be found in Gordon Ray's Thackeray: The Uses of Adversity. In some ways, the best account of these activities and of Thackeray's attitude toward the Muse and literary work at this time is his own fictional account of young Pendennis.

As important as these ventures were in whetting Thackeray's appetite for literary work, they cannot be seen as the beginnings of his professional career. These literary endeavors, on a par with his contributions in 1831 to Ottilie von Goethe's Weimar literary paper, Chaos, were works of amateur enthusiasm. They were not undertaken for pay, nor were they part of any endeavor to forge a literary career, whether "for a living" or as the work of a gentleman of the world, which Thackeray could have been but for his weakness for gambling and, more importantly, the bank failures in India in late 1833 that virtually wiped out his considerable inheritance.

On his return from Weimar in March 1831, having chosen to forgo the rest of his education at college, where he had lost 11, 500 at play, he sampled with distaste the rigors of reading for the law, turned twenty-one on 18 July 1832, dissipated in Paris for three or four months, and tried his hand for three months as a bill discounter. By May 1833 he was ready to invest his money in something more congenial to his tastes and talents. He purchased a periodical, the National Standard, thereby making himself a publisher.

He was also the editor and chief contributor. His motive was only partially economic, as is perhaps clear from the oft-quoted self-satire he printed thirty years later in Lovel the Widower where Mr. Batchelor gave himself "airs as editor of that confounded Museum, and proposed to educate the public taste... and made a gabby of" himself The National Standard lasted till February 1834, by which time Thackeray had learned of the Indian bank failures and knew himself to be a poor man, the bulk of his remaining inheritance having evaporated, for though the estate may still have amounted to £7000, it was encumbered by annuities which left Thackeray financially hobbled.

Even before this misfortune, while still Paris correspondent for the National Standard, Thackeray had undertaken the formal study of art in Paris as "an independent man who is not obliged to look to his brush for his livelihood." But by the end of 1833 all that changed. Thackeray first thought to repair his condition by pursuing with serious intent the calling he had chosen from inclination at a better time; however, he knew by the summer of 1835 that he could not succeed as a painter.

From need he sought out literary assignments, selling at least one article to Fraser's Magazine, working for Galignani's Messenger in Paris, projecting and abandoning a "Picturesque Annual" for which he would both write and draw, producing Flore et Zéphyr, a book of lithographs from which he apparently made nothing, and perhaps starting, editing, or at least working for a Paris rival to Galignani's.

Like painting, writing was a high-risk speculative venture without guaranteed returns. Flore et Zéphyr, Thackeray's first book, has no text beyond captions to the lithographs. It was published in April 1836 in London by John Mitchell while Thackeray was in France. Thackeray's letters to Mitchell betray the confusion characterizing this effort: "I cannot understand from yr. notes what is the drawing wanted," and the next day, "I do not know whether you propose to publish any letter-press with the drawing, will you allow me to see it, before its appearance".

The publication of Flore et Zéphyr was financed by Thackeray's wealthy friend John Bowes Bowes, who held an interest in Galignani's Messenger in Paris and who later wrote Thackeray that he thought Mitchell had fudged on the accounts "and put a lot of money in his pocket." Whether Mitchell made any money is not known, but Thackeray and Bowes did not, though it may not have mattered much to the later. (Time heals all wounds, it seems, for in 1851, Mitchell reappears in Thackeray's affairs as the manager of the London lectures on eighteenth-century humorists.

Thackeray's depression over blasted hopes as a painter was alleviated somewhat by his meeting and falling in love with Isabella Shawe, an event with financial implications requiring an even more assiduous pursuit of literary work.

Thackeray found that writing for a living, which he could do with some success, was far more demanding than writing occasional pieces for fun and glory. So when in early 1836 the opportunity arose to become involved with a politically radical literary paper, the Constitutional and Public Ledger, which was supposed to have a broadly subscribed economic base, Thackeray persuaded his stepfather, Major Carmichael-Smyth, to help him by subscribing the venture and serving as chairman of the company.

Thackeray's salary was set at eight guineas a week. In the flurry of setting up the company and gathering a staff, Thackeray wrote to Isabella that he was to have £450 per year, and serious courtship and plans for marriage became possible in spite of the obstacles provided by his future mother-in-law, Mrs. Shawe. Thackeray's writings for the Constitutional began appearing in September, one month after his marriage. The account given by Ray of those next months suggests that Thackeray thought himself arrived at stability and contentedness, with the leisure to secure and execute additional jobs as illustrator.

But the whole project collapsed by July of the next year, crippling Major Carmichael-Smyth financially and throwing Thackeray once again upon the resources of his free-lance pen, this time with a wife and child to support. Thackeray would not again enjoy the leisure and stability of those few months as Paris correspondent for many years to come, but he had broken into print, he knew how to do it, he had developed some confidence in his abilities, and he set about his work with vigor.

When in 1833 Thackeray had commented to his mother that the National Standard was "very rapidly improving, and will form I have no doubt a property", he was still the investor seeking to acquire and improve a property ready made; now he was to discover that he had "no other saleable property" than his writings.

MAJOR WORKS

English journalist, novelist, famous for his novel VANITY FAIR (1847-48), a tale of two middle-class London families. Most of Thackeray's major novels were published as monthly serials. Thackeray studied in a satirical and moralistic light upper- and middle-class English life - he was once seen as the equal of his contemporary Dickens, or even as his superior. "This I set as a positive truth. A woman with fair opportunities, and without a positive hump, may marry whom she likes." (from Vanity Fair).

William Makepeace Thackeray was born in Calcutta, India, as the only son of Richmond Thackeray, a Collector in the East Indian Company's service. After his father died he was sent to home to England. He was educated at Charterhouse and at Trinity College, Cambridge. Thackeray abandoned his studies without taking a degree, having lost some of his inheritance of twenty thousand pounds through gambling. In the beginning of the 1830s he visited Germany, where he met Goethe.

During 1831-33 Thackeray studied law at the Middle Temple, London, but had little enthusiasm to continue his studies. In 1833 he brought with a large heritage the National Standard, but lost his fortune a year later in the Indian bank failures and other bad investments. According to an anecdote, Thackeray offered to undertake the task of illustrating Dickens's Pickwick Papers in 1836, but the author himself found Thackeray's drawings unsuitable.

After art studies in Paris, Thackeray returned in 1837 to London and started his career as a hard working journalist. Often he used absurd pen names such as George Savage Fitz-Boodle, Michael Angelo Titmarsh, Théophile Wagstaff, and C.J. Yellowplush, Esq. In 1836 he married a poor Irish girl, Isabella Shawe; they had three daughters. Their first child, Anne Thackeray Ritchie (1837-1919), became a writer - her impressionistic texts impressed Virginia Woolf, who drew a portrait of her in Night and Day (1919) as 'Mrs Hilbery'. Ritchie (1837-1919) published several novels, and contributed to an 1898-99 edition of her father's works. A prominent intellectual figure of her time and well-acquainted with a number of the great names of British literature, she also wrote memoirs of her contemporaries, including Tennyson (1809-1892) and Ruskin (1819-1900).

Thackeray began to contribute regularly to Fraser's magazine, morning chronicle, new monthly magazine and the times. His writings attracted first attention in punch, where he satirized English snobbery. These sketches reappeared in 1848 as the book of snobs, in which he stated that "he who meanly admires mean things is a snob." In 1840 Isabella Thackeray suffered a mental breakdown, from which she never recovered, through she survived Thackeray by thirty years. The author was forced to send his children to France to his mother. The children returned to England in 1846 to live with him.

Already in his first novel, Catherine (1839), originally written for Fraser's magazine, Thackeray broke with the literary conventions of his day: "The characters of the tale are immoral, and no doubt of it; but the writer humbly hopes the end is not so.

The public was, in our notion, dosed and poisoned by the prevailing style of literary practice, and it was necessary to administer some medicine that would produce a wholesome nausea, and afterwards bring about a more healthy habit." In the luck of Barry Lyndon (1844), Thackeray portrayed an adventurer, opportunist, and gambler, who serves in the seven years war, first under the English flag and then in the Prussian army, gains wealth, and eventually is punished for his imperfections.

"Suppose in a game of life - and it is but a twopenny game after all - you are equally eager of winning," Thackeray wrote much later in 'autour de mon chapeau' (1863). "Shall you be ashamed of your ambition, or glory in it?" In Vanity Fair, set at the time of the Napoleonic wars, Thackeray created one of the most fascinating immoral female characters, Becky Sharp, who manages to avoid the fate of Barry Lyndon: "I think I could be a good woman if I had five thousand a year." (from Vanity Fair) The book brought Thackeray prosperity and made him an established author and popular lecturer in Europe and in the United States.

Vanity Fair was sub-titled 'A Novel without a Hero'. "Everybody in Vanity Fair must have remarked how well those live who are comfortably and thoroughly in debt; how they deny themselves nothing; how jolly and easy they are in their minds." The vast satirical panorama of a materialistic society centers on Becky Sharp and Amelia Sedley, good-natured but 'silly'.

They are two boarding-school friends, whose destinies are contrasted. Clever and ambitious Becky is born into poverty as the daughter of a penniless artist. Her plans to marry Amelia's brother Joseph fail. She marries Rowdon Crawley, but he is disinherited. Becky manages to live at the height of fashion through the patronage of Lord Steyne.

When her husband discovers the truth, he departs to become the governor of Coventry Island. Becky is ostracized and she moves to the Continent. In the meantime Amelia's stockbroker father is ruined. Amelia is loved by William Dobbin but she marries George Osborne - he dies in the battle of Waterloo. Amelia's son is left into the care of his grandfather, who dies and leaves him a fortune.

Amelia travels in the Continent with his brother and they meet Becky. Dobbin has returned from India and disapproves Amelia's kindness to Becky. Older and disillusioned, Dobbin and Amelia can marry. Becky regains her hold over Joseph, who dies in suspicious circumstances. Becky's husband Rowdon dies, and Becky ends the novel in the guise of a pious widow.

Thackeray's increasing love for Jane Brookfield, the wife of an old Cambridge friend, led to a rupture in their friendship. The history of Henry Edmond, esq., appeared in three volumes in 1852, and reflected the melancholic period in the life of the author. By the end of his career, Thackeray's disillusionment with contemporary culture seems to have deepened. In the adventures of Philip (1862) the protagonist, Philip, is out of place in a world that does not accommodate his vision of masculinity.

Thackeray said that he couldn't start a novel until he knew every aspect of his characters. He called Victorian times "if not the most moral, certainly the most squeamish." Once, as an editor, he rejected an Elizabeth Barrett browning poem because it employed the word harlot. Thackeray became in 1860 the first editor of the Cornhill magazine, for which he wrote his roundabout papers, love the widower, the adventures of Philip and the unfinished Denis Duvall.

Less successful Thackeray was with his attempt to stand for parliament. His contacts with friendly rival Charles Dickens ended in a quarrel, but their daughters continued to be friends. Thackeray died suddenly on Christmas Eve 1863. Just before his death he had reconciled with dickens.

Thackeray was buried in Kensal green cemetery. His bust at the Westminster abbey was made by the Italian sculptor Marachetti. The poet's daughter was not satisfied with the work and let another sculptor to modify her father's stone sideburns until they were the right length.

Sir Pitt brags that there is timber worth six thousand pounds along his driveway and immediately has two little boys flogged for gathering sticks. Although Sir Pitt isn't fit for anything (he can neither read nor spell), yet he is courted by ministers and statesmen. He rates high in Vanity Fair. Part of the twist of Thackeray's plot is that the always correct and stuffy Pitt Crawley, who frowns on his half sisters' laughter, who will neither let them play neither cards nor escape.

Chapter 2

Thackeray's Deep and Fundamental Individual Skepticism

Among the conclusions a study like this one reveals is that books are shaped by the demands they are intended to fulfill. If one is writing for money, as Thackeray quite clearly was, one must write that which will be accepted by publishers. Likewise, this study shows that the production of a book is a multifaceted cooperative affair and that the resulting printed text is not attributable to the author solely.

One is led inevitably, then, to a number of fundamental questions concerning literary works: about competing authorities for the verbal content and visual design of the books, about the authenticity of the text in any given book, about the relative claims as "best text" that could be made for competing editions. Fundamental to any answers is another rather metaphysical question: At what point or points in a continuum from pure, free authorial autonomy to rigid social determinism does the production of literary art take place?

If one thinks art is the product of the artist exercising creative freedom to write as he or she pleases, then the answers to the questions about authority, authenticity, and "the best text" will tend to be answered differently from the way they are answered by one who thinks art is the product of social forces fulfilling external demands for a market. These concepts are more easily adjudicated in the abstract than in specific cases; so this chapter is devoted to an effort to understand the consequences of various answers as they relate to a specific work, Thackeray's Henry Esmond. I try to demonstrate that the questions raised here are of crucial importance to any reader of the novel, not just an editor trying to determine the textual details of a new edition.

A brief orientation regarding theories of textual criticism will help establish their importance. The authority of the text, or more accurately, the authority for the text, is the person, persons, or "force" that has the final responsibility for "getting the text right." Among common notions about authority are, first, that of the author, who originated the linguistic text and read proof, giving authorial approval to additions, deletions, and alterations introduced by other hands. A second centre of authority is the production personnel, for they create the combination of verbal text and visual book that "for the first time really" constitutes the "public work."

A third idea is that regardless of romantic ideals, the final object, often referred to reverentially as "the text itself," is its own authority and, regardless of its provenance, must be treated as "the work." And a fourth is that any thinking, careful, sensitive, knowledgeable person can, through close reading and/or research into the developing text, find and correct flaws and improve the work to better represent its potential ideal artistic form. These views are basically incompatible with one another and appeal variously to different people.

Once a notion of the "properly responsible" authority has been settled, questions about the authenticity of the text in any particular copy of the work can be asked. Identifying typographical errors and unauthoritative interpolations starts the effort to authenticate the text. Locating and restoring or incorporating authoritative readings that "belong" in the text complete the authentication.

Some works, however, do not fit easily into the procrustean bed created by the concepts of authority and authenticity. Authors sometimes revise, or the works become significantly altered in other ways, so that alternate authoritative and authentic versions vie for attention. Persons who think a literary work should be one thing usually push for one text. They would like for statements about a work of art to have a stable referent. In the case of Henry Esmond, such a goal is easier to wish for than to have. There is no one answer to these questions.

What needs to be recognized is that every reader answers them, perhaps not explicitly, in the act of reading by placing some credence in the symbols for the text on the page and by formulating some concept of what kind of thing is being read and what source or sources produced it.

It has been usual for readers to assume that Thackeray wrote Henry Esmond, that Thackeray wrote what is printed on the pages of the book, and that what the readers understand and experience in reading the book came from Thackeray. Some readers, of course, do not have a very clear notion of Thackeray and may think that the text before them is its own authority.

More sophisticated readers may wish to discount Thackeray's authority over meaning and choose instead to read "against the grain" for meanings revealed inadvertently by the text [about the author or about his society or about the means of production that created the physical book.

All of these are common and legitimate readerly acts, and all require some act of faith regarding the authenticity and authority of the text. One of the objects of this book is to explore the foundations for such acts of faith, to see more than is normally seen about the processes, aims, and social forces that influence the particular sequence of symbols on the page.

The problem with this objective is that any historical construct is just that, a construct. Constructs are influenced not just by the evidence of history put together objectively but by the historian's answers to metaphysical questions like, Are works of art the product of individual artistic talent, or are they social acts? For that reason this chapter does not argue in behalf of one point of view, but rather explores the consequences of adopting two or three different points of view.

A working proposition here is the idea that the persuasiveness of any historical construct and of any accommodation of the questions of authority, authenticity, and authorial autonomy or social determinism depends on the context identified as relevant to the construct. Of course, everything is a context for everything else, but historians, editors, and readers usually focus narrowly on "truly relevant" contexts selected from the narrow range of material that survives as evidence.

It is necessary, therefore, to identify the various contexts in which Henry Esmond has been seen and to show the differing consequences to readers and editors. Implicit in the procedure is the idea that coherent explanations can be attempted within defined contexts.

In everyday practice: the meanings of verbal utterances are guided heavily, if not actually established, by contexts. In The History of Henry Esmond, Thackeray, writing in 1851 - 52, had a mid-nineteenth-century audience consisting of book reviewers, circulating-library readers, his mother, his publishers, his friends, and his ex-lady love Jane Octavia Brookfield. These people can be seen as having been addressed by the novel.

But Thackeray said not one word in Henry Esmond, for his narrator, the aged Esmond, and the memoir's editors and commentators, Esmond's wife and daughter, do all the writing. The writing is understood to take place in the second and third decades of the eighteenth century and records events said to have occurred between 1670 and 1720.

Esmond's memoirs are addressed to his grandsons, but his audience clearly includes his wife, who is thought by most critics to resemble Jane Brookfield. The speakers in the novel, in passages of dialogue, also produce their utterances in contexts that help identify their meanings. One can ask what the character meant, what Esmond meant by reporting the character's speech, and what Thackeray meant by having Esmond report it.

One can ask what the passage may have meant to a Victorian totally ignorant of the author and what it may have meant to Jane Octavia Brookfield. And, of course, modern readers produce their own responses to these meanings by contrasting them with their own sense of acceptable beliefs and behaviors. Thus readers contextualize the text in various specific ways as a means of producing what they think are appropriate understandings of the text.

This is only the tip of an iceberg of contexts within which the novel's words can be set and understood. Each context illuminates the text in a different way. Readers know this and act upon that knowledge almost without reflection - they are that good at using and understanding language.

And when a scholar/critic points out to readers an aspect of context they had not considered, they gratefully add it to the mix of factors that influence their understanding of the text. The study of genre, the author's other works, biography, cultural history, the history of ideas, all these are understood to extend the readers' awareness of the contexts within which texts create and convey meaning. Even the physical embodiments of texts, the books themselves as paper, ink, and bindings, influence interpretations.

There is, however, a major flaw in the ordinary idea of authentic texts. If it is assumed that the text of a work is stable, that is, if we work with a text that is thought to have been established, we use the principle of contexts to produce "readings of the text" for contemplation. But if it is recognized that the text itself is not stable, we tend to use the principle of contexts to produce a "reading of the text" that will help establish what the text is by leading us to the right critical choices among variants.

That is clearly circular reasoning and leads to predictable texts that best fulfill the editor's particular contextual construct. But the situation is worse than that. It does not matter that no variant survives at a given point in the text; each word or mark of punctuation is potentially an erroneous witness to the context identified for use in interpreting the text.

That may seem good to the editor, for that is what makes emendation of errors possible. Editors tend to think that some errors, like typographical errors and scribal errors, are "demonstrable," and they emend them. But they may be too quick to believe an error to be demonstrable because they are not sufficiently aware of the influence of the contextualization that they are using to determine the meaning which identifies the textual anomaly as a demonstrable error.

To illustrate the consequences of this approach, a useful example is The History of Henry Esmond, which for these purposes will have to be examined in the original edition, published in London by Smith, Elder and Company in 1852 in three volumes. In what follows I speak as an editor of Henry Esmond, but I mean to imply that in order for an editor to know what is being edited and why it is being edited, he or she must first be a reader, must know how to read, and must know what effect the editing is having on reading. Consequently, everything I say about the editor is applicable also to any careful reader.

To do a contextual reading, one must try to draw together the historical details of authorship as a profession and printing and publishing as a complex of economic traditions and interests in a continuous struggle with innovation - both technical and moral - and with attitudes toward gender, family, and moral conventions, particularly as they reflected the audiences for lending libraries in order to see what Henry Esmond was. Then, perhaps, it can demonstrate more clearly what the reader's and editor's task is, or, at least, what purposes modern scholarly editions serve.

While not forgetting that authors attempt to create something original that will fulfill their own purposes (including the purpose of making money), we will have to examine bibliography, printing history, papermaking, taxes on books and newspapers, copyright law, labour relations, trade guilds relating to printing, publishing, and bookselling, marketing associations, professional societies, the apprentice system, lending libraries, the three-deckers in relationship to parts publication and magazine serials, the growth of the literate public, the development of authorship as a profession, and the developing division of labour into literary agents, publishers, printers, wholesalers, and booksellers.

Each of these can be thought of as a force field influencing what the work became, limiting what the work could say, shaping the work, and thereby influencing reactions to and understandings of the final product. (Incidentally, one of the nice things about scorning historical reconstructions is that there is less work involved.)

Now obviously all of that cannot be detailed here, but it has been done, and its salient details can be summarized (cf. Feltes; Sutherland, Novelists; Harden, edition of Esmond; Altick; Patten; Nowell-Smith; West, "Book Publishing" and "The Chace Act", which explore the development of literary agents and crosscurrents in book production and author/ publisher relations between England and America).

The History of Henry Esmond is Thackeray's only book to appear originally as a three-decker. It was published by a firm whose head, George Smith, was an executive member of the Bookseller's Association. It was Thackeray's second book with Smith, Elder and Company - his first major book with that publisher - and it represented the first significant step in an attempt by George Smith to make Thackeray one of his authors - an object he accomplished thoroughly mid completely in 1859.

Smith descended into publishing from the banking business by way of substantial reference works and scientific publications. His literature list, his fiction, was respectable, yet he was bold and aggressive. He published Charlotte Brontë's Jane Eyre and later went on to acquire as his authors Anthony Trollope and George Eliot.

Esmond, therefore, by virtue of its publishing house belongs to a tradition of book production controlled by establishment wealth and power. To be published by Smith implied certain standards of literary and moral content that Thackeray had never been clearly subject to before, though he was subject in a general way to the Mrs. Grundy censorship affecting all Victorian publications above pulp street literature.

Thackeray rose to the Smith, Elder house from his major publisher, Bradbury and Evans, which in turn had risen into publishing from bookselling, newspaper publishing, and being proprietor of that low comic magazine, Punch, and other comic and sporting publications. In spite of the firm's industry and success, Bradbury and Evans belonged to a decidedly antiestablishment point of view, and in the 1840s Thackeray was one of its chief writers.

Thackeray's sojourn in bohemia as an art student in Paris and as a writing hack in London were social and financial descents from which the economic success of books like Vanity Fair and Pendennis were raising him. Those works and the bulk of his writings in the 1840s (The Book of Snobs, Novels by Eminent Hands, Barry Lyndon, Catherine, The Yellowplush Papers, The Reminiscences of Major Gahagan) all reflect the satirical, antisnob, antiestablishment attitudes of Punch and Fraser's Magazine, the main outlets for his writings.

Esmond was to be different. The author of Esmond was a man financially and socially restored to the level of his upbringing. He was a popular writer and successful public lecturer, having delivered his urbane lectures on the eighteenth-century English humorists to receptive and aristocratic audiences in London, Edinburgh, Oxford, Cambridge, and the larger industrial cities. Esmond was to be his calling card and proof that he could write a thoroughly good, artistically complete, and serious work of art. By and large, Esmond has been seen, both by his contemporaries and by generations of literary critics up to our own day, as a peak in Thackeray's rising career as a writer and artist.

The book belongs to the establishment in otherways, too. The three-decker was in mid-Victorian England a thoroughly establishment commodity, an expensive book made possible and necessary by circulating libraries whose large guaranteed prepublication purchases made three-decker production a book publisher's staple.

It was nearly impossible for a book publisher to lose money on a three-decker that had been adopted by Mudie's library, but the discounts Mudie demanded and the price regulations that kept most ordinary customers from purchasing their own copies instead of subscribing to Mudie's made it equally difficult for a publisher to make very much money on a three-decker.

The price-maintenance system for three-deckers worked

to the benefit of publishers and the circulating libraries from the mid-1840s to the mid-1890s by providing stability; no one was making an inordinate amount of money, but the system could be counted on. This stability depended not only on control of prices but also on certain simple controls over the content and size of the books.

These constraints imposed by Mudie's are now relatively easy to document; their primary focus was on the length of the book and the moral character of the plot and characterizations. An author and publisher who could work within the library constraints and win selection could count on a sound though not spectacular financial return.

But the respectability of the publisher and the library demands are not the only determining or constraining forces observable. Esmond is a historical novel created within a tradition of historical fiction which Thackeray may be said to have modified but not to have invented. Among these constraints was the demand for historical plausibility and the historical research which that demand entailed.

Plausibility was judged by the depth and breadth and accuracy of the historical detail surrounding the fictional characters and events. It was not necessary, however, to maintain historical perspective in moral and intellectual concerns or issues; Sir Walter Scott had made the historical novel both respectable and relevant to current moral and political concerns. But the freedom offered by historical fiction within the establishment contours of the three-decker published by Smith, Elder was a narrow freedom indeed.

N. N. Feltes, in considering Esmond in its marketplace context, has noted that the Booksellers Association and the circulating libraries were fighting a losing battle against an encroaching democratizing, proletarian invasion of the world of books and literature represented by cheap books, serializations in shilling parts, and shilling magazines.

The booksellers' battle was to save the commodity which three-deckers epitomized and thereby save the economic control and stability which they enjoyed primarily through the three-decker. Feltes saw the three-decker as symbolic of the upper-class resistance to progressing economic forces and finds in the three-decker morality and traditional structures a corollary conservatism and reactionary spirit.

He found in Esmond, a historical novel redolent with nostalgia for a past age, the same conservatism and establishment resistance to mass values, mass mores, and mass tastes. He found in Esmond's literary reputation a confirmation of conservative tastes and socioeconomic politics. In the social history of the last half of the nineteenth century, on the other hand, Feltes saw the slow but irresistible subversion of the commodity book by the new cheap, democratizing commodity text.

The triumph of this movement was the demise of the three-decker novel in the 1890s. For Feltes, therefore, Esmond represents a reactionary, establishment work. As such it represents a change or an anomaly in Thackeray's role, which for Vanity Fair and the early journalism was that of satirist of the establishment. Feltes posited the explanation that within the constraints of the three-decker, Thackeray was determined by cultural forces greater than himself and that an examination of these cultural contexts proves that the language and the culture speak the author, that the autonomous author is a figment of the romantic imagination; "reality" is the reality of social determinism.

If this discussion were to stop here, the weight of the social contract might seem irresistible; the social theory of texts would convincingly vest authority for the linguistic text and the meaning of the work in the social context. And the editorial solution for Esmond would be to select the first edition as the copy-text, emend nothing, and present the novel as a commodity book with large margins, heavy paper, and expensive packaging, thus perpetuating its role as representative of the establishment, [standing as an anomaly in Thackeray's literary corpus.

But the author, his text, and his meaning need not disappear behind this sociological arrangement of historical details. It is a significant shortcoming in Feltes's work that he did not apply his critical apparatus to a reading of the text.

Careful rereading of Esmond suggests a conclusion opposite to the one Feltes reached. He skated over the elements in the book that do not confirm his social deterministic theory of book production. The flaw of his approach is the rigidity with which his view of the social contract theory of texts controlled and limited his reading of the work by paralyzing his belief in authorial intentionality.

Social determinism apparently obviates autonomy in Feltes's way of looking. Although all that Feltes pointed out about the cultural milieu surrounding Esmond is true, it is hardly as comprehensive or constraining a view as he suggested.

Though the novel was hailed by many of its original readers (particularly its better-educated and better-heeled readers) as a critical triumph, and though it for many years has been held in high regard even by readers who do not generally admires Thackeray's works, it was and is a profoundly troubling book to many others.

Many of its first readers and reviewers were shaken and angered by the ending, in which Esmond marries the woman he has long treated as his mother. That that denouement was Thackeray's intent from the beginning is perfectly clear on rereading with close attention to Rachel's character - she knew her heart's true relation to Henry well before her husband died and years before naive Esmond himself recognized it.

It shows in her nearly hysterical reaction to the news that Henry has exposed himself to smallpox by visiting Nancy Sievewright, the blacksmith's daughter, although a superficial reading allows one to think that she is reacting merely as a social snob and doting mother.

It also shows in her behaviour to Henry on his third visit home from college when young Frank reveals that she has been fussing over Henry's room for days, having worked a new counterpane for his bed and put fresh-cut roses in his window in anticipation of his arrival, though she pretends not to know if the housekeeper has prepared his room.

It shows in her reaction to the news that "Henry" has been killed in a carriage accident, though the Henry involved turned out to be Melton, not Esmond. It shows in the nearly psychopathic rejection scene in prison after Lord Castlewood has been killed in a duel (bk. 2, chap. 1). And it shows in the news that she has sneaked off to Southampton to watch from hiding as Esmond returns from the Continental wars.

Rachel clearly believes that God has punished her for her disaffection to her husband and her secret affection for Henry by allowing her husband to be killed. She tells Esmond years later when they meet again that God has forgiven her sin: "But I would love you still - yes, there is no sin in such a love as mine now; and my dear lord in heaven may see my heart; and knows the tears that have washed my sin away".

Rachel's secret love was even more disturbing to the Victorian consciousness than the apparent though not real incest at the end of the book, for it portrays a good woman - the heroine angel in the house - in the grip of a powerful and lifelong illicit passion she must and does suppress with visible effort.

Morally the book's psychological realism, though delicately handled, is profoundly subversive to the establishment. It is a measure of Thackeray's artistry that he portrayed these telling scenes in ways susceptible to more conventional interpretations, though to read them as such is to believe Thackeray has overwritten them (cf. Geoffrey Tillotson for a particularly good assessment of Thackeray's "philosophy" and the way it influenced how he write).

But the book is subversive in an even more important way, for Esmond's ostensibly weak character, his apparent vacillation and inability to cast himself passionately and unreservedly behind any cause, religious, political, economic, or amorous - though goodness knows he tries - arguably stems not from a psychological weakness but from a fundamental philosophical uncertainty and humility that is very dangerous to establishment mentality.

The elderly narrator of the book, recounting Esmond's youthful naive enthusiasm for Father Holt's Catholicism, Rachel's Anglicanism, the Dowager Castlewood's Jacobitism, Beatrix's concepts of heroism and honour, constantly reveals

Esmond discovering himself in an assumed and uncomfortable role-playing. Esmond spends his life fulfilling or trying to fulfill other people's expectations for himself and repeatedly discovering that the goals were not worth winning. He ends ashamed of himself as a soldier witnessing his fellows attack nuns, of Father Holt's tawdry lies and deceptions, of Frank Esmond's subjugation to Clotilde, of Beatrix's head-hunting selfishness as courtesan, and ultimately of his own complicity in these other shames he has participated in as a role player rather than in propia persona.

The measure of Esmond's superiority over other characters is that he recognizes his self-delusions and those of his fellow actors. Esmond's way of thinking and suiting action to thought is antiestablisliment.

That is why Beatrix has no permanent use for him. Esmond is constantly giving away [the store on the grounds of scruples; he loses ground for honour and principle without any compensating social or economic or political gain. He is ultimately anti-imperialist and antiroyalist, and he rejects the optimism of the intellectual rationality for which his age, the eighteenth century, is known. At the end of the book he retreats happily enough to the margins of the empire, where he establishes a domestic kingdom of his own.

The question about Thackeray's "intentions" with regard to Esmond and its potentially antiestablishment meanings can be pursued a bit further in two directions. They both bring to bear on the reading of Esmond other contexts than the Marxist economic contexts just examined. The first is the biographical background and in particular the events in the year immediately preceding the writing of Esmond concerning Thackeray's love life.

(By 1851 Thackeray's wife had been confined under special care for insanity for seven years, In the three years before the writing of Esmond his love for Jane Octavia Brookfield, the wife of his best friend, the Reverend William Brookfield, had gotten as heated as a platonic relationship can get. Thackeray was clearly in love, though he was fully aware of the impossibility of the situation.

He imagined that Jane suffered under a sense of repression and lack of appreciation by her husband, which may have been greater in Thackeray's mind than in reality. Whatever the case, in September 1851 William Brookfield, who had tolerated Thackeray's attentions to Mrs. Brookfield with increasing wariness, put his foot down, banning Thackeray from the society of his home and wife. It is not hard to trace Thackeray's melancholy in the Henry Esmond/ Rachel Castlewood relations in the book he was then commencing.

Though he had not written any part of the book, he signed the contract for Esmond in June 1851. It was a story he claimed was boiling up within him as early as January, though his work on his lectures on eighteenth-century English humorists came first. That the rupture with the Brookfields affected the story there can be no doubt.

Thackeray complained to Smith as late as December that he could not get on with the book under the effects of an ailment which time alone could mend. In the book itself there is a romanticized version of what could have been: Lord Castlewood's insensitivity to his wife may be read as William Brookfield's insensitivity to Jane writ large; Rachel's deep love for Esmond, suppressed and denied but tortured and irrepressible, may be Thackeray's portrait of what he saw or wished to see in Jane Brookfield's relation to himself. Thackeray seems to have been much more interested, to judge also from his letters, in assuaging his own sorrow than in upholding establishment social mores.

And in the character of Henry Esmond, Thackeray was able to make Rachel suffer the jealous pangs of seeing her unattainable love object throw himself at the feet of another-Beatrix, who was Rachel's daughter. Nor is it hard to see Thackeray beating his own breast and exploring the ecstasies of rejection while describing the perpetual and nearly unstiflable but unrequited love of Esmond for Beatrix.

The psychological realism of a complicated and confusing network of love and jealousy involving mothers and sons and other forbidden attractions is carefully handled, for in Victorian fiction serious and troubling life passages could be explored only in code. And finally, to focus on the way in which interpretation bears on editing, the rhetorical context of Esmond must be considered. It is a memoir: The History of Henry Esmond, Esq., a Colonel in the Service of Her Majesty Q. Anne. Written by Himself.

It has all the rhetorical characteristics of an extended dramatic monologue, addressed by Esmond to his grandsons. Thackeray, the author, said not one word in propia persona in the whole book; even the introduction is written by Esmond's daughter. As with any first-person narration, the potential for irony and for misapprehending irony is great. Traditionally, critics have read Esmond's narrative as something like the preachments of the author's alter ego. Esmond's opening comments, on the nature of history, strike readers as honest and commonsensical.

"Why shall History go on kneeling to the end of Time? I am for having her rise up off her knees, and take a natural posture: not to be for ever performing cringes and corgees like a Court-chamberlain, and shuffling backwards out of doors in the presence of the sovereign. In a word," Esmond writes engagingly, "I would have History familiar rather than heroic."

It sounds like the sort of attitude Thackeray would adopt; it is like his reviews of pictures in the Academy, knowledgeable but unimpressed. Esmond seems to reflect Thackeray's own attitude also by placing himself and his neighbors on the stage of history and comparing them with the figures normally found there: "I have seen too much of success in life to take off my hat and huzza to it, as it passes in its gilt coach: and would do my little part with my neighbours on foot that they should not gape with too much wonder, nor applaud too loudly.

Is it the Lord Mayor going in stare to mince-pies and the Mansion House? Is it poor Jack of Newgate's procession, with the sheriff and javelin-men, conducting him on this last journey to Tyburn? I look into my heart and think I am as good as my Lord Mayor, and know I am as bad as Tyburn Jack, "In short, the book abounds with reasons not to draw a sharp distinction between the narrator and the author. Moreover, Esmond has a basic distrust of absolutes - that is, of other peoples' absolutes - he does not trust the judgment of priests, military leaders, political leaders, or kings. His love and his loyalty are always tinged with sardonic self-detachment.

As one critic has noted, "Like Vanity Fair, Henry Esmond is a sustained argument against the reality of moral absolutes. Esmond himself does much of the arguing, for he is proficient at identifying illusory values and beliefs. His sophisticated skepticism, however, is itself founded on a dedication to one surviving absolute: truth."

(This personal truth of Esmond's is the foundation of his appeal to the reader in his autobiography. And, as with most monologists, Henry constantly asks the reader to share in his personal recognition and judgment of the self-deception of others. Furthermore, he seldom expects the reader to take him very seriously, and he appears to be disingenuous when he does.

Feltes probably would not rejoice over this coup d'état within the camp of the dying establishment, for the book does not subvert the establishment on behalf of the rising proletariat. Instead, the subversion emanates from the principles of a small intellectual elite, the freethinkers of England's Victorian intellectual class. Some of those freethinkers were ideologues, but Thackeray's religious and philosophical ideas did not develop in a cell of like-minded philosophers or so-called freethinkers (though it was not insignificant that he was a close friend of Edward FitzGerald, the translator of Omar Khayyám's Rubáiyát).

Thackeray's philosophy is revealed in his letters and private papers as a deep and fundamental individual skepticism about causes of every sort. It got him into trouble with many proponents of causes in need of money or moral support who approached Thackeray.

If the cause was individual, to honour an admirable writer's family, to provide charity on nonsectarian bases, Thackeray was a patsy. But if it was to establish a guild for literature or to propose an evangelical school or cause, his purse and ear alike were closed. He did not trust institutionalized schemes.

Esmond is subversive to the establishment it represents, but not on behalf of emerging socioeconomic ideologies. Even the fact that both Thackeray and his publisher made a good bit of money from Esmond, which was all unusually good seller despite its price, does not indicate that its themes or its production was [determined or dominated by either a vested production tradition or an emerging public taste. Both of those "ideologies" claim the book by ignoring its subversive elements.

So much for Feltes's establishment interpretation of Esmond; this "establishment" book has a strikingly antiestablishment text - it is a wolf in sheep's clothing. And this interpretation makes the social contract solution to the editorial problem unacceptable. To take the first edition as copy-text for the linguistic text of all edition would be to accept the work of the minions of the establishment. Now, it so happens that in 1852, George Smith did not own his own printing establishment, so he sent Thackeray's manuscript to Bradbury and Evans to be typeset and printed.

There may be comfort to be found, then, in the fact that the compositors of Thackeray's "proletarian serial novels" also typeset his "establishment commodity book," but the principle of authorial autonomy which the antiestablishment interpretation tends to support leads one to question the whole production process. That is to say, belief in the possibility of authorial autonomy, even of a limited sort, requires the rejection of any blanket rules for editing.

Rejecting Feltes's conclusions about the meaning of Henry Esmond in three volumes and rejecting the conclusion that a social contract requires special respect from an editorial view I do not mean that the three-volume format and the production process are unimportant. Quite the contrary. The book could not be a wolf in sheep's clothing without the sheep's clothing, and such a wolf means far different things from regular wolves or regular sheep.

The novel is quite definitely a collaboration, or at least a joint venture between the author and the social institutions of book production and marketing. And that identifies serious editorial problems.

A close look at Esmond reveals an extensive network of evidence suggesting an intentional subversion of the narrator by the author. Thackeray seems not to have trusted Esmond's foundation rock of personal truth, Elaine Scarry in a 1975 article compiled an extensive list of errors in the book. These she invariably attributed to Esmond, claiming that Thackeray put them there on purpose.

Scarry was not the first to notice that [Esmond occasionally contradicts himself or forgets what he has said earlier in the narrative, but she was the first to attribute these errors to Esmond instead of to Thackeray or to the publishers. John Sutherland's Penguin edition annotations, for example, point out scores of historical and plotting errors, but Sutherland encouraged the readers to ignore them as understandable though regrettable characteristics of Thackeray's fiction.

Scarry identified an astonishing array of errors and anomalies, including an undermining of the rhetorical force of Esmond's own protestations - as when, having renounced the doctrine of divine right of kings and declared himself a republican, he nevertheless couches his adoration for Beatrix in the language of subjugation to royalty - and other more direct contradictions - as when he declares that an event so impressed him that memory would never fail him, whereupon he recounts the event in such a way as to contradict or distort his own earlier account of it. I believe Scarry is right to say that Esmond, "who has taken truth for his motto," was ironically undercut by Thackeray, "who has taken the absence of truth for his theme."

J. Hillis Miller, following a different line of reasoning altogether, arrived temporarily at the same conclusion Scarry reached. Miller brilliantly revealed the older Henry's ironic stance with respect to the younger Henry and then showed the ironic self-destruction of the self that Henry Esmond the narrator has constructed. Miller saw Thackeray's presence behind the narrator undercutting his claims to memory's sovereignty and the basis upon which Esmond allows himself to become "king" of the Virginia Castlewood and to accept the "worship" of Rachel and his daughter. Miller did not use any references to the "narrative errors" in the book to detect this irony.

But his view of Thackeray undercutting the narrator was a temporary stop an Miller's deconstructive way through the novel, for he then undercut or deconstructed this third level of irony by arguing that Thackeray was trying to "understand and control his life by taking ironic authority over that assumed role and by showing the imagined person to have made a false interpretation of himself."

Miller was more interested in his theory of irony as "infinite absolute negativity" than he was in the meaning of Henry Esmond, the book being in the final analysis only an illustration for what Miller had to say about irony. Furthermore, his conclusion about the novel could not stop with resolution, for it is the nature of deconstructive criticism to deconstruct the deconstruction. Resolution would put an end to the fun and games.

However, Miller's point is not without seriousness. Resolution - say, the conclusion Miller considered at one point, that Thackeray undercut the narrator through telling references to Oedipus Rex and Hamlet which the reader with the help of Freud's Interpretation of Dreams can use to see Thackeray's ironic distance from his narrator - cannot be reached with any conviction if one is fully cognizant of the slippery ground such a resolution must take for its base. Miller implied that Thackeray, like his narrator, revealed himself rather than justified himself in the endless cycle of ironic undercuttings.

This view makes Henry Esmond "one of the best texts in English fiction by means of which to explore the workings of irony in narrative." But in order to get boxed up, as Miller wanted the reader to be, one must agree that Thackeray was seeking "authority over his own life by way of a detour representing that life in ironically displaced form in a fiction." Miller's conclusion that Beatrix is a sad mirror image of

Esmond, revealing unconsciously the "corrosive power" of both characters and of their author, was based on the idea that Thackeray was seriously trying to present a "Pretense of mastery."

It would be possible - in fact, preferable - to conclude that Thackeray was not trying any such thing. Instead, he was demonstrating the inability to exercise any such mastery. Beatrix, in her cold-blooded, calculating attempts, which from the cynic's point of view should succeed, fails just as truly as does Esmond, whose machinations the reader is led to believe are wholly unconscious. The melancholy nihilism of the book can and has been seen as Thackeray's cynicism. But it is one thing to recognize the lack of control implied by nihilism and quite another to give in to it.

Beatrix recognizes it and gives in to it. Henry Esmond recognizes it up to a point; that is, he recognizes it for others but not for himself, and the sensitive reader of his memoirs is bruised by Esmond's lack of self-awareness, revealed, for example, in the way he punishes Rachel for "unfaithfulness" to him in the prison while excusing his own blatant and egregious "unfaithfulness" to her during the years of his infatuation with Beatrix.

It is inconceivable that Thackeray failed to see Esmond's self-deception or the dual view of nihilism implied by Beatrix's and Esmond's stories. Thackeray did not give in to it, as the cynical view would have it, [nor did he close his eyes to it, reverting blindly to an assertion of good that would be no more than a repetition of Esmond's quest for something worth believing in at one further level of self-deception. Anyone who has read Thackeray's own story - in the Letters and Gordon Ray's two-volume biography - can see the melancholy acceptance of uncertainty, as opposed to mastery, that characterized his mature years.

But two things mitigate against Miller's reading of Esmond, which was after all based on a reading of the text alone. One is Thackeray's determination expressed in conversation to John Chapman in 1851, thirteen days before he signed the contract to write Henry Esmond, that he did not feel "called upon to martyrise himself for the sake of his views" by expressing them too clearly to his reading public. The second is, that Thackeray's personal reaction to his nihilistic ideas was to resist the temptation to give in. His personal intense desire not to hurt anyone, not to take advantage of anyone, not to manipulate others out of a sense that his version of "the truth" was the right version of it all reveals the light in which he created in Esmond the views Miller has described.

That is to say, in view of the emptiness of institutionalized values such as royalty, inherited rank, honour, party and country loyalty, marriage, and institutional religion, Thackeray chose not to sneer and not to pontificate, but to assert a sardonic kindliness and gentleness that are as far from sentimentality as those qualities can get. Nihilism in Thackeray bred humility about his politics, religion, and responsibilities.

It did not, of course, keep him from reacting rather dangerously when his dignity was bruised by Edmund Yates's caricature of him in 1858. That episode may appear to give the lie to the portrait sketched here, but in spite of what the episode ultimately turned into, Thackeray's actions began as self-defence against what he saw as unprovoked attack. That, at least, is not antithetical to the view that Thackeray in Henry Esmond, was giving up mastery over his life rather than desperately trying to gain control of it.

Now the point of all that is this: The contexts we identify as relevant to the text we read determines our interpretation, and the interpretation that is adopted determines the text we establish or edit. If N. N. Feltes's interpretation is adopted, one chooses the first edition as copy-text and makes the reading text ape the result of the social contract that originally produced it. The emendations policy will be documentary and conservative.

If, however, John Sutherland's interpretation is adopted, one selects the manuscript (or possibly the first edition) and emends the text to conform as closely as possible to one's notion of Thackeray's intentions by correcting as many errors as possible and writing notes for all the rest to explain them away or de-emphasize any damage they might do to the reader's enjoyment of Thackeray's tour de force historical pastiche. And if Elaine Scarry's interpretation is adopted, one chooses the manuscript as copy-text and emends the text so that it effectively undermines the narrator's credibility, thus emphasizing Thackeray's rejection even of Esmond's attachment to personal truth. But if J. Hillis Miller's interpretation is adopted, there is no need to edit the text since his reading is untrammeled by information of any sort from Thackeray's life, the period in which he lived, the production institutions which enabled the book to become a book, or the genesis of the text.

If our goal is to read the text as a finished product, edited according to a "better way," then we must take a stand or abide by the editor's stand on answers to the following questions: To what extent was the author aware of and in control of the book's potential ironies? Did Thackeray intend to undermine Esmond's trust in personal truth, or did he share Esmond's view? Did Thackeray deliberately undercut Esmond's credibility by introducing obvious errors and memory lapses into Esmond's memoirs, or are the errors those of the novelist, Thackeray? To what extent did the production crew understand the author's intention and enhance or inhibit it?

These questions are to be answered by critical inquiry, not by ascertaining discoverable facts. This situation illustrates well what is critical about critical editing. But it also illustrates the way any single text edition of the book is capable of distorting it and hiding its possible meanings by privileging one context over others as the determiner of meaning. It does not take genius to see that an editorial approach to Esmond which sets about correcting errors may well be thwarting the author's intentional and meaningful introduction of those errors.

On the other hand, not to correct the errors also may thwart authorial intention. Only persons who regard their personal solutions to these imponderables as universally acceptable would say that editing can be done by anyone correctly. The economic, biographical, and rhetorical contexts in the cultural envelope where Esmond became a three-decker historical novel all influenced what that book became; but it is a gross oversimplification to conclude that the book became inevitably what it is through determining forces over which the author had no control.

A concept of the editorial task is not helped by the glittering generalities that suggest "the language [speaks the artist" or "the social complex employs authors to produce books" or "the author is dead." These conclusions are half-truths. Likewise, it does not help one to understand the business of editing if one concludes that the author is autonomous, the sole authority over text. That view tends to cast the editor in the role of rescuer and restorer. But the illustration just detailed demonstrates that it is impossible to say with any certainty what Thackeray is to be rescued from or what needs to be restored.

This brief survey of the complexities of Esmond's text seems to indicate that the author's communication to the reader is not only individual and free but constrained and directed by external forces. That is not a contradiction, nor is it a tragedy. It is a fact. Nothing understandable can be said or thought without the contextual frame of language and society and genre and custom and economic realities. But all establishments and power structures have within them the capacity to be satirized, subverted, criticized, and amended - that is to say, the author is free within the limits allowed by the medium.

The power of some texts is that their subsurface purposefully subverts the surface meanings. The question about the reader's and editor's dual responsibility to authorial intention and the social contract can be answered by saying they are both operative. It follows that a critical theory that ignores either is a lopsided theory, and it also follows that an editorial practice that edits away the evidence of either is equally lopsided.

The concept of editions which emphasize the importance of process and avoid extravagant claims for the correctness of the product is gaining ground, but not without resistance - resistance stemming from editors who are reluctant to give up power over the texts, from critics who want a stable text, and from publishers who, market driven, wish to save expense.

Editions such as Hans Gabler's of Ulysses, Michael Warren's of King Lear, and the Garland Thackeray edition are attempts in different ways to emphasize alternative texts, or multiple texts, or indeterminate texts, but all these editions are controversial.

Resistance to them in preference for editions with supposedly unproblematic, stabilized texts accounts for the polemics of textual theory. Any single solution requires commitment to one of several orientations toward texts which are mutually exclusive. At that level there is considerable debate among editors about the right way to edit or the right goal or end product to present as the established text.

The alternative to a single text solution represents not an extension of polemic but a resolution. It represents a more comprehensive view of textual criticism, which, though probably not stable, at least does not stagger distractedly from one polemic to another. What then is the function of a scholarly edition? In the Garland edition of Vanity Fair, the famous last paragraph of chapter 32, in which Jos takes flight and the war is brought to a close, reads: "No more firing was heard at Brussels - the pursuit rolled miles away. The darkness came down on the field and city, and Amelia was praying for George, who was lying on his face, dead, with a bullet through his heart."

The effect is both thrilling and chilling, and even first readers of this passage as it appears here can feel the tear of opposing passions as the pleasure of seeing George dead combats the sorrow for sudden death and for poor Amelia, while at the same time the reader feels she is a sap for turning on the ever-ready waterworks for what one already knows is a "selfish humbug", a "low-bred cockney-dandy," and "padded booby," though Becky does not provide these words to describe George till chapter 67.

First-time readers will also, no doubt, sense the clean, crisp, efficient, and flat (i.e., nonpejorative, nonheroic) diction which gives the account its force and gives free play to the reader's conflicting feelings. If readers were inclined to contemplate the passage, they might note that the phrase "The darkness came down" probably means primarily that night fell, but it allows the potential reverberations of the thought that "the darkness" has ominous symbolic overtones.

There is little to encourage such a speculation, however, except the juxtaposition of Amelia's own sorrow - which one can only partially share - and perhaps a twentieth-century propensity to see symbols everywhere. Should these readers turn to the "Record of Composition and Revision" in the Garland edition, they will find that the printed text reflects the reading of the first edition (1847) and that in 1853 someone (it is not entirely definite that it was Thackeray) revised the phrase to "Darkness came down."

Now, if the revised reading had been in the text in the first place, the sense of potential ominous symbolic overtones to the descent of "Darkness" (now fortuitously capitalized) might have struck readers more forcibly. Some might say, because this reading is "stronger," it should have been chosen for the Garland edition. It was not chosen because such aesthetic judgments were not part of the editorial strategy. To choose readings that correspond with the historical integrity of Thackeray's text at the time of first publication is not to reject the 1853 revisions. The point is not which of these readings is the correct one. The fact is that no one knows if either is correct or if both are correct.

The point is that in a scholarly edition both are available and have their various effects on the reading of Vanity Fair. Having read "The darkness came down," readers then find that a change was made to "Darkness came down."

Either reading, by itself, conveys the fall of night, or both reveal the potential for a symbolic reading, the revised reading perhaps more so. But discovering that the reading was revised is the strongest indication that something was being attempted here beyond indication that night fell. The changing itself is a stronger indication of meaning than either phrase is alone.

That is a crucial point in understanding the importance of a scholarly edition. The aim of the editorial work should not be to produce a pristine, correct, reliable text, a product. It should instead be to trace the growth and development of the work and to place the reading text in its developing context, a process. The effect is lost on readers who insist on reading the text as product, but the potential is there for serious, sensitive reading directed in part by reaction to what the author did - as opposed just to what the author said.

This paragraph from Vanity Fair reveals a flaw in the Garland edition. The edition fails to include a parallel account of George's death from a letter Thackeray wrote to his mother who had complained about Amelia s selfishness. Thackeray's response is pretty well known, but it all should have been quoted in the edition, including his anticipation of the time two months ahead when Amelia's "scoundrel of a husband is well dead with a ball in his odious bowels".

With that highly inflammatory and emotionally laden phrase ringing in one's ears, one cannot read the printed passage in the book without trying to account for the clean, flat, efficient diction found there in terms of Thackeray's narrative strategies and, perhaps, the demands of serial publication.

Scholarly editions should encourage and make possible such intertextual readings. The richness and satisfaction of such reading complexities go up when the countertexts are understood for what they are: parallel texts in letters, revisions in manuscripts, or alternative printed texts emanating either from revision or from compositorial or editorial intervention.

The sources and relative dates of countertexts have a great deal to do with a reader's assessment of their significance. It seems, then, that the duty of a scholarly edition is not arbitrarily (and stealthily) to reduce the complexity and richness of a work of art to one correct and established standard text, but rather to lay out the materials as clearly and usefully as possible.

Chapter 3

Thackeray's Illustrations For Vanity Fair

Thackeray, who intended his illustrations to be an integral part of the novel, filled it with drawings. The first letter of every chapter is incorporated into a drawing; almost every chapter includes a full-page drawing with an inscription at the bottom and one or more drawings of various sizes.The drawings supplement or complement the text in various ways. He was not entirely pleased with the final result in print.

Firstly, he regarded them as "tenth or twentieth rate performances having a meaning perhaps but a ludicrous bad news of execution." Secondly, the methods of reproducing graphics in the nineteenth century tended to produce less accurate renderings than modern methods. I have included several drawings to illustrate some of the ways that they contribute to the meaning of the novel.

EXAMPLE 1

Thackeray's drawing of himself holding a mask and a fool's scepter is relevant to the discussion of the narrator: is Thackeray to be equated with the narrator and the narrator's views, or is Thackeray the deliberate creator of a persona whom we call the narrator? Does the mask suggest the possibility of changing guises or identities? (A poor copy of this drawing appears on the title page of your text.)

EXAMPLE 2

The meaning of the initial drawing for Chapter 4 is

obvious; Becky is angling for a fat fish, Jos. There is irony in the fact that Jos, who distinguishes himself by how much he eats and drinks, is himself in danger of being caught and eaten by Becky. Continuing the fish metaphor, Mr. Sedley tells his wife, "But mark my words, the first woman who fishes for him, hooks him".

Besides flattering Jos with references to his knowledge of foods, Becky lures Jos by knitting a green purse, the purse symbolizing money and the green perhaps suggesting Becky's envy of the Sedley's affluence;

She shyly implies that she is making it for him. Though Becky is in a natural setting in the drawing, Thackeray's emphasis on society is maintained by the buildings in the background.

EXAMPLE 3

The initial drawing for Chapter 5 deflates the "epic" fight between Cuff and Dobbin. The boys carry wooden swords, wear paper hats, and Cuff rides a rocking horse. Interestingly, in a novel which deals with the Battle of Waterloo, a watershed in European history, their fight is one of the most violent actions presented.

EXAMPLE 4

Some drawings are less flattering to Becky than the text is. The drawing which most affects our view of Becky represents Becky as Clytemnestra at the end of the book. I will discuss it after you have finished the novel. The point I am making can readily be seen in the drawing of Becky using the dolls as puppets to mimic Miss Pinkerton and her sister. Note Becky's malicious expression.

The posture and dress of the men is somewhat disreputable. Does the picture also suggest why, as an adult, she gets along so well with men? why the Bohemian life appeals to her? and why she enjoys being with people?

EXAMPLE 5

Thackeray uses a drawing to support the reason he offers

for using contemporary dress for his characters, even though the novel is set a generation earlier, when styles were quite different:

It was the author's intention, faithful to history, to depict all the characters of this tale in their proper costume, as they wore them at the commencement of this century.

But when I remember the appearance of people in those days, and that an officer and lady were actually habited like this I have not the heart to disfigure my heroes and heroines by costumes so hideous; and have, on the contrary, engaged a model of rank dressed according to the present fashion.

Chapter 4

Thackeray's Attitude Toward Women

I have listed a number of passages about the role of women in Vanity Fair, for you to consider in deciding what Thackeray's attitude is, toward women in general and toward Amelia in particular, who fits the stereotypical image of woman and of the Angel in the House.

PASSAGE 1

The narrator is discussing the jealousy and condescending attitude of women toward Amelia, who is greatly admired by men. He also discusses the intimidating treatment she receives from the Miss Osbournes and their governess Miss Wirt, who wonder what George sees in her.

How is this? some carping reader exclaims. How is it that Amelia, who had such a number of friends at school, and was so beloved there, comes out into the world and is spurned by her discriminating sex.

My dear sir, there were no men at Miss Pinkerton's establishment except the old dancing-master; and you would not have had the girls fall out about him? When George, their handsome brother, ran off directly after breakfast, and drifted from home half-a-dozen times a week, no wonder the neglected sisters felt a little vexation.

When young Bullock, who had been making up to Miss Maria the last two season, actually asked Amelia to dance the cotillion, could you expect that the former young lady should be pleased?

PASSAGE 2

The narrator is describing the early days of Becky's marriage and her successful efforts in pleasing Rawdon and hiding her opinion of his abilities. What is Thackeray's attitude toward the women's hypocrisy? How does this passage apply to Becky and to Amelia as wives?

The best of women (I have heard my grandmother say) are hypocrites. We don't know how much they hide from us: how watchful they are when they seem most artless and confidential: how often those frank smiles which they wear so easily, are traps to cajole or elude or disarm I don't mean in your mere coquettes, but your domestic models, and paragons of female virtue. Who has not seen a woman hide the dulness of a stupid husband, or coax the fury of a savage one? We accept this amiable slavishness, and praise a woman for it: we call this pretty treachery truth. A good housewife is of necessity a humbug; and Cornelia's husband was hoodwinked, as Potiphar was only in a different way.

PASSAGE 3

The narrator is referring to Miss Briggs and Miss Crawley's abusive treatment of her, all which attacks the poor companion bore with meekness, with cowardice, with a resignation that was half generous and half hypocritical with the slaving submission, in a word, that women of her disposition and station are compelled to show. Who has not seen how women bully women? What tortures have men to endure, comparable to those daily repeated shafts of scorn and cruelty with which poor women are riddled by the tyrants of their sex? Poor victims!

PASSAGE 4

Amelia has been blaming herself for selfishness in not giving up Georgy to his grandfather and thereby denying him an education, pleasures, and luxuries. The narrator comments:

I know few things more affecting than that timorous debasement and self-humiliation of a woman. How she owns that it is she and not the man who is guilty; how she takes all the faults on her side; how she courts in a manner punishment for the wrongs which she has not committed and persists in shielding the real culprit. It is those who injure women who get the most kindness from them they are born timid and tyrants and maltreat those who are humblest before them.

PASSAGE 5

Amelia's grief is submerged or lessened by her nursing her dying mother. The illness of that old lady had been the occupation and perhaps the safeguard of Amelia. What do men know about women's martyrdoms? We should go mad had we to endure the hundredth part of those daily pains which are meekly borne by many women. Ceaseless slavery meeting with no reward; constant gentleness and kindness met by cruelty as constant; love, labour, patience, watchfulness, without even so much as the acknowledgment of a good word; all this, how many of them have to bear in quiet, and appear abroad with cheerful faces as if they felt nothing. Tender slaves that they are, they must needs be hypocrites and weak.

PASSAGE 6

Amelia accepts money from Osbourne, after giving up Georgy to his wealth. The narrator comments on her lack of pride, which stems from her being naturally simple and needing protection, her suffering, poverty, humility and privations since her marriage. Many women similarly sacrifice themselves. O you poor secret martyrs and victims, whose life is a torture, who are stretched on racks in your bedrooms, and who lay your heads down on the block daily at the drawing-room table; every man who watches your pains, or peers into those dark places where the torture is administered to you, must pity you and and thank God that he has a beard.... if you properly tyrannize over a woman, you will find a h'p'orth of kindness act upon her and bring tears into her eyes, as though you were an angel benefiting her.

PASSAGE 7

The narrator describes Amelia's routine of watching for

Georgy and tending the sickbed, to suffer the harassment and tyranny of querulous disappointed old age. How many thousands of people are there, women for the most part, who are doomed to endure this long slavery? who are hospital nurses without wages sisters of Charity, if you like, without the romance and the sentiment of sacrifice who strive, fast, watch, and suffer, unpitied, and fade away ignobly and unknown.

The hidden and awful Wisdom which apportions the destinies of mankind is pleased so to humiliate and cast down the gender, good, and wise, and to set up the selfish, the foolish, or the wicked. Oh, be humble, my brother, in your prosperity! Be gentle with those who are less lucky, if not more deserving. Think, what right have you to be scornful, whose virtue is a deficiency of temptation, whose success may be a mere change, whose rank may be an ancestor's accident, whose prosperity is very likely a satire.

PASSAGE 8

The narrator describes Amelia's kindness to her father, her taking care of him, and her listening to the same stories over and over as "affectionate hypocrisy".

BECKY'S INNOCENCE

Intelligent and outrageous, self-reliant and alone, resourceful and courageous, meeting the world on its own terms and succeeding time and again, refusing to be defeated Becky engages us with her vitality and aliveness and arouses our admiration for her resilience. An unscrupulous trickster, a liar and a cheat, a schemer and manipulator, a swindler, a hypocrite, a betraying wife and friend, a callous mother, a gambler, and possibly a murderer Becky has her dark side which we (and Thackeray?) have to come to terms with. Who is Becky Sharp? How finally are we to feel about her and to think about her? If our feelings and our reason produce contradictory responses, how do we reconcile them?

BECKY AND LORD STEYNE

Becky's innocence becomes a major issue in the novel

when Rawdon discovers her alone with Lord Steyne. A great deal of planning goes into making Steyne's tete-a-tete with Becky possible; her son is placed in a boarding school, Miss Briggs is sent to Steyne's country house, and Rawdon is arrested for debt. Her indifference to his welfare becomes clear to Rawdon when he receives her letter beautiful in appearance (pink paper, light green seal, highly scented), heartless and superficial in content. Rawdon's suspicions of Becky are reawakened and he is desperate to be released.

His suspicions are confirmed when he finds Steyne and Becky alone. Becky, frightened, cries, "I am innocent, Rawdon" (. Is it significant that the snake image appears at this point, her hands being covered with "serpents, and rings, and baubles"? Rawdon strikes Steyne twice, throwing him to the ground. Becky sees her husband in a new light: "She admired her husband, strong, brave, and victorious".

Thackeray was enormously proud of this detail: "When I wrote the sentence, I slapped my fist on the table, and said, 'that is a touch of genius!'" Why does she have this response when all her plans and her success are destroyed at the moment of achievement? Does she perhaps get some satisfaction in seeing the powerful, wealthy Steyne humiliated, in seeing the man who repeatedly sneered at her and held the power to fulfill her social ambitions powerless? Or is Thackeray being ironic?

Steyne vehemently denies her innocence; he has spent thousands of pounds on her. Does this necessarily mean they have slept together? Would Steyne have waited years and spent thousands of pounds without some sexual return from Becky? Did he enjoy her company enough, did she interest him enough and was she clever enough so that he waited?

If they have been lovers, why go to all the bother of setting up this evening for them to be alone and to get her son and Miss Briggs out of the house? Is Steyne's word about her guilt necessarily accurate? He erroneously accuses Rawdon of being part of a scheme to shake him down. And does Steyne live in a world and have a view of life in which innocence is possible?

Even if she has not physically betrayed Rawdon, are there

other kinds of betrayal that she might be guilty of? Did she intend to sleep with Steyne? Would an unfulfilled intention make her guilty? Christ taught that a man who lusts in his heart after a woman is guilty of adultery. Does this moral principle apply to Becky?

A similar question arises in her flirtation with George at Brussels. When Amelia accuses Becky of trying to take George away from her and of being a false friend, Becky protests, "I have done my husband no wrong". So far as physical infidelity goes, Becky is accurate; that she intends to run off with George, who is poor and whom she holds in contempt, is unlikely. Is she stringing him along so that Rawdon can fleece him gambling? Amelia raises a different offense, betrayal of friendship, "Have you done me no wrong, Rebecca? You did not succeed, but you tried. Ask your heart if you did not" (. Is Rebecca guilty of this offense? If so, is it serious moral and/or emotional offense?

Has she betrayed Rawdon's trust and love? When he discovers the money she has squirreled away in the desk Amelia gave her in friendship (an irony?), he says, "You might have spared me a hundred pounds, Becky, out of all this I have always shared with you". Rawdon refuses a reconciliation, "If she's not guilty, Pitt, she's as bad as guilty, and I'll never see her again never". How can Becky be not guilty but "as good as guilty"? Is Rawdon judging morally or emotionally? Is Rawdon qualified to cast moral stones at Becky, in view of his accepting the governorship which Steyne got him because of Becky? Thackeray leaves the question the question of her innocence open:

What had happened? Was she guilty or not? She said not, but who could tell what was truth which came from those lips, or if that corrupt heart was in this case pure? All her lies and her schemes, all her selfishness and her wiles, all her wit and genius had come to this bankruptcy.

Society's judgment of her guilt is unreliable, because it is not based on the facts or concern for the truth but on rumor, a priori assumptions, and corrupt values: "Was she guilty or not? We all know how charitable the world is, and how the verdict for Vanity Fair goes when there is a doubt". Should much meaning be attached to a comment Thackeray dryly makes when Becky sees Steyne and other people she remembered from "happier days, when she was not innocent but not found out".

BECKY'S INNOCENCE AND THE SERVANTS

Previous to Rawdon's confrontation with Steyne, the servants had judged her guilty, "the awful kitchen inquisition which sits in judgment in every house and knows everything" (. Later in this passage, Thackeray explains that Lord Steyne's visits reassured the servants and Raffles into giving Becky credit. Are servants in a position to know what is happening in a household? are they likely to know their employer's secrets? The reliability of their knowledge is called into question. The narrator warns employers, "If you are not guilty, have a care of appearances, which are as ruinous as guilt". Of Becky specifically, he comments that she was "guiltless very likely".

THE GENTLEMAN AND THE LADY

A concern in Thackeray's writing, as in the writing of many other middle-class Victorian novelists, is the question of who and what a gentleman is. The traditional concept of a gentleman is a man of family and fortune who does not work; it is a class-based concept which excluded most middle class men.

Having in mind this definition, Thackeray said that it took three generations to make a gentleman. The middle classes, which were growing in number, wealth, and power, did not want to wait to be accepted as gentlemen. To make the concept of the gentleman more inclusive, writers identified character and moral values as the criteria for recognizing a gentleman. Thackeray uses both concepts of the gentleman in Vanity Fair. He uses the older definition ironically in connection with characters like Lord Steyne and Sir Pitt Crawley, the father; the new definition is applied to the honorable and honest William Dobbin.

THE GENTLEMAN AS MAN OF FAMILY AND WEALTH

Fashionable society accepts Lord Steyne as indisputably a gentleman even though his immoral lifestyle is notorious. Despite his open womanizing and other vices, his "distinguished courtesy" toward his wife in public "caused the severest critics to admit how perfect a gentleman he was, and to own that his Lordship's heart at least was in the right place". Appearance and status are what matter in determining who is a gentleman, not character or virtue or the whole life of a man.

In private, where society cannot see or hear his treatment of his wife or other female dependents, Steyne is heartless or ungentlemanly. He savagely abuses his wife, Lady Steyne, and daughter-in-law, Lady Gaunt, verbally to force them to invite Becky to their home.

Moreover, "To see his wife and daughter suffering always put his Lordship into a good humour". To emphasize the irony, Thackeray uses Steyne's title, "his lordship." When Lady Gaunt defies him to strike her, he replies, "I am a gentleman, and never lay my hand upon a woman, save in the way of kindness".

He is brutal in his advice to Becky, when she reveals that she has cheated Miss Briggs out of her money and ruined her financially: "'Ruined her? Then why don't you turn her out?' the gentleman asked". In both of these incidents, the term "gentleman" is used ironically for satiric purpose; Steyne is simultaneousl and ironically a sadistic brute and a perfect gentleman. This concept of the gentleman contrasts with the newer one Thackeray espouses.

THE GENTLEMAN AS MAN OF CHARACTER AND VIRTUE

Thackeray explicitly identifies what the true gentleman is and who of his characters is a true gentleman. On the one hand, his concept democratizes the concept of the gentleman because a man of any class who has the requisite character and integrity could be a gentleman. On the other hand,

Thackeray sets such a high standard for the gentleman that very few men actually fit his definition of true gentlemen, though there are many who regard themselves and are regarded as gentlemen using the standards of Vanity Fair. Thackeray distinguishes between the few true gentlemen and the more numerous group whose claim to being gentlemen is based on externals, not ideals:

> Perhaps these are rarer personages than some of us think for. Which of us can point out many such in his circle men whose aims are generous, whose truth is constant, and not only constant in its kind but elevated in its degree; whose want of meanness makes them simple; who can look the world honestly in the face with an equal manly sympathy for the great and the small?
>
> We all know a hundred whose coats are very well made, and a score who have excellent manners, and one or two happy beings who are what they call in the inner circles and have shot into the very centre and bull's-eye of the fashion; but of gentlemen how many? Let us take a little scrap of paper and each make out his list.
>
> My friend the Major I write, without any doubt, in mine. He had very long legs, a yellow face, and a slight lisp, which at first was rather ridiculous. But his thoughts were just, his brains were fairly good, his life was honest and pure, and his heart warm and humble.

THE NEW CONCEPT OF THE GENTLEMAN CORRUPTED

The new concept of the gentleman can degenerate into the recognition of appearance, position, wealth, and a conformity to decorum. Sir Pitt Crawley, the son, is the model of the prig who places money and advancement before generosity, honour, and kindness. He is able to listen to Rawdon's request for help and sympathize with him after Rawdon assures him he is not asking for money.

On this occasion, Thackeray describes Sir Pitt, ironically, as "a real old English gentleman, in a word a model of neatness and every propriety". He is wearing a starched cravat with his dressing gown! Mr. Osborne, made brutal and self-righteous by egotism and pride of success, represents the middle class capitalist who sees the world in terms of money, judges people by their wealth, and uses his children to fulfill his social ambitions and enhance his sense of self-worth.

He raises his son to be a gentleman and not surprisingly turns out a self-centered, self-satisfied, superficial snob. He is in the process of ruining his grandson with extravagant indulgence.

Ironically the chapter which describes Georgy's life in the Osborne mansion is titled "Georgy is Made a Gentleman"; in reality, his crass, ignorant grandfather is making Georgy less of a gentleman than he starts out as by encouraging his self-importance and by not providing boundaries to guide him. Fortunately Georgy is redeemable.

It is true that he has been indulged by his mother, that his egotism has been fostered by her idolizing him, and that he is being turned into his father even by her. Nevertheless he has benefitted morally and emotionally by being raised by a true lady who has many excellent qualities; he is, after all, the recipient of her love, kindness, humility, selflessness, and tenderness.

Obnoxious as Georgy can be, he nevertheless has sterling qualities, as shown by his generosity to and tender feeling for the beggar boy whom he gives money to before his attendant can chase the boy away. Circumstance favors his being saved from his father's character with the elder Osborne's death and the guidance of Dobbin, whose sterling nature George is gentleman enough to perceive.

LADY REDEFINED

Redefining the gentleman requires redefining the lady, so that the lady, too, is no longer a class-based concept. Like the gentleman, the lady must have character and be virtuous, though the nature of her character and her specific virtues differ from those of the gentleman. Amelia exemplifies the true lady for Thackeray, in a passage discussing her raising Georgy:

He had been brought up by a kind, weak, and tender

woman, who had no pride about anything but about him, and whose heart was so pure and whose bearing so meek and humble that she could not but needs be a true lady. She busied herself in gentle offices and quiet duties; if she never said brilliant things,

She never spoke or thought unkind ones; guileless and artless, loving and pure, indeed how could our poor little Amelia be other than a real gentlewoman!" Lady Steyne, suffering, pure, and passive, is a true lady; Lady Jane Sheepshanks, who develops more depth and character as the novel progresses, comes to be another true lady.

THE NEW CONCEPT OF THE LADY CORRUPTED

The new concept of the lady, like that of the gentleman, can degenerate into the recognition of appearance, position, wealth, and a conformity to decorum. As Amelia exemplifies the new true lady, so Becky expresses the corrupted concept of a lady, a concept whose criteria would be easier to meet and would undoubtedly be more widely acceptable:

"It isn't difficult to be a country gentleman's wife," Rebecca thought. "I think I could be a good woman if I had five thousand a year. I could dawdle about in the nursery and count the apricots on the wall. I could water plants in a green-house and pick off dead leaves from the geraniums. I could ask old women about their rheumatisms and order half-a-crown's worth of soup for the poor.

I shouldn't miss it much, out of five thousand a year. I could even drive out ten miles to dine at a neighbor's, and dress in the fashions of the year before last. I could go to church and keep awake in the great family pew, or go to sleep behind the curtains, with my veil down, if I only had practice. I could pay everybody, if I had but the money.

This is what the conjurors here pride themselves upon doing. They look down with pity upon us miserable sinners who have none. They think themselves generous if they give our children a five-pound note, and us contemptible if we are without one".

Becky's idea of a lady is based on externals money, clothes, and socially-acceptable behaviour, without the virtues and character which should motivate that behaviour.

The satire is clear. But Thackeray introduces ambiguity by wondering in the rest of this paragraph whether Becky is right: And who knows but Rebecca was right in her speculations and that it was only a question of money and fortune which made the difference between her and an honest woman?

If you take temptations into account, who is to say that he is better than his neighbour? A comfortable career of prosperity, if it does not make people honest, at least keeps them so. An alderman coming from a turtle feast will not step out of his carriage to steal a leg of mutton; but put him to starve, and see if he will not purloin a loaf.

Is this Thackeray speaking or a narrator, a persona who is not expressing Thackeray's view? Is Thackeray expressing a pessimistic view about human nature and our capacity for goodness and honesty? The small number of gentlemen would be explained by such a view. Or is he challenging the smug, reasuring belief his readers may hold of their own righteousness? This passage upset many contemporaries, because it assumes that honesty comes from self-interest and sufficient wealth not to be tempted rather than innate goodness. Thackeray justified this passage to G.H. Lewes, who was offended by it:

I am quite aware of the dismal roguery wh goes all through the Vanity Fair story and God forbid that the world should be like it altogether: though I fear it is more like it than we like to own. But my object is to make every body engaged, engaged in the pursuit of Vanity and I must carry my story through in this dreary minor key, with only occasional hints here and there of better things of better things wh it does not become me to preach.

Thackeray felt some unease with the role of moralist and preacher because he seldom lost sight of his own flawed nature and regrettable past actions. He had personally experienced Becky's view and feelings. In 1839, when he was facing poverty after the loss of his inheritance, he wrote his mother about a wealthy "good, sobre, and religious" friend, "a fine English squire"; he added that "if I had 3,000 a year I think I'd be so too."

THE NARRATOR, THE READER, AND AMBIGUITY IN VANITY FAIR

Thackeray's contemporaries equated Thackeray with the narrator, whom they saw as omniscient; as a result, they often missed the irony, read Thackeray's satire as his actual beliefs, and attacked him for cynicism and worse. A more careful reading of the novel indicates that the narrator is not consistently or even mainly omniscient. His character constantly shifts to fallibility, to ignorance, and even to incomprehension.

His identity changes too. He is the stage manager, introduced in "Before the Curtain"; even in this guise, his role shifts from directing the performance, to controlling the actions of the characters or puppets, as he calls them, to helplessly watching them do as they wish. (So, even when Thackeray adopts the guise of the stage manager, questions arise; is he the creator of the story, the teller, or a hapless observer?)

He metamorphoses into critic, clown, satirist, commentator, preacher, reporter, and participant. His situation changes, for example, from being married to being single, from having no children to having children. His relationship to the characters shifts from being a friend to being a hostile judge. His attitude too undergoes breathtaking transformations, being by turns wise, sentimental, worldly, cynical, amused, sad, inane, smug, and pleased at showing the characters up.

This shifting in the narrator has led some readers to accuse Thackeray of being inconsistent. This is a serious charge and would be a major flaw in any novel. The charge implies that Thackeray lacked the skill to create a consistent narrator, that he was too careless to create a consistent narrator, or that he was too intellectually lacking to be aware of the narrator's inconsistency (Thomas Carlyle, for instance, questioned Thackeray's capacity for serious thought).

The charge of inconsistency is particularly serious because

of the pervasive presence of the narrator; he is everywhere with his comments and his reactions and even appears as a character who has met Amelia and Dobbin.

We see the characters through his eyes and know them through his words, though Thackeray also presents myriad other voices and views. For these reasons, the narrator is a major source of the ambiguity or difficulty in determining Thackeray's intention and meaning throughout the novel. When are the narrator's comments and attitudes ironic? when are they to be taken literally? and when or how often do they express Thackeray's attitudes and values?

Not everyone concedes that Thackeray is unintentionally inconsistent. If the narrator is seen as a fictional persona, then he does not necessarily speak for or as Thackeray. He becomes one more character, different in kind and in function from the other characters, certainly, but a character nonetheless. Therefore, Thackeray is free to manipulate him to achieve particular effects at different points in the novel. Viewing the narrator as a persona raises another set of considerations and assessments. Are the narrator's shifts justified by achieving special effects, or are they confusing? Do they, in other words, add to or detract from the novel?

The views of critics differ significantly on these issues, as the following sampling of opinions suggests:

E.D.H. Johnson attributes the shifts in the narrator to Thackeray's ambiguous relationship to his world. Johnson believes that Thackeray had difficulty in combining his satiric bent and his moral purpose, a difficulty which resulted in confused aims:

> The curious alternations of attraction and repulsion manifest in Thackeray's handling of Becky and Amelia characterize his attitude towards the entire world of the novel. As a satirist, he castigates the manners and morals of that world; as a moralist, he is more taken in by its standards than he is presumably aware. Unlike Fielding, he was never able artistically to harmonize his twin purposes, because again unlike Fielding he lacked any compelling vision of forces making for unity and poise within the social organism.

Johnson explains that the eighteenth-century Henry Fielding lived in a stable society with intact institutions underpinned by a robust religious faith. But in Thackeray's society, religion was losing its authority. In Johnson's view, one result of this loss was that love as a generalized form of brotherhood and charity no longer held society together but existed only as a bond between individuals.

Arnold Kettle, on the other hand, attributes the difficulty in determining Thackeray's intention and views to his cowardice, "from a desire to expose illusions and yet keep them." Harold Bloom calls Thackeray's narrator "that supreme fiction" and sees the point of view as one of the strengths of the novel. Many readers see the narrative shifts as part of Thackeray's subtlety, a device whereby he indicates the difficulty, if not the impossibility of arriving at the whole truth. If determining the truth is problematic, then making judgments becomes an issue; in this view, the narrator's shifts challenge our right to judge since we are all corrupted, in some way and to some degree.

Kathleen Tillotson believes that the narrator's commentary serves other purposes. It bridges past and present. Furthermore, Without Thackeray's own voice, the melancholy and the compassion of his attitude to Vanity Fair might escape us. It is needed merely as relief, from a spectacle that might otherwise be unbearably painful. And not only morally painful, but mentally impoverished. The characters, the best as well as the worst, are almost without ideas; the intellectual atmosphere of the novel is provided by the commentary.

By presenting the narrator's comments and reactions as well as the characters' feelings and reactions, Thackeray gives the novel a richer, more complex, and subtle texture. Juliet McMaster believes that the narrator's commentary, which she calls alternately inane, snug, cloying, or cynical, forces the reader to react, thereby giving the characters a kind of life and making them feel like autonomous beings. You will have to decide these issues for yourself based on your reading and understanding of the novel.

Chapter 5

The Narrator and the Reader in Vanity Fair

Just as the narrator's identity shifts, so does the reader's identity. The narrator addresses a succession of different readers e.g., a supercilious clubman, a lady, women in general, "you" to whom he attributes specific attitudes and whom he characterizes as behaving in certain ways. Behind these fictional readers there are the actual readers of the novel. What do you see as the functions of the fictional readers addressed by the narrator? And what is the relationship between the fictional readers and the actual readers, that is, between them and you?

For example, do they create a bond between you, the actual reader, and the narrator? or a bond between you, the actual reader, and the characters? Are your feelings and your judgment about the characters, their actions, and their world affected by Thackeray's use of fictional readers? When Thackeray addresses "you," is he addressing the actual reader, or is the "you" a fictional persona? or is the identity of "you" sometimes the actual reader and sometimes a fictional persona?

THE TECHNIQUE AND STYLE IN VANITY FAIR

The story is presented by summarized narrative, bits of drama, interpolated essays, without much recourse to the minds of the characters. If there is any doubt as to how the reader should judge an individual, the author steps in and makes appropriate comment. For example, when the Sedleys lose their money, the chief critic and enemy is old Osborne, whom Sedley has started in business. Thackeray comments on the psychology of old Osborne's attitude:

When one man has been under very remarkable obligations to another, with whom he subsequently quarrels, a common sense of decency, as it were, makes of the former a much severer enemy than a mere stranger would be... a persecutor is bound to show that the fallen man is a villain otherwise he, the persecutor, is a wretch himself.

Here is an example of dramatic presentation. Amelia visits Becky to find out if she can help her. Becky has hidden her brandy bottle in the bed, and is putting forth every effort to engage Amelia's sympathy by way of little Rawdon:

"My agonies," Becky continued, "were terrible (I hope she won't sit down on the bottle) when they took him away from me I thought I should die; but I fortunately had a brain fever, during which my doctor gave me up, and and I recovered, and and here I am, poor and friendless."

"How old is he?" Emmy asked.

"Eleven," said Becky.

"Eleven!" cried the other. "Why, he was born the same year with George who is "

"I know, I know," Becky cried out, who had in fact quite forgotten all about little Rawdon's age. "Grief has made me forget so many things, dearest Amelia. I am very much changed: half wild some times. He was eleven when they took him away from me. Bless his sweet face, I have never seen it again."

"Was he fair or dark?" went on that absurd little Emmy. "Show me his hair."

Becky almost laughed at her simplicity...

Usually Thackeray just describes what happens. George and Becky are talking about how Becky can get next to Briggs, Miss Crawley's maid, and thereby see Miss Crawley and regain her favor for Rawdon. Becky says she will find out when Briggs goes to bathe; she will dive in under Briggs' awning and "insist on a reconciliation".

The idea amuses George, who bursts out laughing,

whereat Rawdon shouts at them to ask what the joke is. Thackeray does not say Amelia is jealous, he shows the reader what she does: "Amelia was making a fool of herself in an absurd hysterical manner, and retired to her own room to whimper in private."

Instead of showing, sometimes the author tells what the situation is. Of Sir Pitt's second wife, he says, "Her heart was dead long before her body. She had sold it to become Sir Pitt Crawley's wife. Mothers and daughters are making the same bargain every day in Vanity Fair." Although Thackeray claims to write about real people, at the close of the book, he says, "Come, children, let us shut up the box and the puppets, for our play is played out." Thackeray does write about real people; Amelia is drawn from Mrs. Thackeray. However, in the writing of a story, there is a transformation and adaptation which justifies also the figure of the manipulation of puppets.

The author calls his characters ironic or patronizing names such as "Our poor Emmy," or "Our darling Rebecca." The modern reader may think his writings full of clichés. One must remember, however, that Thackeray makes fun of just such patronizing expressions, and one cannot be sure that he uses such expressions seriously. Thackeray likes certain words such as "killing." Sometimes his punctuation seems old-fashioned, like his use of the colon instead of a period in sentences like: "William knew her feelings: had he not passed his whole life in divining them?"

Sentence structure ranges from a few words to a whole paragraph. The variety tends to make the story readable, slows the pace or quickens it; variation may come in the form of a question or direct address. Essay or narration alternates with dialogue and dramatic action. Because the story was written as a serial, Thackeray didn't have the whole manuscript in hand for completion and correction.

As a result the story rambles; essays have been inserted as padding; there is a certain amount of confusion in regard to names, places, and time. For example, Mrs. Bute Crawley is sometimes Martha, sometimes Barbara. Georgy sees Dobbin in London at a time when he is in Madras.

The reader has a complete picture of Joseph's visit with his father and Amelia, his reassurance as to their welfare. Then Amelia gets a letter from Jos saying he will be delayed he hasn't yet left Southampton. Whatever his faults in producing a sprawling, sometimes inaccurate manuscript, Thackeray has never missed a chance to point out the futility, the snobbery of Vanity Fair.

STRUCTURE OF VANITY FAIR

Thackeray's original title, Pen and Pencil Sketches of English Society, indicates his intention to describe a succession of social situations. As he was writing his novel, the idea of society as a Vanity Fair came to him, and he changed both his plan for the novel and the title.

Though the name Vanity Fair comes from John Bunyan's Pilgrim's Progress, Thackeray uses the concept in a very different way from Bunyan. For Bunyan, Vanity Fair comprises all the worldly activities which distract the Christian from salvation and lead to damnation; they are vanities for this reason. At risk is the Christian's immortal soul.

The phrase "vanity fair" came to mean "a place where all is frivolity and empty show; the world or a section of it as a scene of idle amusement and unsubstantial display". For Thackeray, everyone lives in Vanity Fair or society; vanity has become the desire for society's approval and rewards; the individual seeks, not spiritual salvation, but the rewards of this world success, status, and wealth.

The change from sketches about society to society as a vanity fair raises a major critical question; is the novel rambling and formless? To paraphrase the subtitle, is it a novel without a structure?

This issue was raised by contemporary reviewers. Robert Rintoul, who praised Thackeray's realism, saw the novel as episodic: "if putting Vanity Fair aside as a fiction of high art, we look at it as a series of bits from life, it is entitled to the first ranks as a set of sketches lifelike and natural".

Supporting this view is the time difference in the first half and the second half of the novel; the first half covers two years before Waterloo and is compact while the second half sprawls over the next twenty-five years.

Even if the novel lacks form, is that necessarily a serious flaw? The Victorians did not perceive structure and unity in a novel the same way as modern readers, who have been raised on James and Conrad and critical theories focusing on structure.

But is the perception that the novel lacks unity accurate?

Do major themes, like selfishness, give it form?

Do the parallel lives of Becky and Amelia structure the novel? They leave school together, to enter the world; their subsequent careers, which include marriage, motherhood, and financial struggles, intersect several times; the tender, loving, and passive Amelia contrasts with the ruthless, ambitious, and active Becky.

Is his portrayal of society, with its crippling, perverted values and its lovelessness, the centre which holds the novel together?

Does the narrator hold the novel together and structure it?

Is Vanity Fair a panoramic novel, i.e., a novel which presents a broad view of a society? Percy Lubbock uses Vanity Fair as an illustration of the panoramic novel; he says that Thackeray creates the impression of a world, a society, a time certain manners of life within a few square miles of London, a hundred years ago.

Thackeray flings together a crowd of the people he knows so well, and it matters not at all if the tie that holds them to each other is of the slightest... The light link is enough for the unity of his tale, for that unity does not depend on an intricately woven intrigue. It depends in truth upon one fact only, the fact that all his throng of men and women are strongly, picturesquely typical of the world from which they are taken that in all their different ways can add to the force of its effect.

The book is not the story of any of them, it is a story which they unite to tell, a chapter in the notorious career of well-to-do London. Exactly how the various "plots" evolve is not the main matter; behind them is the presence and the pressure of a greater interest, the mass of life which Thackeray packs into his novel.

THE PLOT OF VANITY FAIR

The plot appears complex because of the multitude of characters and because the stated motives are seldom the true ones. Moreover, the author digresses so often in essays on related subjects that the casual reader may lose the thread of the story. The story, however, is as modern as tomorrow the struggle to establish oneself in society.

Whereas the tale seems disjointed and diverse, it is held together by the one theme: the foibles and deceptions of the inhabitants of Vanity Fair. No matter how minor a character, Thackeray identifies that person perhaps by the significance of his name only as living or not living in Vanity Fair. This continuous focus on human nature in all aspects from motherhood to death, from poverty to prosperity, makes the plot both probable and unified.

The conflict is always man against man for the joys and advantages of Vanity Fair. There is little soul-searching. The reader does not often enter the minds of the characters. He watches what they do, he hears what the author tells about them, and then with some direct prompting from the author, judges them.

Any conflict with nature is conflict with human nature. Thackeray wishes to impress on the reader the futility of Vanity Fair but he does not underestimate its values either. He admits that roast beef is good, although it vanishes like all pleasures of Vanity Fair. He points out the duplicity, the dishonesty, the double crossing of human beings all under the guise of doing good, being neighborly, or saving souls; but actually the purpose is to get money or position or advantage.

Most of the characters bow down to wealth and position regardless of the persons who have them. This worship of false values makes it possible for Rebecca to climb to the top, and if she had possessed sufficient money she would not have fallen on account of the discovery of her affair with Lord Steyne. For, although citizens of Vanity Fair may have a low opinion of the morals of their leading personages, this scruple will not deter them from attending balls, dinners, or any affair where one may get a free meal or sit beside nobility.

SOCIETY

Like Austen in Emma, Thackeray identifies the place or status characters have in society and the nature of their relationship to society in Vanity Fair. Unlike Austen, who portrays the limited world of Highbury, Thackeray fills his novel with people, places, and travel.

Almost all his characters are individualized, no matter how briefly they appear. We know their attitudes, their values, their hypocrisies and pettiness, their class, their desires and feelings. Taken together they make up the society that Thackeray calls Vanity Fair.

His characters also satirize the institutions they serve or represent: Lord Steyne and Sir Pitt Crawley (both the father and the son) show up Parliament, the rotten election system, and the aristocracy; religion is satirized with the Rev.

Bute Crawley (the Church of England) and Mr. Pitt Crawley and Lady Southdown (Dissent); the army leadership is satirized with General Tufto; the Colonial and foreign service, with Joseph Sedley, Rawdon Crawley, Mr. Pitt Crawley, and Tapeworm; the financial system, with Osborne senior. One class, however, is excluded, the poor. In view of his characters' vitality and their representing major institutions, is it tenable to suggest that society is the real protagonist of Vanity Fair?

THE HERO

Even though Thackeray subtitles his novel A Novel Without a Hero, readers in Thackeray's day and in ours want a hero, and many assign the role to Dobbin. Does Thackeray in fact regard him as the hero of the novel or even as a hero? If you see Dobbin as the hero, then the subtitle and the narrator's references to the novel's having no hero are part of Thackeray's satire of novelistic conventions and manipulation of the unthinking or careless reader. Is there any doubt that George Osborne is used to satirize the conventional hero?

AMELIA

The question of whether the novel has a heroine is more complex. Amelia seems to be the conventional heroine sweet, passive, self-sacrificing, gentle, tender, and loving. And Thackeray calls her a heroine at times, but he contradicts himself at other times and says she is not a heroine (he also refers to Becky as a heroine and not a heroine). In addition, he repeatedly calls Amelia "weak" and "selfish." Of Dobbin's faithful love and decades-long submission to her, Thackeray wrote to a friend that finally "he will find her not worth having." Thackeray wrote his mother that

"My object is not to make a perfect character or anything like it. Don't you see how odious all the people are in the book (with the exception of Dobbin) behind whom all there lies a dark moral I hope. What I want is to make a set of people living without God in the world (only that is a cant phrase) greedy pompous mean perfectly self-satisfied for the most part and at ease about their superior virtue."

Does this judgment apply to Amelia? Does Thackeray admire her wholeheartedly or admire some of her traits and behaviour but not others? If she is not the heroine, is Thackeray using her to expose the selfishness of the conventional heroine?

BECKY

Becky has much more appeal than Amelia for most readers, as Thackeray acknowledged:

The famous little Becky Puppet has been pronounced to be uncommonly flexible in the joints, and lively on the wire; the Amelia Doll, though it has had a smaller circle of admirers, has yet been carved and dressed with the greatest care by the artist... (x).

Born with no advantages, in a society that values rank and wealth, Becky makes her way to the highest levels of society through her own resources, with determination, intelligence, hard work, and talent. She is resourceful and bounces back from every reversal. At the same time, her behaviour and character are morally indefensible; she constantly manipulates others, she lies, she cheats, she steals, she betrays Amelia, and perhaps she even commits a murder.

As the novel progresses, some readers feel that she becomes more dangerous and villainous. If so, was Thackeray upset that so many readers found her attractive? Does the change in her portrayal reflect ambivalence toward Becky? was he both attracted to her energy and courage and repelled by some of her actions, for instance? Or is the perception that her characterization changes false?

Dyson explains Becky's appeal in terms of the corrupt nature of society and her role in that society:

Surely we do admire Becky, and legitimately, however glad we are to be outside the range of her wiles? The fact is that she belongs to Vanity Fair, both as its true reflection, and as its victim; for both of which reasons, she very resoundingly serves it right.

Like Jonson's Volpone, she is a fitting scourge for the world which created her fitting aesthetically, in the way of poetic justice, and fittingly moral, in that much of her evil is effective only against those who share her taint. Dobbins is largely immune to her, since he is neither a trifler, a hypocrite nor a snob. The other characters are all vulnerable in one or other of these ways, and we notice that those who judge her most harshly are frequently the ones who have least earned such a right.

A question arises about Becky's innocence in the last portion of the novel. Specifically, is she innocent of adultery? and/or of murder? Thackeray offers a variety of opinions from self-interested and self-righteous observers, who range from the servants to the highest levels of fashionable society; the narrator's opinion remains ambiguous.

It is important to keep in mind that though what characters say about one another is significant, their judgments may reveal more about the speaker or society's values than about the person being discussed; the opinion offered may not be trustworthy. The question of Becky's personal innocence raises a larger question; how important or meaningful is the question of her innocence, in view of how universally corrupt society is and how selfish the people judging her are? Who in this society is innocent?

CHARACTER DEVELOPMENT

Do the characters change or develop in any significant way? or do we merely come to know them better as Thackeray reveals more details about them? Edwin Muir describes Thackeray's presentation of his characters as a gradual "unfolding in a continuously widening present"; the characters have the same weaknesses, vanities and foibles throughout, the only change being "our knowledge of them." The character who seems to change most is Rawdon Crawley, but how great is his change actually? If he does change significantly, are his love for Becky and his love for his son a sufficient, convincing reason for his change?

A REVIEW

In the novels of Thackeray, essay is so much mixed up with narrative, and comment with characterization, that they can hardly be thoroughly appreciated in poor editions. The temptation to skip is almost irresistible, when wisdom can be purchased only at the expense of eyesight. We are therefore glad to welcome the commencement of a new edition of his writings, over whose pages the reader can linger at his pleasure, and quietly enjoy the subtleties of humor and observation which in previous perusals he overlooked.

The present volumes, published by the Harpers, are among the most tasteful and comely products of the Cambridge University Press. Printed in large type of tinted paper, elegantly bound in green cloth and with a fac-simile of the author's autograph on the cover, every copy has the appearance of being a presentation copy.

No English edition of Vanity Fair is equal to this American one in respect either to convenience of form or beauty of mechanical execution. The illustrations are numerous, well engraved, and embody the writer's own conceptions of his scenes and characters, and are often deliciously humorous. Vanity Fair, though it does not include the whole extent of Thackeray's genius, is the most vigorous exhibition of its leading characteristics.

In freshness of feeling, elasticity of movement, and unity of aim, it is favorably distinguished from its successors, which too often give the impression of being composed of successive accumulations of incidents and persons, that drift into the story on no principle of artistic selection and combination. The style, while it has the raciness of individual peculiarity and the careless case of familiar gossip, is as clear, pure, and flexible as if its sentences had been subjected to repeated revision, and every pebble which obstructed its lucid and limpid flow had been laboriously removed.

The characterization is almost perfect of its kind. Becky Sharp, the Marquis of Steyne, Sir Pitt Crawley and the whole Crawley family, Amelia, the Osbornes, Major Dobbin, not to mention others, are as well known to most cultivated people as their most intimate acquaintances in the Vanity Fair of the actual world.

It has always seemed to us that Mr. Osborne, the father of George, a representation of the most hateful phase of English character, is one of the most vividly true and life-like of all the delineations in the book, and more of a typical personage than even Becky or the Marquis of Steyne. Thackeray's theory of characterization proceeds generally on the assumption that the acts of men and women are directed not by principle, but by instincts, selfish or amiable that toleration of human weakness is possible only by lowering the standard of human capacity and obligation and that the preliminary condition of an accurate knowledge of human character is distrust of ideals and repudiation of patterns.

This view is narrow, and by no means covers all the facts of history and human life, but what relative truth it has is splendidly illustrated in Vanity Fair. There is not a person in the book who excites the reader's respect, and not one who fails to excite his interest. The morbid quickness of the author's perceptions of the selfish element, even in his few amiable characters, is a constant source of surprise. The novel not only has no hero, but implies the non-existence of heroism.

Yet the fascination of the book is indisputable, and it is due to a variety of causes besides its mere exhibition of the worldly side of life. Among these, the perfect intellectual honesty of the writer, the sad or satirical sincerity with which he gives in his evidence against human nature, is the most prominent. With all his lightness of manner, he is essentially a witness under oath, and testifies only to what he is confident he knows.

Perhaps this quality, rare not only in novel writing, but in all writing, would not compensate for the limitation of his perceptions and the repulsiveness of much that he perceives, were it not for the peculiar charm of his representation. It is here that the individuality of the man appears, and it presents a combination of sentiments and powers more original perhaps than the matter of his works.

Take from Vanity Fair that special element of interest which comes from Thackeray's own nature, and it would lose the greater portion of its fascination. It is not so much what is done, as the way in which is is done, that surprises and delights; and the manner is always inimitable, even when the matter is common.

A MAN OF EXPERIENCE

It is perhaps easy to make too much of the tone with which stray remarks are written in casual correspondence, but it is interesting to note an apparent shift in Thackeray's self-portrayal in his letters to Chapman and Hall and Bradbury and Evans in the months following the appearance of The Irish Sketch-Book, on 15 May 1843, from Brighton, he wrote the former, "I came down here to be alone, and avoid good dinners and do some magazine work".

The letter is otherwise about reviews of, and advertisements for, the Irish book, In August, just before setting out on a tour of the Low Countries, he wrote Chapman and Hall again, lamenting briefly that an article he wrote for the Foreign Quarterly Review did not appear, asking for any money due to him, and devoting the bulk of his letter to proposing a German sketchbook:

I wish I could persuade you to think that Titmarsh in Germany devoting himself to the consideration of the fine arts there, and with a score or two of ballads to decorate the volumes, and plenty, of etchings and a great deal of [52/53] fantastical humour and much nurture of the poetical and the ludicrous - I say I wish you would think such a book popular, and offer me the same terms for it as the Irish book.

People (as I hope and trust) have only to become better acquainted with Titmarsh to like him more and the success of a German Sketch Book would help off very likely the few remaining copies of the Irish one. I am also in "the interesting situation" with respect to a novel: but I want to produce a very good one and a good work of art, and such a w[ork] demands a deal of time and thinking. original in possession of Peter Rhodes, Esq.; transcript supplied by Nicholas Pickwoad.

To Bradbury and Evans he wrote in February 1844:

I do not know whether you pay anything extra for great services (as all wise persons do) but I should not be surprised at hearing that any sum of money had been paid to my bankers as a reward for the astonishing late enclosed.

If you publish it again in a little book there will be a deal of extra profit for all of us.

In short, Thackeray now fancied himself primarily an author of books who also wrote for the magazines, and he now often thought of the potential book version of his magazine contributions. Though nothing ever came of the German sketchbook, it is interesting to note Thackeray's warning to the publisher that "such a work demands a deal of time and thinking" - this from the man who on 10 September 1841 signed a contract to deliver by the end of December a two-volume work which he had not even started.

The professional author had learned some things from the fact that serious work on the Irish book took four months of touring and writing in Ireland and four more months of writing, illustrating, and proofreading. His expenses from July 1842 to March 1843 (estimated by himself for an account to his mother and therefore, like Pendennis's accounts of college expenses, probably conservative) were £370, including £110 spent in Ireland.

His income, not counting the £120 advance that had long since been spent, came to £110 for magazine work and under £200 for the book, which seems to have sold fairly well. Although for the purpose of the account to his mother Thackeray counted the £120 advance and figured his income on the book to be near £300, he did have to admit that the "childrens' nest egg is broken in upon as you say". The pressure was clearly still on; and while a visible property was accumulating, Thackeray's fortune was still largely in the inkwell.

Another indication that Thackeray's sense of his profession and of his own position in it had come to a turning point after The Irish Sketch-Book and after agreeing with Fraser's for twelve installments of Barry Lyndon comes in a December 1843 letter of advice to his cousin Richard Bedingfield, who recently had published a book called The Miser's Son. It was advice which Thackeray clearly drew from his own experience and which was given as from one "old in the trade now."

I sent on Tuesday week last a very pressing note to Jerdan regarding the "Miser's Son," with a little notice which I myself had written so as to save him trouble. It was, I need not tell you a favourable one as the story deserved; it has a great deal of talent of a great number of kinds, and many a man has made a fortune with a tithe of the merit. But in spite of this, Jerdan has not inserted my article. Have you ever advertised in his paper or elsewhere? A laudatory paragraph here and there will do you no earthly good, unless the name of your book is perpetually before the public.

The best book I ever wrote I published with an unknown publisher, and we got off two hundred and fifty copies of it, and this was after the success of the Paris book, with some thirty pounds of advertisements, and hugely laudatory notices in a score of journals. Shakespeare himself would not get a hearing in Gray's Inn Lane.

Unless your publisher actually offers you money for a future work, I beg you to have nothing to do with him. Write short tales. Make a dash at all the magazines; and at one or two of them I can promise you, as I have said, not an acceptance of your articles, but a favourable hearing. It is, however, a bad trade at the best. The prizes in it are fewer and worse than in any other professional lottery; but I know it's useless damping a man who will be an author whether or no - men are doomed, as it were, to the calling.

Make up your mind to this, my dear fellow, that the "Miser's Son" will never succeed - not from want of merit, but from want of a publisher. Shut it up without delay, and turn to some work that will pay you. Eschew poetry above all (you've had too much of it), and read all the history you can. Don't mind this patriarchal tone from me. I'm old in the trade now, and have lived so much with all sorts of people in the world that I plume myself on my experience.

Bedingfield followed Thackeray's advice, but a new work eighteen months later fared no better than the first with Thackeray, who wrote, "I can suit the magazines (but I can't hit the public, be hanged to them), and, from my knowledge of the former, I should say you will never get a good sale for commodities like these... your system may be the right one and mine wrong, but I'm sure I'm right as to the state of the market" (Letters 2: 193).

In mid-1843 Thackeray's literary accounts stood thus: two substantial travel books (the Paris and Irish sketchbooks - the second an actual success); one collection of novellas and short stories (Comic Tales - not a success); three ephemeral pamphlets (Fiore et Zéphyr, An Essay on the Genius of George Cruikshank, and The Second Funeral of Napoleon - all of greater critical than financial note).

Catherine and The History of Samuel Titmarsh had been written with book publication in mind, but the former never got beyond magazine publication, and the latter was not published at all until after Vanity Fair. The odious magazine work was still the mainstay of his professional income.

Within three years he would be the author of Vanity Fair;

but for the present art criticism, travel, and observations on manners, dished out periodically, seemed his forte. The latter two veins of his genius would be extended in From Cornhill to Grand Cairo (1845-46) and "The Snobs of England" (1846-47). But at the same time Thackeray was gearing up for greater things. Catherine (1839) and Barry Lyndon (1844) develop the satiric fiction; A Shabby Genteel Story (1840), Samuel Titmarsh (1841), and A Legend of the Rhine (1845) develop the sentimental pathetic line. All these elements would find their way into Vanity Fair.

Though Thackeray had not produced a best-seller, he was steadily gaining attention. The Irish Sketch-Book was reprinted in America, the pirate being J. Winchester of New York. It became, in 1844, Thackeray's second American book, but like the first, it added nothing to Thackeray's coffers. The most substantial property to come front Thackeray's pen in the remaining months of 1843 was the serial form of Men's Wives by George Fitzboodle in Fraser's. And in January 1844 the first installment of Barry Lyndon under the same pseudonym appeared in the same magazine.

Though Men's Wives seems to have grown in response to favorable reactions to Fitzboodle's Confessions of late 1842, Barry Lyndon was a deliberate attempt to write a novel for eventual book publication. Despite the success of The Irish Sketch-Book, however, Wives and Lyndon both finally became books with no help from, and no immediate benefit to, Thackeray when in 1852 they became parts of a series of small books pirated by Appleton and Company of New York to take advantage of the publicity surrounding the author's first lecture tour of America.

In the short term, however, Barry Lyndon gave Thackeray a steadiness of income he was not used to: "it is a comfort to think that there is a decent income arranged for 1844 (please God my health hold good) and actually a prospect of saving money at the year's end.... I have begun a story wh. is to last through the year in Fraser, and am to have my own way with the worthy Mr. Punch, whose pay is more than double of that I get anywhere else".

It was with the confidence instilled by this financial prospect, as well as the assurance in his "experience," of which he had written Bedingfield, that one month later he declined to sign a contract for ≤ 108 per year with an American periodical publisher (a man named Henry Wikoff whose periodical has yet to be identified) because it required that Thackeray stay in Paris to write two articles a month on Paris and France. Unwilling to "sacrifice my liberty,"

Thackeray offered instead that "as I take your word for the payment of the articles you must please to take mine for supplying them."

He outlined a plan for the American to pay a monthly salary and for himself to submit the two monthly articles, concluding: "I am a bad man of business, and only settle with you as I would with any other publisher. If I don't hear from you I shall conclude the negociation at an end". Thackeray's account book for 1844 shows receipts of £4 and £3.10 for "Indiaand American letters" in January and February and 4s. 10d. for an American letter in February; none of these has been identified.

We hear no more of the American publisher but need not conclude Thackeray was right to characterize himself as a bad businessman. True, he did not close a deal with Wikoff, but neither did he commit himself to a course he could not or would not follow.

Though Thackeray was still in a sense "writing for his life" and still occasionally had to remind friends that he was a "poor day-laborer in the vineyard and must work often when I would like to be taking my diversion", he was not clutching desperately at every chance of work as he had been only a year earlier.

Thackeray's conception of himself as a bad businessman stemmed in large part from his sense of his own lack of steady, disciplined, organized work habits. Capable of enormous work binges, he thought himself lazy for procrastinating. And he could not shake the effects of the unfortunate experiences with the National Standard and the Constitutional. His "failure" to close with Wikoff may have contributed to that sense, as perhaps did also his failure four days later to get the publisher Giraldon to pay for his translation of Eugene Sue's Mystères de Paris, a work he threw over because he was not paid.

But the same evidence shows a businessman who knew, perhaps from bitter experience, when to cut his losses and who had a clear sense of himself, his profession, and what he was and was not willing to do. The letters to Wikoff and Giraldon were not written in financial complacency; in spite of the steady work on Barry Lyndon and the Punch contributions, Thackeray wrote the same month offering Fraser a burlesque originally titled "The Childe of Godesberg"; he proposed substantial reviews for Chapman and Hall's Foreign Quarterly Review (only one of which was accepted) and asked if they would "send me to any other country to travel"; and he wrote Bradbury and Evans proposing a collection of his shorter pieces.

He was prompted to write to Bradbury and Evans under the mistaken notion that Comic Tales had been sold out, though in fact the 1848 reissue of Comic Tales was an attempt to sell off remaining copies of the 1840 impression with a new title page. At the same time he offered to edit a new gentleman's journal with "a decided air of white kid gloves... I know of no man in Europe who would handle <it better>"

The tone of these proposals has changed: the appeals with side references to family obligations and friendship that suggested an undercurrent of desperate need are gone. The letters now have an air of "take it if you will; don't if you won't," suggesting perfect willingness on the author's part to face reality with equanimity.

He was grateful, it is true, that Bradbury and Evans approved of his latest Punch contribution, "The History of the Next French Revolution," and he thanked the firm for its remittance, but at the same time his friendly and familiar relations with the publisher are revealed in his mock serious tone when, on reading the first installment in print, he complained:

"Having confided to you a few chapters of my forthcoming work on the next French revolution - you are bound in justice to print my words fairly - and I protest in the most solemn manner against several liberties which have been taken with my text. What is a historian without accuracy? A mere romancer and I hold such a creature in the utmost contempt" He pointed out three specific errors, which because "The Next French Revolution" was never reprinted in Thackeray's lifetime have never been corrected.

While Thackeray began as an enthusiastic amateur, a gentleman/author, and had become, because of financial and domestic disasters, a desperate literary hack dependent on the largess of relatively powerful publishers, nevertheless the relations between author and publisher by 1844 had become those between equals, literary tradesmen in the best meaning of the term as Thackeray had redefined it. This relationship did not characterize only Thackeray's dealings with Bradbury and Evans; he wrote in the same tone to Henry Colburn on 15 May, "Here is a very little article but in revenge I think a very good one"), and Colburn printed it.

The point is worth emphasizing, for it contradicts another misapprehension that has grown up about Thackeray's relations with publishers. Sir William Fraser, recollecting Thackeray years after the author's death, wrote:

Thackeray's resentment towards the trade of Publishers was deeply rooted. I believe that sixteen publishers refused him the pittance required to print his immortal work, Vanity Fair. Not one of them was capable intellectually of appreciating it.

He pours out the vials of his wrath upon them in Pendennis: painting them to the world as the most stupid, the most selfish, and the most vulgar, class of tradesmen.... Calling on a publisher Thackeray waited with a friend, who told me the story: the carpet of the drawing-room was of a gaudy design of red and white: on the host appearing, the author of Vanity Fair said, "We have been admiring your carpet: it is most appropriate! You wade it, the blood and brains of authors,".

Aside from the exaggeration represented by sixteen publishers without the brains to appreciate Vanity Fair and the distorted overstatement of Warrington's characterization of publishers, both of which reveal more about Sir William than about Thackeray, the final anecdote can be seen as typical of Thackeray's ironic humor rather than as the bitter commentary Fraser obviously took it for.

Other commentators refer to Thackeray's haughty attitude toward publishers and usually point to the portraits of Bacon and Bungay in Pendennis as indications of Thackeray's general attitude.

But if one can see Bentley and Colburn in these two portraits, one cannot see Chapman and Hall, Bradbury and Evans, or George Smith in them. I doubt if one can see James Fraser, John Macrone, or Hugh Cunningham there either, though there is precious little factual material with which to build a picture of Thackeray's personal relations with these three publishers.

Chapter 6

W.E. Henley on Thackeray

According to Henley's "Prefatory," which self-deprecatingly descibes Views and Reviews (1890) as "less a book than a mosaic of scraps and shreds recovered from the shot rubbish of some fourteen years of journalism", this essay was "pieced together" from articles in London, Vanity Fair, The Athenaeum.

In editing this text for the Victorian Web, I have retained orginal spelling and punctuation, and I included numbers in brackets to indicate page breaks in the print edition in order to enable users of VW to cite or locate the original page numbers.

HIS WORSHIPPERS

Some regard him as the greatest novelist of his age and country and as one of the greatest of any country and any age. These hold him to be not less sound a moralist than excellent as a writer, not less magnificently creative than usefully and delightfully cynical, not less powerful and complete a painter of manners than infallible as a social philosopher and incomparable as a lecturer on the human heart.

They accept Amelia Sedley for a very woman; they believe in Colonel Newcome ' by Don Quixote out of Little Nell' as in something venerable and heroic; they regard William Dobbin and 'Stunning' Warrington as finished and subtle portraitures; they think Becky Sharp an improvement upon Mme. Marneffe and Wenham better work than Rigby; they are in love with Laura Bell, and refuse to see either or caricature in their poet's presentment of Alcide de Mirobolant.

Thackeray's fun, Thackeray's wisdom, Thackeray's knowledgee of [9/10] men and women, Thackeray's morality, Thackeray's view of life, 'his wit and humour, his pathos, and his umbrella,' are all articles of belief with them. Of Dickens they will not hear; Balzac they incline to despise; if they make any comparison between Thackeray and Fielding, or Thackeray and Richardson, or Thackeray and Sir Walter, or Thackeray and Disraeli, it is to the disadvantage of Disraeli and Scott and Richardson and Fielding. All these were well enough in their way and day; but they are not to be classed with Thackeray. It is said, no doubt, that Thackeray could neither make stories nor tell them; but he liked stories for all that, and by the hour could babble charmingly of Ivanhoe and the Mousequetaires.

It is possible that he was afraid of passion, and had no manner of interest in crime. But then, how hard he bore upon snobs, and how vigorously he lashed the smaller vices and the meaner faults! It may be beyond dispute that he was seldom good at romance, and saw most things art and nature included rather prosaically and ill-naturedly, as he might see them who has been for many years a failure, and is naturally a little resentful of other men's successes; but then, how brilliant are his studies of club humanity and club manners! how thoroughly he understands the feelings of them that go down into the west in broughams!

If he writes by preference for people with a thousand a year, is it not the duty of everybody with a particle of self-respect to have that income? Is it possible that any one who has it not can have either wit or sentiment, humour or understanding? Thackeray writes of gentlemen for gentlemen; therefore he is alone among artists; therefore he is 'the greatest novelist of his age.' That is the faith of the true believer: that the state of mind of him that reveres less wisely than thoroughly, and would rather be damned with Thackeray than saved with any one else.

HIS CRITICS

The position of them that wear their rue with a difference,

and do not agree that all literature is contained in The Book of Snobs and Vanity Fair, is more easily defended. They like and admire their Thackeray in many ways, but they think him rather a writer of genius who was innately and irredeemably a Philistine than a supreme artist or a great man.

To them there is something artificial in the man and something insincere in the artist: something which makes it seem natural that his best work should smack of the literary tour de force, and that he should never have appeared to such advantage as when, in Esmond and in Barry Lyndon he was writing up to a standard and upon a model not wholly of his own contrivance.

They admit his claim to eminence as an adventurer in 'the discovery of the Ugly'; but they contend that even there he did his work more shrewishly and more pettily than he might; and in this connection they go so far as to reflect that a snob is not only 'one who meanly admires mean things,' as his own definition declares, but one who meanly detests mean things as well.

They agree with Walter Bagehot that to be perpetually haunted by the plush behind your chair is hardly a sign of lofty literary and moral genius; and they consider him narrow and vulgar in his view of humanity, limited in his outlook upon life, inclined to be envious, inclined to be tedious and pedantic, prone to repetitions, and apt in bidding for applause to appeal to the baser qualities of his readers and to catch their sympathy by making them feel themselves spitefully superior to their fellow-men.

They look at his favourite heroines at Laura and Ethel and Amelia; and they can but think him stupid who could ever have believed them interesting or admirable or attractive or true. They listen while he regrets it is impossible for him to attempt the picture of a man; and, with Barry Lyndon in their mind's eye and the knowledge that Casanova and Andrew Bowes suggested no more than that, they wonder if the impossibility was not a piece of luck for him.

They hear him heaping contumely upon the murders and adulteries, the excesses in emotion, that pleased the men of

1820 as they had pleased the Elizabethans before them, and they see him turning with terror and loathing from these which after all are effects of vigorous passion‹to busy himself with the elaborate and careful narrative of how Barnes Newcome beat his wife, and Mrs. Mackenzie scolded Colonel Newcome to death, and old Twysden bragged and cringed himself into good society and an interest in the life and well-being of a little cad like Captain Woolcomb; and it is not amazing if they think his morality more dubious in some ways than the morality he is so firmly fixed to ridicule and to condemn.

They reflect that he sees in Beatris no more than the makings of a Bernstein; and they are puzzled, when they come to mark the contrast between the two portraitures and the difference between the part assigned to Mrs. Esmond and the part assigned to the Baroness, to decide if he were shortsighted or ungenerous, if he were inapprehensive or only cruel.

They weary easily of his dogged and unremitting pursuit of the merely conventional man and the merely conventional woman; they cannot always bring themselves to be interested in the cupboard drama, the tea-cup tragedies and cheque-book and bandbox comedies, which he regards as the stuff of human action and the web of human life; and from their theory of existence they positively refuse to eliminate the heroic qualities of romance and mystery and passion, which are as they have only to open their newspapers to see essentials of human achievement and integral elements of human character.

They hold that his book contain some of the finest stuff in fiction: as for instance, Rawdon Crawley's discovery of his wife and Lord Steyne, and Henry Esmond's return from the wars, and those immortal chapters in which the Colonel and Frank Castlewood pursue and run down their kinswoman and the Prince But they hold, too, that their influence is dubious and that few have risen from them one bit the better or one jot the happier. Genius apart, Thackeray's morality is that of a highly respectable British cynic; his intelligence is largely one of trifles; he is wise over trivial and trumpery things.

He delights in reminding us with an air! that everybody is a humbug; that we are all rank snobs; that to misuse your aspirates is to be ridiculous and incapable of real merit; that Miss Blank has just slipped out to post a letter to Captain Jones; that Miss Dash wears false teeth and a wig that General Tufto is almost as tightly laced as the beautiful Miss Hopper; that there's a bum bailiff in the kitchen at Number Thirteen; that the dinner we ate t'other day at Timmins's is still to pay; that all is vanity; that there's a skeleton in every house; that passion, enthusiasm, excess of any sort, is unwise, abominable, a little absurd; and so forth.

And side by side with these assurances are admirable sketches of character and still more admirable sketches of habit and of manners are the Pontos and Costigan, Gandish and Talbot Twysden and the unsurpassable Major, Sir Pitt and Brand Firmin, the heroic De la Plache and the engaging Farintosh and the versatile Honeyman, a crowd of vivid and diverting portraitures besides; but they are not different in kind at least from the reflections suggested by the story of their several careers and the development of their several individualities. Esmond apart, there is scarce a man or a woman in Thackeray whom it is possible to love unreservedly or thoroughly respect.

That gives the measure of the man, and determines the quality of his influence. He was the average clubman plus genius and a style. And, if there is any truth in the theory that it is the function of art not to degrade but to ennoble not to dishearten but to encourage not to deal with things ugly and paltry and mean but with great things and beautiful and lofty then, it is argued, his example is one to depreciate and to condemn.

HIS STYLE

Thus the two sects: the sect of them that are with Thackeray and the sect of them that are against him. Where both agree is in the fact of Thackeray's pre-eminence as a writer of English and the master of one of the finest prose styles in literature. His manner is the perfection of conversational writing. Graceful yet vigorous; adorably artificial yet incomparably sound; touched with modishness yet informed with distinction; easily and happily rhythmical yet full of colour and quick with malice and with meaning; instinct with urbanity and instinct with charm it is a type of high-bred English, a climax of literary art. He may not have been a great man but assuredly he was a great writer; he may have been a faulty novelist but assuredly he was a rare artist in words. Setting aside Cardinal Newman's, the style he wrote is certainly less open to criticism than that of any other modern Englishman.

He was neither super-eloquent like Mr. Ruskin nor a Germanised Jeremy like Carlyle; he was not marmoreally emphatic as Landor was, nor was he slovenly and inexpressive as was the great Sir Walter; he neither dallied with antithesis like Macaulay nor rioted in verbal vulgarisms with Dickens; he abstained from technology and what may be called Lord Burleighism as carefully as George Eliot indulged in them, and he avoided conceits as sedulously as Mr. George Meredith goes out of his way to hunt for them.

He is a better writer than any one of these, in that he is always a master of speech and of himself, and that he is always careful yet natural and choice yet seemingly spontaneous. He wrote as a very prince among talkers, and he interfused and interpenetrated English with the elegant and cultured fashion of the men of Queen Anne and with something of the warmth, the glow, the personal and romantic ambition, peculiar to the century of Byron and Keats, of Landor and Dickens, of Ruskin and Tennyson and Carlyle. Unlike his only rival, he had learnt his art before he began to practise it.

Of the early work of the greater artist a good half is that of a man in the throes of education: the ideas, the thoughts, the passion, the poetry, the humour, are of the best, but expression is self-conscious, strained, ignorant. Thackeray had no such blemish. He wrote dispassionately, and he was a born writer. In him there is no hesitation, no fumbling, no uncertainty. The style of Barry Lyndon is better and stronger and more virile than the style of Philip; and unlike the other man's, whose latest writing is his best, their author's evolution was towards decay.

HIS MISSION

He is so superior a person that to catch him tripping is a peculiar pleasure. It is a satisfaction apart, for instance, to reflect that he has (it must be owned) a certain gentility of mind. Like the M.P. in Martin Chuzzlewit, he represents the Gentlemanly Interest. That is his mission in literature, and he fulfils it thoroughly. He appears sometimes as Mr. Yellowplush, sometimes as Mr. Fitzboodle, sometimes as Michael Angelo Titmarsh, but always in the Gentlemanly Interest.

In his youth (as ever) he is found applauding the well-bred Charles de Bernard, and remarking of Balzac and Dumas that the one is 'not fit for the salon,' and the other 'about as genteel as a courier.' Balzac and Dumas are only men of genius and great artists: the real thing is to be 'genteel' and write as Gerfeuil (sic) is written 'in a gentleman-like style.'

A few pages further on in the same pronouncement (a review of Jérome Paturot), I find him quoting with entire approval Reybaud's sketch of 'a great character, in whom the habitué of Paris will perhaps recognise a certain likeness to a certain celebrity of the present day, by name Monsieur Hector Berlioz, the musician and critic.'

The description is too long to quote. It sparkles with all the fadaises of anti-Berliozian criticism, and the point is that the hero, after conducting at a private party (which Berlioz never did) his own 'hymn of the creation that has been lost since the days of the deluge,' 'called for his cloak and his clogs, and walked home, where he wrote a critique for the newspapers of the music which he had composed and directed.'

In the Gentlemanly Interest Mr. Titmarsh translates this sorry little libel with the utmost innocence of approval. It is The Paris Sketch-Book over again. That Monsieur Hector Berlioz may possibly have known something of his trade and been withal as honest a man and artist as himself seems never to have occurred to him.

He knows nothing o£ Mousieur Hector except that he is a 'hairy romantic,' and that whatever he wrote it was not Batti,

batti; but that nothing is enough. 'Whether this little picture 'is a likeness or not' he is ingenuous enough to add, 'who shall say?' But, and here speaks the bold but superior Briton 'it is a good caricature of a race in France, where geniuses poussent as they do nowhere else; where poets are prophets, where romances have revelations.'

As he goes on to qualify Jérome Paturot as a 'masterpiece,' and as 'three volumes of satire in which there is not a particle of bad blood,' it seems fair to conclude that in the Gentlemanly Interest all is considered fair, and that to accuse a man of writing criticisms on his own works is to be 'witty and entertaining,' and likewise 'careless, familiar, and 'sparkling' to the genteelest purpose possible in this genteelest of all possible worlds.

Chapter 7

The Influence of Vanity fair Upon Thackeray's Reputation and Prosperity

It is inaccurate to speak of Thackeray's American publishers as though there was a formal relationship, for every American edition was a reprint of material originally published in England, and until 1852 every American edition was unauthorized. Conventional analysis of American literary piracy notes that there was no international copyright law until 1891, that cross-Atlantic literary piracy was not a legal crime, and that American protectionism and isolation stood in the way of international legislation for literary rights.

Cynics are fond of noting in addition that whatever effect it had on authors, the absence of the law did not hurt American publishers until such a time as there was an American literature they might be able to sell to an international market. The absence of an international law was not so much a cause as it was a symptom of conditions in the publishing world that prevailed on both sides of the Atlantic, but which publishers on the American side managed to enjoy for a longer time and with fewer inhibitions than did those on the English side.

The first surprising fact is that Thackeray himself found those early unauthorized American appearances of his work interesting and important. The wisdom of his way of looking at the situation is supported by the fact that he eventually came to benefit financially from an American market in spite of the absence throughout his lifetime of any copyright protection for his works in America. Aside from the author-subsidized publication of Flore et Zéphyr, a book of twelve lithographs with captions produced in London in 1836, American publishers were the first to recognize in the magazinery of the struggling journalist the stuff for book work.

The Yellowplush Correspondence, which Thackeray had written as a loosely connected series for Fraser's Magazine in 1837, became, early the next year, in the hands of Cary and Hart of Philadelphia, his first book. The company's "Cost Books" indicate the production of 1,000 copies at a cost of twenty-four cents per copy (PHS). That cost, of course, included no payment to the author. I have not found what the books were sold for or how many were actually sold, but there was apparently no demand for a reprint, for none is recorded.

English authors and publishers might rant and rave about American literary piracy, but Americans had, at least in the 1830s and 40s, nothing to fear and no incentive to care what the English establishment thought is part, Thackeray began by looking with sardonic curiosity and a philosophical attitude at his American successes.

He may have rued the failure to get any payment for Yellowplush or for the putative reprinting of The Historical Reminiscences of Major Gahagan (a work as yet unseen by any bibliographer), but he benefited, nonetheless, by these piracies, for he used their existence to convince his first English book publishers, John Macrone and his successor Hugh Cunningham, to publish Yellowplush and Gahagan along with a few other items in a two-volume collection called Comic Tales.

In the preface to the collection he remarked on the popularity of The Yellowplush Papers in America "where they have been reprinted more than once," adding that Gahagan was "received by our American brethren with similar piratical honours; and the editor has had the pleasure of perusing them likewise."

Though Thackeray's journalism continued to be reprinted in American magazines, a lull in book publication set in and lasted until 1844, a condition no doubt irritating to Thackeray who was having a hard time getting anything into book form anywhere. It is possible that in 1844 J. Winchester, a New York publisher, reprinted The Irish Sketch-Book, without formal arrangements with its author, of course. In the next few years before Vanity Fair, American publishers in New York, Baltimore, and Philadelphia reprinted Notes on a Journey from Cornhill to Grand Cairo and Jeame's Diary with impunity.

Throughout his career, in fact, Thackeray expressed willingness to take half a loaf when there was no whole loaf to be had or to dine on mutton when there was no venison. But with the publication of Vanity Fair, January 1847-July 1848, Thackeray's attitude changed along with the shift in his economic situation.

In the early days of Vanity Fair, he wrote that the book "did everything but sell, and appears really immensely to increase my reputation if not my income", But when, in August 1848, he could write that "Vanity Fair is doing very well commercially I'm happy to say at last", he knew he had gained bargaining power, and he quickly developed the ability and habit of persuading publishers to raise his fees.

At first this power did not extend over American publishers. Harper and Brothers was the first to cash in freely on the economic strength of the new superstar, but that firm was in no hurry. Its two-volume paperbound edition of Vanity Fair was published in July and August 1848, after the entire serial had run its course in England.

In December, Harper coolly added The Great Hoggarty Diamond to its list by lifting it from Fraser's Magazine, thereby, apparently by coincidence rather than malice aforethought, predating the authorized English reprinting by three months. With Pendennis, as with Vanity Fair, there was no rush of competition among the American pirates.

The first of Harper's eight-part reprint appeared on 14 August 1849, ten and a half months after the London publication of the first serial part. Surviving Harper and Brothers records show no payments to English author or publishers for these three works, though the company's record of reprints over the next twenty-five years indicates how lucrative the piracy of superstars could be. While lack of competition for Vanity Fair might be attributed to the fact that Thackeray was not yet a popular author, that for Pendennis might have resulted, instead, from the operation of a self-imposed but not very binding "courtesy of the trade" practiced among the more established American publishers.

These large publishing houses knew that competition for marginal books was detrimental to profits. In fact, the only book by Thackeray that was published simultaneously by two American publishers was The Virginians. Thackeray attributed the reluctance of American pirates to publish his works to the fact that Harper and Brothers was too difficult to compete with. Probably, however, The Virginians was the first of Thackeray's works thought to be worth fighting over.

When, in October 1852, Thackeray met the Harper brothers in New York at their homes, he reportedly greeted James Harper's daughter with the words, "So this is a 'pirate's' daughter, is it?" But on 26 November, Thackeray could write to his English publisher George Smith that "Messrs.

Harper through your friend Mr. Low have communicated with me and to-night after the Lecture made me an offer of 1,000$ for the publication of my Lectures, simultaneously with the re-issue in England - I shall thankfully accept the same and keep this little sum for myself this time". He went on to describe New York as "the only city in wh. piracy is, I think, most to be feared".

And early in January he eased Smith's anxiety about getting the English edition of the lectures in print, saying, "I should not like the Lectures to go to press without reviewing, and here and there altering them; there's no danger now of their being pirated in this Country, the Harper's being the chief buccaneers, and the perfect terror of all their brethren in these seas". Thackeray's confidence in the horror of American publishing pirates is evident in the tone with which he declined a rival offer for the lectures from George P. Putnam of Philadelphia:

"All things considered, I think it best that I should accept their liberal proposal. I thank you very much for your generous offer; and for my own sake, as well as that of my literary brethren in England, I am sincerely rejoiced to find how very kindly the American publishers are disposed towards us".

Of course, kindness may have had nothing to do with it. There were, for one thing, no printed copies of the lectures available for pirating, so any publisher in this case would have to deal directly with the author or work from transcripts made at the lectures. And in the second place, it might have been the opinion of the American publishers that while one edition of the lectures could be produced profitably, the market would not bear two.

Such a judgment, combined perhaps with the workings of trade courtesy, probably kept Putnam from issuing a pirated edition. The Harper records do show payments for all of Thackeray's books beginning with Henry Esmond, but, curiously, they also show a December 1848 payment of £3.3 for Dr. Birch, a Christmas book published in England by Chapman and Hall, which Harper never published.

The second American publisher to cash in on Thackeray's growing reputation was William Appleton. In 1852, under the direction of Evert Duyckinck, Appleton launched its Popular Library. Thackeray's name topped the list of proposed authors in the prospectus, and Yellowplush was the first of his works in the series. It is probable that the people at Appleton knew or hoped at the outset of this project that Thackeray would be coming to America in October of that year. Thackeray's first mention of a possible lecture trip to America appeared in a letter written to his mother on 3 January 1851, though one thing after another intervened to postpone the trip until the end of October 1852.

The lecture series in London began in May 1851, and in June he signed the contract with George Smith for Henry Esmond, which was not completed until the end of May 1852. However, in May 1852 Thackeray responded to the New York Mercantile Library Association's invitation to lecture there; so, no doubt, word had by then gotten around that Thackeray was planning to come to America. The trip was actually worked out for Thackeray by James T. Fields, of Ticknor and Fields in

Boston, a publishing house which failed to cash in on Thackeray until 1855 when it reprinted a small book of ballads. It seems likely then that the trip was well known far in advance and that Duyckinck planned Appleton's Popular Library with the impending trip in mind. When Thackeray arrived in Boston on 13 November, the fledgling Appleton Popular Library already contained The Yellowplush Papers, The Paris Sketch Book (in two volumes), The Book of Snobs, Men's Wives, and A Shabby Genteel Story.

Four more volumes were announced as "nearly ready" in the week Thackeray arrived in New York, though only three of them were published (The Luck of Barry Lyndon, in two volumes, and The Confessions of Fitz-Boodle and Some Passages in the Life of Major Gahagan). In all, nine volumes were produced in the series without a by-your-leave or any planned financial arrangement with the author. Appleton, to its credit, [was quick to redress the moral wrong, though there had been no legal wrong committed. Of course, the redress of moral wrongs is never as expensive as that for legal ones; Appleton approached Thackeray with £100 "to edit a couple of volumes out of Punch".

Thackeray recounted that while on board ship just out from Liverpool en route to Boston and before the passengers had acquired sea legs, a young man representing the firm of Appleton approached him with a publishing proposal. What the proposal was or what the outcome, Thackeray did not disclose, for at that moment the ship gave an unusually large heave and the two gentlemen were obliged to approach the rail and bring up accounts of a different nature.

There can be little doubt, however, that the proposal was to make up two or three volumes from his contributions to Punch for the Popular Library and to write a preface. Thackeray's response as reported to his daughters in a letter home was, "So you see here is the harvest and let us reap it against the winter comes". In 1853 Appleton published four new volumes of Thackeray's miscellaneous works and produced a second edition of A Shabby Genteel Story.

Thackeray's preface to the first Punch volume in the

Appleton series remarks on the authority of the texts and reveals fairly honestly his attitude toward the American appropriation of his work. On coming into this country I found that the projectors of this series of little books had preceded my arrival by publishing a number of early works, which have appeared under various pseudonyms during the last fifteen years.

I was not the master to choose what stories of mine should appear or not: these miscellanies were all advertised, or in course of publication; nor have I had the good fortune to be able to draw a pen, or alter a blunder of author or printer, except in the case of the accompanying volumes, which contain contributions to Punch, whence I have been enabled to make something like a selection.

Later in the preface he adds:

That extreme liberality with which American publishers have printed the works of English authors, has had at least this beneficial result for us, that our names and writings are known by multitudes using our common mother tongue, who never had heard of us or our books but for the speculators who have sent them all over this continent.

It is, of course, not unnatural for the English writer to hope, that someday he may share a portion of the profits which his works bring at present to the persons who vend them in this country; and I am bound gratefully to say myself, that since my arrival here I have met with several publishing houses who are willing to acknowledge our little claim to participate in the advantages arising out of our books; and the present writer having long since ascertained that a portion of a loaf is more satisfactory than no bread at all, gratefully accepts and acknowledges several slices which the book purveyors in this city have proffered to him of their free will.

If we are not paid in full and in specie as yet, English writers surely ought to be thankful for the very great kindness and friendliness with which the American public receives them; and if he hopes some day that measures may pass here to legalize our right to profit a little by the commodities which we invent and in which we deal, I for one can cheerfully say, that the good will towards us from publishers and public is undoubted, and wait for still better times with perfect confidence and humour.

If I have to complain of any special hardship, it is, not that our favourite works are reproduced,... but that ancient magazines are ransacked, and shabby old articles dragged out, which we had gladly left in the wardrobes where they have lain hidden many years. There is no control, however, over a man's thought - once uttered and printed, back they may come upon its on any sudden day.

The Appleton preface shows Thackeray as a deft diplomatist, expressing his pleasure in the evident pleasure of American publishers and public alike. Thackeray's sincerity in this regard can be measured by remarks he made at about the same time in letters to England- "Even the publishers are liberal one gives me a thousand dollars and another 500 or perhaps 1000 more for books to be republished". "I have made 1200£ by coming here already - 800 by the lectures and 4 by my books, money wh.

I shouldn't have had had I staid home" "It would have been worth my while even for my books to come out here: the publishers are liberal enough and will be still more so with any future thing I may do" "Appleton Harper and others all give or offer me money. I shall be able to add something like 40 per Cent to the value of my future books". To the Boston publisher Fields, Thackeray wrote from New York: "The publishers here are acting most generously with regard to my works, past, present, and to come; in fact it was a lucky Friday when I set foot in the country".

However, the possibility of a whole loaf remained very attractive, too. While lecturing in Washington, he dined and talked with a great many persons in government, including the incumbent president, Millard Fillmore, and incoming president, Franklin Pierce. From the American capital he wrote, "I hear the most cheering accounts (but this is a secret I believe) of the International Copyright bill, wh. upon my conscience will make me 5000 dollars a year the richer". The attempt Thackeray referred to as "a secret I believe" was surely something he learned upon his arrival in Washington. The first strategy in the movement to promote an international agreement about copyright had been to jockey a copyright bill through the House of Representatives.

It was being promoted by John F. Crampton, British foreign minister to Washington, who had recently taken over that position and project from Edward Bulwer Lytton's brother, Henry. It was a secret because the attempts to orchestrate the necessary support just to get the bill introduced and approved at committee level were complicated, expensive, and drawn out. Its supporters did not want

American book publishers, book manufacturers, and that part of the American book-buying population that thrived on low-priced, unauthorized reprintings of British writings to mount a lobby against the bill until it had gotten a head of steam.

Thackeray may have known about it before, for an appeal had been made early in 1852 to English authors and publishers for financial support for the effort. Smith, Elder and Chapman and Hall had contributed £50 each; Bradbury and Evans and Charles Dickens gave £100 each. In all, a variety of authors, publishers, and booksellers contributed £1,000 finance the legislation. Thackeray, however, is not among those recorded as contributors.

In addition to his secret efforts to promote a copyright bill in the House, Crampton was secretly negotiating an Anglo-American copyright treaty with the secretary of state, Daniel Webster. Crampton had to keep information about the proposed treaty from those involved with the House bill because a treaty, since it did not require House action, might be seen in the House as an attempt to circumvent its authority.

And then, apparently to Crampton's surprise, a separate petition for a copyright bill was introduced in the Senate by Senator Charles Sumner, with the support of senators Andrew Butler of South Carolina and M. T Hunter and James M. Mason of Virginia. The fact was that there was considerable support in America, particularly among its writers, for a fair copyright agreement. The opposition came primarily from publishers and even more from book manufacturers - typesetters, type foundries, stereotypers, and bookbinders.

By the time Thackeray reached Washington in February 1853, Daniel Webster had died; his successor Edward Everett seemed less keen on dealing with Crampton, whom he apparently did not like; and the publishers had gotten wind of the proposed agreement and had submitted a list of objections to the copyright treaty.

Thackeray met Crampton, and together they drafted a response to those objections. The effect must have been good, for on 17 February 1853 Everett signed the treaty, which then had to be delivered to the Senate for ratification. Delay followed delay; the Senate adjourned for the summer; other Anglo-American treaties and crises intervened; proposed amendments were negotiated by the Americans and objected to by the British; and worse, the American opposition lobby gained momentum.

In August 1852 President Fillmore had written to Harper and Brothers asking for its opinion regarding an international copyright treaty. The response was ambiguous and evasive, declining to try to influence the government on a matter affecting so many different kinds of people. In May 1853 a similarly oracular statement was published in the editor's "Easy Chair" of Harper's Magazine:

"We may not pass by silently the new stir in relation to an international copyright. And however the question may finally be settled, we welcome the discussion, and the interest in the discussion, as so many tokens of the increased consideration which is given, both by people and by government, to the making and printing of books.

Twenty odd millions of people in our commonwealth are furnishing a host of readers; and it behooves government and people to consider wisely what sort of reading is to be furnished, and what sort of pay the furnishers are to receive.". Having lobbed this bit of wisdom from a firm position on the fence, the editor went on to cloud the issue with irrelevant arguments about whether authors could or could not make a decent living and to poke fun at Edward Bulwer Lytton for guessing at the amount of money he could have made had there been an international law. The fact is that Harper and Brothers, whose history of piracy and whose system of small payments for advance sheets from English authors must have overcome their sense of the fairness of paying full rates in a regulated trade, stood to gain nothing by a copyright treaty. The treaty failed in 1854. There would be no international copyright law until 1891.

Nevertheless, by 1853 Thackeray's power and confidence as a major economic commodity made it possible for him practically to write his own ticket with the publishers in ways unavailable to many of his contemporaries, yet that power did not mean that his relations with publishers went smoothly. In 1851 the author of Vanity Fair and Pendennis discovered with some astonishment that the lecture circuit was more lucrative in the short run than book publication.

The contract for Esmond had stipulated that Thackeray would not publish anything anywhere within six months of the publication of that book, but he did not publish anything except Esmond in the whole of 1852. Yet his income from lecturing and the sale of "moral rights" to his books in America made it the most financially satisfying year he had ever had since 1832 when he came into his patrimony.

It should not escape notice that the unauthorized Appleton editions were dragged into the mainstream of textual history when Thackeray used them as the basis for the authorized Miscellanies produced by Bradbury and Evans in London. And it is questionable whether Thackeray actually took the opportunity to select and correct the texts of the three volumes of Punch material; one can only assume that he selected or at least reviewed the selection of items for those three Appleton volumes.

Two of the volumes Appleton had announced as nearly ready in November 1852 did not appear as advertised; their alterations may well have been influenced by Thackeray. Furthermore, the parody of James Fenimore Cooper in Punch's Prize Novelists was emitted either by Thackeray who was already embarrassed by the Bulwer satire or by Evert

Duyckinck who may have been more sensitive on behalf of American than British writers.

But it is known that Thackeray did little if any correcting, and he did no revising for Appleton. The text of Mr. Brown's Letters to a Young Man about Town, for example, differs from the Punch text only in spelling and punctuation. Some Punch errors were corrected, but a number of new errors were introduced. No change bears the unmistakable stamp of authority.

Most of the alterations are neither errors nor corrections, though unlike Harper and Brothers, which systematically house-styled Thackeray's spelling and punctuation for its reprints, Appleton did not. The effect, therefore, on the authority of the Bradbury and Evans reprints of the mid-1850s, even though Thackeray did revise slightly at that time, is that of progressive minor deterioration of textual authority.

In April 1853 Thackeray returned to England and soon agreed with Bradbury and Evans, the publishers of Vanity Fair and Pendennis, to write The Newcomes in twenty-four monthly parts. In June he wrote to Harper that "it will appear as soon as possible after the termination of Mr. Dickens' serial, and I hope you will be inclined to treat with me for the republication of my story in America, upon the same terms wh. you give Mr. Dickens and Sir Bulwer Lytton.

I do not intend to begin to publish until several numbers are completed, and propose to devote the whole of the next 12 months to this story... please to tell me that you have paid to my account... the $1000 I am to receive from you for the publication of my lectures. I hope they have been as successful with you as in London, where we sold the whole of the first edition of 2500 (at 10/6) in a week."

During the next few months Thackeray visited with his family, toured the Continent, and wrote four numbers of The Newcomes with which he returned to London on the first of September where he discovered that in his absence Harper and Brothers had offered him £10 per number. Thackeray immediately wrote to Bradbury and Evans noting Harper's condition that "they could get my numbers 6 weeks before it was printed here - so unless we put off till Nov. I lose £240". Bradbury and Evans did not put off the projected publication, the first number appearing in London on 1 October. Later that month Thackeray wrote Bradbury and Evans again: "I just find a letter from Mr. Low... proposing still to treat with me on behalf of Messrs. Harper, and to secure you."

By this time his tone is plaintive, perhaps on the edge of irritation: "Could one of you see Mr. Low without delay to day if possible as a Steamer starts tomorrow wh. might take out no 3 if you so chose.

They did not publish no 1. No Briton has pirated it - it is impossible that it should now be touched and I have the consolation of thinking that my [£]300 have been lost from a panic where there was no danger. Some of it however may be recovered if you'll have the goodness to go to Lowe. Do [133/134] try to day". The Harper "Priority List" of payments made to English publishers for advance sheets indicates that Harper paid only it £150 ($750) for The Newcomes, which appeared in Harper's Magazine from November 1853 through October 1855.

Whether or not a lesson in international relations had been learned from the experience with The Newcomes is impossible to know, but the arrangements for The Virginians, which began publication in London on 1 November 1857, seem to have worked out a little better from Thackeray's point of view and worse from Harper's.

As before, the negotiations with Harper's agent, Sampson Low, were carried out by Thackeray, but the business of collecting the money and sending the advance proofs was left to the publisher. When in early October 1857 news of bank failures in America reached England, Thackeray wrote to his American friends the Baxters fearful "that all the American savings were gone to smash, including the 500£ from Harper Brothers for the Virginians".

It was with some relief that he wrote a note to Bradbury and Evans on 3 December saying: "I hear that Messrs. Harper of New York have forwarded funds to meet their engagements in this country, and shall be glad to have payment for my 2 numbers of the Virginians. Will you or Mr. Joyce call on Messrs. Low and receive the monthly money on behalf of Yours very Faithfully W M Thackeray".

Meanwhile, a sticky situation was developing for the chief of American literary buccaneers. Serialization in Harper's Magazine began in the issue dated December, which appeared in the middle of November. A few days later The Virginians reappeared in the New York Semi-Weekly Tribune. Harper immediately appealed to Thackeray through Sampson Low to do something; on 11 December he replied:

I am sorry to hear from you that the N Y. Tribune is reprinting the Virginians, and no doubt hurting the Messrs, Harpers' Issue of the story, who pay me 100$ per month for early impression. But I do not see what good any remonstrances of mine can effect.

If American houses choose to reprint our books we can't prevent them, and the Tribune will doubtless take it's own course, in spite of any objections of mine or Messrs. Harper. Could English writers have remonstrated with any effect we should have done so years ago: but I am sure an outcry at present would neither be useful nor dignified; and can only express my regret that I dont see how, in the present instance, I can be of any service to a House wh. shows itself inclined to act in a kind and friendly manner to English literary men.

A postscript in a scribal copy of this letter notes, "I am just advised of your payment for No I and II and hope to send you no III next week". This letter is barbed (which may account for why the postscript was deleted from the letter actually sent): the reference to English authors being unable to prevent American houses from printing their works and the explanation that the unhappiness of the situation was one which English writers had been frustrated about for years are pointed reminders that there was no international copyright agreement.

Thackeray must have known of the Harper firm's failure to take any active role in support of the copyright initiatives in 1853-54, though the firm had assured President Fillmore in 1853 that an international copyright arrangement "becomes more and more manifest."Thackeray probably could not help hinting to the company that it was merely suffering the consequences of its own complacency and receiving, besides, only what it had dished out so generously over the years in which it had gained the reputation of a pirate. On the other hand, Thackeray's letter shows his deft diplomacy in the reference to Harper's freely chosen attempts to be kind and friendly to English literary men.

Harper and Brothers continued to chaff ineffectually at the Tribune, accusing the newspaper of lifting the story from Harper's and remarking sarcastically that the Tribune "had been leading advocates of an International Copyright Law," The Tribune claimed on 26 November that the novel was "carefully reprinted from a London copy" and that readers could expect it "in the Weekly and Semi-Weekly Tribune, usually a few days in advance of its appearance in any other American publication."

Harper's printed response was: "This is simply untrue - Harper's magazine for January was published on the 17th of December; it contained part ii of Mr. Thackeray's novel, in which three slight corrections were made from the London copy. The Virginians was 'carefully reprinted,' with these alterations in the semi-weekly tribune the next day. When the editor of the tribune receives a London copy, he will be able to ascertain what these alterations are." Confronted with this damning evidence, the tribune countered that the Harper's was contaminating the text and thus breaking faith with the public. The legalities were a moot point, a fact not lost on the newspaper, which had nothing to fear but a little bad publicity.

Once George Smith had fished for and netted Thackeray, a series of complicated and restrictive contracts organized his financial fortunes from 1860 until his death in 1863.

In these contracts Smith specified that the income from foreign editions would go to the publisher, and Thackeray no longer concerned himself with the proper fulfillment of these foreign agreements. But until then the frequently frantic negotiations on his own behalf which characterized Thackeray's dealings with his publishers on both sides of the

Atlantic may be an indication that the absence of all international copyright law was merely a symptom, not a cause, of the turmoil and uncertainty in the transatlantic profession of authorship in the 1840s and 1850s.

The cause seems to have been the laissez-faire economics that made a free-for-all in which the devil might take the hindmost on both sides of the Atlantic even in the case of popular authors.

In such conditions the publishers had the upper hand; the history of copyright legislation from that time forward was the history of increased protection of authors' rights, not publishers' rights.

Chapter 8

Critically Analyse on Vanity Fair

Vanity Fair: A Novel without a Hero, the first major work published by William Thackeray under his own name, was published serially in London in 1847 and 1848. Previously, under various comic pseudonyms (such as Michael Angelo Titmarsh and George Savage Fitzboodle) Thackeray made clear, both in his role as the narrator of Vanity Fair and in his private correspondence about the book, that he meant it to be not just entertaining, but instructive. Like all satire, Vanity Fair has a mission and a moral.

The first published installment had an illustration on its cover of a congregation listening to a preacher; both speaker and listeners were shown with donkey ears. In the pages, Thackeray explains the illustration thus: my kind reader will please to remember that these histories.... have "Vanity Fair" for a title and that Vanity Fair is a very vain, wicked, foolish place, full of all sorts of humbugs and falseness and pretentions.

And while the moralist who is holding forth on the cover (an accurate portrait of your humble servant) professes to wear neither gown nor bands, but only the very same long-eared livery in which his congregation is arrayed: yet, look you, one is bound to speak the truth as far as one knows it.

That Becky is allowed to live, and to live well, is perfectly consistent with Thackeray's view of life and morality.... Losing is vanity, and winning is vanity. By the halfway point in its serial publication, Thackeray's long, rambling tale of relentless and corrupt social climbing, told with biting humor and cynicism, was the talk of London. Readers eagerly awaited new episodes in the life of Thackeray's deeply immoral, self-serving anti-heroine, Becky Sharp, who has since become one of the most well-known and most argued-about characters in literature. The novel secured Thackeray's place among the literary giants of his time; and the giants of his time, among them Charles Dickens, the Brontë sisters, Thomas Hardy, and Alfred Tennyson, have endured as giants to this day. Vanity Fair is considered a classic of English literature and one of the great works of satire in all history.

Vanity Fair was a turning point in Thackeray's life and career. A gentleman by birth and education, Thackeray was forced to earn his living by writing because most of his money had been lost in a financial crash. The articles, reviews, essays, and sketches he produced for magazines and newspapers did not provide sufficient income either to support a gentleman's status or to provide for the futures of his two daughters. In addition, writing for a living made his status as a gentleman somewhat tenuous.

The serialization of Vanity Fair, which was a financial success, quickly established Thackeray's literary reputation. Thackeray was jubilant, "There is no use denying the matter or blinking it now. I am become a sort of great man in my way all but at the top of the tree: indeed there if the truth were known and having a great fight up there with Dickens." Though Thackeray's novels never sold at the rate of Dickens's novels (in the tens of thousands), he became financially secure with Vanity Fair. Also his social status as a gentleman was assured because of his acknowledged genius, he was no longer an amusing, talented hack writer, just one of a crowd of London journalists.

CONTEMPORARY RESPONSE TO VANITY FAIR

Contemporary reviewers and novelists appreciated the brilliance of the novel. John Forster wrote, "Vanity Fair is the work of a mind, at once accomplished and subtle, which has enjoyed opportunities of observing many and varied circles of society... his genteel characters... have a reality about them... They are drawn from actual life, not from books and fancy;

and they are presented by means of brief, decisive yet always most discriminative touches" (1848). Charlotte Bronte, whose admiration for his genius was boundless, called him "the legitimate high priest of Truth":

The more I read Thackeray's works, the most certain I am that he stands alone alone in his sagacity, alone in his truth, alone in his feeling (his feeling, though he makes no noise about it, is about the most genuine that ever lived on a printed page), alone in his power, alone in his simplicity, alone in his self-control. Thackeray is a Titan, so strong that he can afford to perform with calm the most herculean feats; there is the charm and majesty of repose in his greatest efforts; he borrows nothing from fever, his is never the energy of delirium his energy is sane energy, deliberate energy, thoughtful energy.

George Eliot's praise was more restrained, "I am not conscious of being in any way a disciple of his, unless it constitute discipleship to think him, as I suppose the majority of people with any intellect do, on the whole, the most powerful of living novelists" (1857).

Not all reviewers and readers agreed. Some were repelled by his realism and his focus on society's moral corruption. Robert Bell complained:

The people who fill up the motley scenes of Vanity Fair, with two or three exceptions, are as vicious and odious as a clever condensation of the vilest qualities can make them. The women are especially detestable. Cunning, low pride, selfishness, envy, malice, and all uncharitableness are scattered amongst them with impartial liberality. It does not enter into the design of Vanity Fair to qualify these bitter ingredients with a little sweetness now and then; to shew the close neighbourhood of the vices and the virtues as it lies on the map of the human heart, that mixture of good and evil, of weakness and strength, which in infinitely varied proportions, constitutes the compound individual. (1848)

An anonymous reviewer wondered, "is it advisable to raise so ruthlessly the veil which hides the rottenness pervading modern society?" (1848). Harriet Martineau could not finish the novel "from the moral disgust it occasions" (1848).

From Thackeray's day to the present, Vanity Fair has generally been regarded as a masterpiece and as his best novel. What has changed is the flaw Thackeray, as well as Vanity Fair, is most commonly charged with. Critical readers of his day called him cynical and even depraved; comparable readers today call him sentimental and even cloying.

THEMES IN VANITY FAIR

Vanity. Vanity, which takes a variety of forms, is a major motivation of individuals and characterizes society. Consider the following definitions of vanity from the OED: "Vain and unprofitable conduct or employment of time"; "The quality of being foolish or of holding erroneous opinions"; "The quality of being personally vain; high opinion of oneself; self-conceit and desire for admiration." Another meaning of vanity could possibly be the vanity mirror; this meaning relates to the use of mirrors in the text and the drawings.

Society's values. Individuals and society are driven by the worship of wealth, rank, power, and class and are corrupted by them. Consequences of this worship are the perversion of love, friendship, and hospitality and the inability to love.

Selfishness. Everyone is selfish in varying degrees. As little Georgy ironically writes in an essay. "An undue love of Self leads to the most monstrous crime and occasions the greatest misfortunes both in States and Families" (page 698). The selfishness of characters like Becky, Jos Sedley, and Lord Steyne is obvious; however, even apparently selfless characters like Amelia, Dobbin, and Lady Jane are selfish.

Illusion and reality. Is it possible to distinguish between illusion and reality? Motivated by self-interest, the characters practice hypocrisy, they misrepresent themselves both to others and to themselves, and they lie. Some characters deliberately choose their illusions or fantasies over the truth. Thus, every character deludes others and/or is self-deluded.

Heroism. Men and women are not heroic; the heroic poses and pretenses of characters, literature, and society are consistently deflated. Fiction versus reality. The false portrayal of human nature and activities in novels, romance, and literary conventions is distinguished from real life. The subtitle, A Novel Without a Hero; Thackeray's identifying various characters as the hero or heroine; the marriages of Amelia and Becky early in the novel all violate novelistic conventions. George Osborne parodies the conventional hero. Is Thackeray's shifting narrator a satire of the literary convention that "novelists know the truth about everything".

Married and parental relationships. In a novel of domestic life, there are no happy marriages because of the egotism, selfishness, folly, and false values of individuals and of society. Similarly, selfishness, vanity, snobbery, and/or materialism affect every child-parent relationship.

The gentleman. Thackeray rejects the older concept of a gentleman as a man of rank and leisure, i.e., a member of the gentry or aristocracy. The true gentleman, as well as the true lady, is recognized by moral character, being considerate, benevolent, and diligent. Amelia, Lady Jane, and Dobbin are among the few real ladies and gentlemen in this novel.

Time. Thackeray's concern with time has caused him to be called the novelist of memory. The action is set in the past, and the narrator compares and contrasts the past with the present as he moves between them; occasionally he tells us a future event or outcome. The characters' memories of the past help to characterize them in the present. Thackeray shows the effect which the passage of time has on the characters. The concern with time is reflected in the structure; the narrator occasionally interrupts the chronology, jumps back in time, and returns to the point where he stopped the chronology.

VARIOUS ASPECTS OF VANITY FAIR

The setting so far as physical place is concerned, moves from London to Brighton, to the Continent including Paris, Rome, Brussels, and "Pumpernickel," a small German principality. The reader moves from city house to country estate, from private academy to the sponging house, or debtors' jail. But there is also a social setting. The story unfolds against the back ground of the estates and attitudes of the landed aristocracy such as the Lord Steynes and the Crawleys;

the houses of the city merchants such as the Sedleys, the Osbornes, and the Dobbins the colonial order and money of Miss Swartz and Joseph Sedley, the collector of Boggley Wollab; the military protocol in Brussels before Waterloo and in India; the Anglo-Irish in the persons and prejudices of the O'Dowds and the lesser fringes of Vanity Fair embodied in the Clapps, Raggles, Briggs, and others.

The book, then, has not only a setting as to place but also, and more important, as to position and power. It emerges as a social document, accurate in terms of history, sociology, and psychology. The highest point in the social strata is the Court, where Becky finally is presented. The lowest is the Fleet prison, where fate sends poor Raggles. The two characters more concerned with human relationships than with position or power are Amelia and Dobbin.

Vanity Fair, then, is not so much a story told against a setting, as a state of mind, a state of mind still prevalent in the twentieth century. The title suggests the idea: Vanity Fair. The treasures of Vanity Fair, that is, money and position, are desirable but transient. The gaiety, the mask of the ball, does not stay with the person when he faces death. Thackeray does not underestimate the importance of having a home, clothes and food; but he does expose the cruelty, the deception, the futility of making possessions and power the only aim in life.

The book is so saturated with the vanity of Vanity Fair, the duplicity of social climbers, and the weakness of human nature, that it would be impossible to separate idea from plot or plot from characters. If the book appears to ramble, it never strays from the focus of attention on the foibles of human nature in its struggle to reach the highest strata of Vanity Fair. The setting could be changed to modern times and the observations would be true today.

The vanity of man is universal and ever present. Women still berate and betray women; relatives still fight over money; mothers still sell their daughters for popularity, money, or position. Yet, there are some people, the reader hopes and Thackeray indicates, who do not bow down to the idols of Vanity Fair.

The winners at the end of the story are those who cherished human relationships first: Amelia, Dobbin, and Lady Jane, with the children Georgy and little Rawdon. Thackeray's idea, then, is that although one may live in Vanity Fair, one need not be a slave to its values, which in the final analysis turn into futility and emptiness. The reader feels that Georgy and little Rawdon will be better men than their grandfathers. Thackeray takes symbols from everyday life, from the classics, and from the Bible.

He shows Rebecca ensnaring Joseph in a tangle of green silk, at their first acquaintance. As Becky climbs the social stairway, she is likened to a spider. At the close of the book, she has literally entangled and destroyed Joseph just as a spider would its victim. She sucked his money, his vitality, his personality from him. She did not reduce Rawdon to such a shell, but she played Delilah to his Samson.

At the charade party Rebecca plays Clytemnestra, symbolic of her destruction first of Rawdon, second of Joseph. (Clytemnestra killed her husband, Agamemnon, when her lover's courage failed.) Rebecca is also called Circe, the siren who lured men to their death. Sir Pitt refers to the Bute Crawleys as Beauty and the Beast, a symbolic hint that Bute has married a battle-axe, which he has.

The Osborne household keeps time by a clock representing the sacrifice of Iphigenia. Iphigenia, daughter of Clytemnestra and Agamemnon, was sacrificed by her father for success in war, another route to power and position. Old Osborne tries to sacrifice George to a marriage for money; he destroys Miss Jane's one romance for his own selfish convenience. The Iphigenia clock, then, symbolizes the complete subordination of the Osbornes to money and social success.

Amelia's giving up Georgy is compared to Hannah's giving up Samuel. The Bible story has religious significance; Hannah gives up her son to the Lord. In Vanity Fair, Amelia, though she is not of Vanity Fair, surrenders her son to advantages that money and position can provide. The symbol here may be ironic.

The symbolism described in the foregoing paragraphs constitutes one form of imagery. To continue with similar figures which may not be considered broadly symbolic, one reads of Miss Pinkerton, "the Semiramis of Hammersmith." Sermiramis was an Assyrian queen noted for beauty, wisdom, and voluptuousness. Hammersmith was a metropolitan borough of London. Obviously the figure is ironic. When Pitt lures James into trouble by urging him to drink and smoke in Miss Crawley's house, Thackeray calls Pitt, Machiavel, a name synonymous with political cunning, duplicity, and bad faith.

Old Sir Pitt, called Silenus, leers at Becky like a satyr. In mythology Silenus is a fat old man, jolly, intoxicated, an attendant of Bacchus. Satyrs are goat-like men, attendants of Bacchus, the god of wine. Men and women are compared to trees and birds:

"While Becky Sharp was on her own wing in the country, hopping on all sorts of twigs and amid a multiplicity of traps, and pecking up her food quite harmless and successful, Amelia lay snug in her home..." He compares George to a tree where Amelia can built her nest but says it is not safe. When Dobbin has at last won Amelia, the author says, "The bird has come in at last. There it is with its head on his shoulder, billing and cooing close up to his heart with soft outstretched fluttering wings..." He calls Dobbin the "rugged old oak to which you cling."

Dobbin, the "uproused British lion," tells his sisters they "hiss and shriek and cackle... don't begin to cry. I only said you were a couple of geese." Thackeray compares Amelia to a violet, speaks of her nursing the corpse of Love, after George seems to have abandoned her In caring for her father, she appears to Dobbin to walk "into the room as silently as a sunbeam."

Pitt Crawley is "pompous as an undertaker." Lady Crawley is a "mere machine in her husband's house." Amelia is a "poor little white-robed angel," who fortunately can't hear George and his fellows roaring over their whiskey-punch. When the ladies cry, the author says, "The waterworks again began to play." Miss Swartz, in fancy garments, is dressed "about as elegantly... as a she chimney-sweep on May Day." Dobbin, on contemplating Becky's flirtation, has "a countenance as glum as an undertaker's." When Amelia comes out, just before George's departure for battle, holding his sash against her bosom, Thackeray says "the heavy net of crimson dropped like a large stain of blood," a possible symbol of George's fate.

The note George gives Becky asking her to run away with him, lies "coiled like a snake among the flowers." When Becky exploits her fellow men, she is like the mermaid feeding below the surface of the water on the pickled victims. The "sheep-dog," or female companion necessary to the vivacious social climber in Vanity Fair, reminds Thackeray of "the death's head which figured in the repasts of Egyptian bon-vivants..." Mrs. Bowls, formerly Firkin, maid to Miss Crawley, extends her hand to Becky and "her fingers were like so many sausages, cold and lifeless." Mrs. Frederick Bullock's kiss is "like the contact of an oyster."

One of the most humorous comparisons is that of cleaning a woman's reputation by presenting her at Court as one would clean dirty linen by putting it through the laundry. A countess of sixty is compared with faded street lights. She has "chinks and crannies" in her face. The calling cards from the ladies of Lord Steyne's family are "the trumps of Becky's hand." But Steyne says, "You poor little earthenware pipkin, you want to swim down the stream along with the great copper kettles."

When Georgy's nose is hurt, one does not see blood, but "the claret drawn from his own little nose." Becky calls herself a mouse, perhaps able to help the lion, the second Sir Pitt. To indicate that the servants are gossiping about Becky, Thackeray personifies Discovery and Calumny as the waiters who serve the food and drink. When Dobbin comes home, the English landscape "seems to shake hands" with him. Dobbin's desire is a "bread-and-butter paradise." Becky is a hardened Ishmaelite who halts at Jos' tents and rests.

Samuel Chew notes that Thackeray spent much of his time "parodying and satirizing romantic sentiment" and that he "possessed a terrible power to detect and expose men's self-deceptions, shams, pretenses and unworthy aspirations." Also, Thrall and Hibbard in the section on satire in their Handbook refer to Thackeray as one of the "later satirists," along with Byron, following in the great tradition of the "golden age of satire" characterized by the writings of Dryden, Swift, Addison, Steele, Pope, and Fielding. Thackeray as satirist, then, should not be overlooked even in a cursory review of Vanity Fair.

Considered standard among a good many students and teachers of literature is the Thrall and Hibbard definition of satire "A literary manner which blends a critical attitude with humor and wit to the end that human institutions may be improved." Accepting this definition the student of Thackeray would do well to examine some of the ways Thackeray employs satire mainly by (1) the use of names, (2) irony, and (3) humorous situations.

Some of the names have symbolic significance and some apparently are used for humor or irony's sake. For certain occupations the author chooses "killing" names: Lance, the surgeon; Mrs. Briefless, the barrister's wife; Sir Thomas Coffin, the celebrated hanging judge; Dr. Ramshorn, the preacher; Mr. Bawler, minister of the Darbyites. The Miss Scratchleys fight; Mary Box is always thumping her small brother; Mr. Hammerdown is the auctioneer; Quill is a cashier; Dipley is a candlemaker; Miss Grains is the brewer's daughter; Pestler is an apothecary; Mr. Quadroon writes on the slave question.

To portray characteristics there are names such as Mr. Smirk, Miss Toady, the Reverend Mr. Crisp, and the Reverend Mr. Flowerdew. Mrs. Flamingo dresses in a crimson silk gown. Lord Methuselah is an old man, and Mrs. Highflyer is a social climber. Lady Slingstone is a notorious gossip. Madame de St. Amour would be affectionate, while Madame de Belladonna might be quite deadly. Becky outwits the brilliant Lady Stunnington and the witty Mr. Wagg. The situation, at the time the name is mentioned, frequently augments the satire. Becky is riding with Sir Pitt to Queen's Crawley. Rain is pouring. The towns along the way are Leakington, Mudbury and Squashmore.

Lord Steyne (stain is the symbolic meaning) lives in Gaunt House. Wealthy, honored, and bored, he fills his life with sensuous pleasure, but actually his existence is empty, as Gaunt indicates. Becky Sharp is not named Sharp by accident. Neither are the Crawleys, who use every means to crawl up the social and monetary ladder. Some names are apparently just for fun: Lord Heehaw, Mrs. Hook Eagles, Swanky, Trotter, Lady Vere Vane, Mrs. Rougemont, Miss Hawky. Bowls is the butler; Heavytop, is the colonel; Knuckles is the private; Cackle is the assistant surgeon; Ensigns Spooney and Stubble are young officers; Mr. Chopper bandies the Osbornes' money; Deuceace is a gambler.

IRONY

Thackeray's irony takes a wide range sometimes biting, sometimes playful, but always pertinent. A sample of comment on money follows: "I for my part, have known a five-pound note to interpose and knock up a half-century's attachment between two brethren; and can't but admire, as I think what a fine and durable thing Love is among worldly people." "What a charming reconciler and peacemaker money is!" "The good quality of this old lady has been mentioned... She had a balance at her banker's which would have made her beloved anywhere."

When Becky and Rawdon look for George in order for Rawdon to gamble with him, the author remarks, "I hope the reader has much too good an opinion of Captain and Mrs. Crawley to suppose that they ever would have dreamed of paying a visit to so remote a district as Bloomsbury, if they thought the family whom they proposed to honour with a visit were not merely out of fashion, but out of money, and could be serviceable to them in no possible manner."

Women come in for a good share of Thackeray's sarcasm. He has his tongue-in-cheek as he describes Becky's need of a mother. "All she wanted was the proposal, and ah! how Rebecca now felt the want of a mother! a dear, tender mother, who would have managed the business in ten minutes..." "All old women were beauties once, we very well know."

Miss Pinkerton writes Mrs. Bute that Miss Tuffin is sweet, young, eighteen, and therefore, probably not suitable. She illustrates Thackeray's idea that "natural jealousy... is one of the main principles of every honest woman." Mrs. Bute is reluctant to forgive the begging Miss Horrocks. "But those who know a really good woman are aware that she is not in a hurry to forgive, and that the humiliation of an enemy is a triumph to her soul." Mrs. Bute, in her treatment of Miss Crawley "... ground down the old lady in her convalescence in such a way as only belongs to your proper-managing, motherly, moral woman."

Becky's friendship with Lady Jane is such that "... these two ladies did not see much of each other except upon those occasions when the younger brother's wife, having an object to gain from the other, frequented her. They my-loved and my-deared each other assiduously, but kept apart generally..." In ironical comments on society and life in general, Thackeray lets the reader know that even those in modest circumstances love their children. Dobbin writes his mother "... who was fond of him, although she was a grocer's wife and lived in a back parlour in Thames St."

Captain Dobbin makes conversation "... like a consummate man of the world... some topic of general interest such as the opera... or the weather that blessing to society." Gossips have not changed since Vanity Fair "The tartwoman hints to somebody, who took an affidavit of the fact to somebody else, that there was a great deal more than was made public regarding Mr. Crisp and Miss Sharp..."

Of deaths and funerals, Thackery comments, "Could the best and kindest of us who depart from the earth, have an opportunity of revisiting it, I suppose he or she... would have a pang of mortification at finding how soon our survivors were consoled..." Of weddings, he says, "After three or four ceremonies, you get accustomed to it, no doubt; but the first dip, everybody allows, is awful." And of the fighting in Belgium, he says, "For a long period of history they have let other people fight there."

Thackeray's characterizations are often ironic. The rich

Miss Crawley says of herself, Rebecca, and Rawdon: "'We're the only three Christians in the county my love,' in which case it must be confessed that religion was at a very low ebb in the county of Hants." George broke up Becky's marriage to Joseph and "she loved George Osborne accordingly." Miss Crawley "showed her friendship by abusing all her intimate acquaintances to her new confidante (than which there can't be a more touching proof of regard)."

Joseph's eating is "the delightful exercise of gobbling." As an invalid, he takes two-thirds of the bottle of champagne. Mr. Sedley says that if Joseph should receive word of the death of the rest of the family, he would say "Good Gad!" and go on with his dinner.

Mr. Osborne's disposition has suffered because "... he has not been allowed to have his own way. To be thwarted in this reasonable desire was always very injurious to the old gentleman... "Maria Osborne Bullock "... felt it her duty to see her father and sister as little as possible."

Mr. Osborne called kicking a footman downstairs a "hint" to leave. Lord Steyne says his wife is as gay as Lady Macbeth and calls his home a "temple of virtue." Lady Fits-Willis is of the "best people." Her patronage helps Becky. The lady "asked her to her own mansion, and spoke to her twice in the most public and condescending manner... The important fact was known all over London that night..." At Vauxhall "our young people made the most solemn promises to keep together... and separated in ten minutes afterwards."

Joseph, embarrassed when he first meets Rebecca, turns red, can't talk, and yanks the bell rope loose. Sir Pitt is a stingy, dirty, disreputable boor who can't spell, doesn't read, eats boiled mutton, and has but one candle in the house; but it stands in an ornate silver candlestick, and three footmen serve the boiled mutton. Old Sir Pitt proposes marriage to Becky:

"I'm an old man, but a good'n. I'm good for twenty years. I'll make you happy, see if I don't. You shall do what you like; spend what you like; and 'av it all your own way. I'll make you a settlement. I'll do everything regular. Look year!" and the old man fell down on his knees and leered at her like a satyr.

Rebecca started back a picture of consternation. In the course of this history we have never seen her lose her presence of mind; but she did now, and wept some of the most genuine tears that ever fell from her eyes. "Oh, Sir Pitt!" she said. "Oh, sir I I'm married already."

When the party gets ready to leave Brighton, Amelia rises to pack, while her husband lies in bed "deploring that she had not a maid to help her." When Becky wants to impress someone with her domesticity and her love for her child, she pulls out a little shirt that she is sewing for little Rawdon, but he outgrows it long before it is finished. Jos calls on Becky in her room at the "Elephant." She has to do some quick house cleaning:

In that instant she put a rouge-pot, a brandy-bottle, and a plate of broken meat into the bed... she placed herself on the bed not on the bottle and plate, you may be sure... she put her hand to her heart with a passionate gesture of despair, burying her face for a moment on the bed.

The brandy-bottle inside clinked up against the plate which held the cold sausage. Both were moved, no doubt, by the exhibition of so much grief... that spotless being that miserable unsullied martyr was present on the bed before Jos on the bed, sitting on the brandy-bottle.

MONEY AND MATRIMONY IN VANITY FAIR

In his novel Vanity Fair, William Thackeray exposes and examines the vanities of 19th century England. His characters pursue wealth, power, and social standing, often through marriage or matrimony. The present essay looks at Thackeray's use of the institution of marriage in Vanity Fair to comment on how these vanities often come at the expense of the true emotions of passion, devotion, and love.

PARENTAL AMBITIONS

In Vanity Fair, money is central to nearly all of the characters' relationships. Thackeray connects England's merchant families, the lesser nobility, and the high aristocracy through money and matrimony, and parents are frequently the chief negotiators in these business transactions. Mr. Osborne is perhaps the novel's most avaricious parent; money and social eminence are all-important to Mr. Osborne, and he is willing to sacrifice his children's happiness to connect his family name with these vanities. He forbids his daughter Jane to marry an artist with whom she has fallen in love with, swearing to her "that she should not have a shilling of his money if she made a match without his concurrence" (p416). For Mr. Osborne love has little to do with matrimony, and marriage is simply a transaction that should increase family wealth and prestige.

This concept was by no means uncommon during the 19th century: the rise of industrialism and colonialism meant an influx of wealth into England, and marriage was seen by many as a way of either rising in station or cementing business ties. This latter theme is seen in Mr. Osborne's interference in his son George's relationship with Amelia. Their courtship is arranged, the "two young people [having] been bred up by their parents" for love and marriage.

George and Amelia's relationship is encouraged because of the business connection between Mr. Sedley and Mr. Osborne, and their feelings are not really an issue to be considered. As Mr. Sedley's fortunes fall, Mr. Osborne questions George if the match is not now beneath the Osborne family's station: "Why shouldn't you marry higher than a stockbroker's daughter, George, that's what I want to know?"). George replies that it is a "family business," and that "you and Mrs. Sedley made the match a hundred years ago".

The terminology of business is frequent in discussions of marriage in Vanity Fair, and money, not love, is the motive for matrimony. Mr. Osborne states these feelings very clearly to his son: "Unless I see Amelia's ten thousand down you don't marry her".

Mr. Sedley's misfortunes are a convenient way for Mr. Osborne to force the cancellation of the engagement, for he sees an opportunity to marry his wealth (which was only acquired through Mr. Sedley's facilitation) through George to Miss Swartz, a young heiress with connections to the aristocracy. It is important to notice that these aspirations are Mr. Osborne's and not George's, for George ignores his father's order to marry Miss Swartz, believing that he is in love with Amelia. Thackeray's characterization of Mr. Osborne shows us how love can be subverted by parental aspirations for the many vanities that exist.

THE ECONOMICS OF MATRIMONY

Parental scheming for wealth and power is of course only one side of the issue of marriage for money. Thackeray's characters are often only too willing to forsake true love for money and social eminence. The arrangement between Mr. Osborne's daughter Maria and Fredrick Bullock centers on this theme, with the author noting that in such a marriage whom you marry is quite irrelevant.

Maria would just as equally marry Frederick's father: "...She would have taken Bullock Senior, just the same, her mind being fixed as that of a well-bred young woman should be, upon a house in Park Lane, a country house at Wimbledon, a handsome chariot, and two prodigious tall horses and footmen, and a fourth of the annual profits of the eminent firm of Hulker and Bullock...". Again, love is unimportant, and money is the issue upon which such engagements revolve.

Frederick, too, is more concerned with the "economics" of matrimony: George being dead and cut out of his father's will, Frederick insisted that the half of the old gentleman's property should be settled on his Maria, and indeed, for a long time, refused "to come to the scratch" (it was Mr. Frederick's own expression) on any other terms. Osborne said Fred had agreed to take his daughter with twenty thousand, and he should bind himself to no more.... [Fred] thought himself infamously swindled by the old merchant, and for some time made as if he would break off the match altogether.

Fred consents to marry Maria only after his business partners have persuaded him of "the chances of the further division of property" at the death of Mr. Osborne. Theirs is certainly not a match based on love, but it is perhaps a perfect match, for both Maria and Frederick are willing to sell the ideal of true or romantic love for money. Love has no place in the business of marriage, but as we shall see, Thackeray is very clear in pointing out that happiness is frequently sacrificed in the transaction.

THE PURSUIT OF THE VANITIES

The relationship of Sir Pitt Crawley and Lady Crawley is another based on the pursuit of the vanities. There is certainly little happiness in their marriage: Sir Pitt is generally rude to Rose, he often leaves her completely alone, and he frequently hits her. Thackeray contrasts their relationship with what might have been had Rose given her hand in youth to a truer, purer love: O Vanity Fair Vanity Fair! This might have been, but for you, a cheery lass; Peter Butt and Rose a happy man and wife, in a snug farm, with a hearty family, and an honest portion of pleasures, cares, hopes, and struggles: but a title and a coach and four are more precious than happiness in Vanity Fair.....

Here Thackeray hints that the lower classes, far less concerned with social standing, perhaps are happier than those with wealth and power. The people of the Fair are willing to sell their happiness for social prestige. The author returns to this idea upon the death of Lady Crawley: "Her heart was dead long before her body. She had sold it to become Sir Pitt Crawley's wife. Mothers and daughters are making the same bargain every day in Vanity Fair". While this commentary seems to be provided in a matter-of-fact tone, there can be little doubt that it is a stark condemnation of the "business" of marriage.

ADVANCEMENT THROUGH MATRIMONY

Perhaps the most interesting character in Vanity Fair engaged in the transactions of matrimony is Rebecca Sharp. Thackeray's anti-heroine is continuously scheming to advance her position in life through marriage. She laments at the outset of the novel that she has no mother to arrange an engagement for her, "a dear, tender mother who would have managed the business in ten minutes, and, in the course of a little delicate confidential conversation, would have extracted the interesting avowal...". Rebecca's own considerable wits and schemes, however, are more than enough to captivate several men. Her first attempt at advancing in society through marriage centers on Joseph Sedley. Even before she has met him, Rebecca decides that she will attempt to wed him:

"If Mr. Joseph Sedley is rich and unmarried, why should I not marry him? I have only a fortnight, to be sure, but there is no harm in trying". Becky doesn't even hesitate to consider that there might be something more to marriage than money, and her artifices in attempting to win Jos. are worthy of the most skilled business negotiator. She cares little for him, quietly laughing at his pompousness and inflated airs behind his back. For Becky marriage is simply a way to rise to a new station in life, and when Jos. suddenly takes leave after his embarrassing drunkenness at Vauxhall, she is forced to begin her artful negotiations anew.

By involving herself in the intricacies of Sir Pitt Crawley's affairs, Rebecca manages to become indispensable to him. Upon the day of the death of his wife, Sir Pitt proposes to Becky. She is somewhat devastated by this, of course, because she is already married to his son, Rawdon Crawley. Like Maria Osborne, we see that Rebecca would have married the father just as quickly as the son; she is only interested in the wealth and access to society that either man can offer.

She marries Rawdon only because she believes that he will inherit his aunt's money upon her death. Rawdon, on the other hand, loves his wife: "the admiration, the delight, the passion, the wonder, the unbound confidence, and frantic adoration with which...[he] got to regard the little Rebecca, were feelings which...were not altogether discreditable to him". Rawdon's emotions would seem to be of the type found in the happiest of marriages, but they are unfortunately not returned.

The difference between the two in their emotions for each other is seen as Rawdon is off to battle. He takes inventory of what Becky will be left with should he die, showing love and concern for his wife. Rebecca, too, takes a similar inventory, but she displays little emotion for the possibility that her husband may be killed: Every calculation made of these valuables Mrs. Rebecca found, not without a pungent feeling of triumph and self-satisfaction, that should circumstances occur, she might reckon on six or seven hundred pounds at the very least, to begin the world with; and she passed the morning disposing, ordering, looking out, and locking up her properties in the most agreeable manner.

Becky shows little emotion for her husband except contempt, and her implied affair with Lord Steyne exposes her lack of devotion. When Rawdon leaves her, she sheds no tears but instead contemplates the lack of return on her investment in the relationship: "He was gone for ever.... She thought of her long past life, and all the dismal incidents of it. Ah, how dreary it seemed, how miserable, lonely, and profitless!...All her lies and her schemes, all her selfishness and her wiles, all her wit and genius had come to this bankruptcy" (. Thackeray hints at the unhappiness inherent in relationships based on the pursuit of vanities, but Becky ignores the lesson and continues to scheme until the novel's end, "writhing and pushing onward towards what they call 'a position in society'".

The novelist comments on how Becky could have been happy: It may perhaps have struck her that to have been honest and humble, to have done her duty, and to have marched straightforward on her way, would have brought her as near happiness as that path by which she was striving to attain it. But...if ever Becky had these thoughts, she was accustomed to walk round them, and not look in. She eluded them, and despised them or at least she was committed to the other path from which retreat was now impossible.

Thackeray points out that Becky could have led a simple, happy life, but for her relentless desire to achieve wealth and social status. She never comes to this realization, however, and through Rebecca the author shows us how our desires for the vanities can blind us to more truer, simpler emotions. The marriages and mésalliances of the characters in Vanity Fair show us the folly and futility of chasing wealth, power, and social eminence at the expense of love and passion. Thackeray's novel reminds us that there are frequently hidden costs when we make such a bargain, and the true expense is often more than we can afford.

Chapter 9

Victorian Publishing and W.M. Thackeray

Among the professional Victorian writers who made a living, or even a fortune, from writing without the aid of outside sources of income, there were a fair number who were incompetent businessmen. Of those who made a fortune, Thackeray probably has the reputation of being the least businesslike.

He is known as a lucky, careless genius, a lazy giant with great powers and equal weaknesses. Although he squandered a considerable part of his £17,000 inheritance through a weakness for gambling and in two ill-fated investments in periodicals, the Constitutional and the National Standard, the loss that threw him absolutely upon the resources of his pen appears to have been a bank failure in India - no fault of his own. Having struggled back to fiscal competence from his initial ruin, he invested £500 in the railroad mania in which he lost again in the general collapse of 1845. The success of Vanity Fair made his life easier but did not restore his lost fortunes.

His lecture tours in America netted approximately £5,000, which Thackeray invested in American railroads and sold out during the Civil War for only £3,895. Nevertheless, he left his daughters an estate nearly equaling the £ 10,000 apiece that he repeatedly said was his goal.

Explaining the differences between Thackeray and Dickens as professional writers, Anthony Trollope - certainly one of the most business-manlike of authors - wrote:

The one was steadfast, industrious, full of purpose, never doubting of himself always putting his best foot foremost and standing firmly on it when he got there; with no inward trepidation, with no moments in which he was half inclined to think that this race was not for his winning, this goal not to be reached by his struggles.

The sympathy of friends was good to him, but he could have done without it. The good opinion which he had of himself was never shaken by adverse criticism; and the criticism on the other side, by which it was exalted, came from the enumeration of the number of copies sold. He was a firm reliant man, very little prone to change, who, when he had discovered the nature of his own talent, knew how to do the very best with it. It may almost be said that Thackeray was the very opposite of this.

Unsteadfast, idle, changeable of purpose, aware of his intellect but not trusting it, no man ever failed more generally than he to put his best. foot foremost. Full as his works are of pathos, full of humour, full of love and charity, tending, as they always do, to truth and honour and manly worth and womanly modesty, excelling, as they seem to me to do, most other written precepts that I know, they always seem to lack something that might have been there.

There is a touch of vagueness which indicates that his pen was not firm while he was using it. He seems to me to have been dreaming ever of some high flight, and then to have told himself, with a half-broken heart, that it was beyond his power to soar up into those bright regions. I can fancy as the sheets went from him every day he told himself, in regard to every sheet, that it was a failure. Dickens was quite sure of his sheets.

It is not quite clear if Trollope was aware of the potential double meaning of that last assertion, but Thackeray was. In any case, this passage is the sort of realistic fiction for which Trollope is justly famous. But though it is misleading, if not an outright falsehood, Trollope's Thackeray has stuck in the popular mind.

The image Trollope evoked corresponds generally with the one promoted by Thackeray himself in such things as his vignette drawing of a printer's devil waiting at the door to carry his manuscripts to a presumably impatient printer and by stories like the one James T. Fields told of Thackeray coming to one of his own dinner parties well over an hour late with ink on his fingers announcing the completion of the last sheet of The Virginians.

It is indisputable that Thackeray produced much of his work under the pressure of deadlines. That need not mean he was lazy. John Sutherland has argued that Thackeray may even have written better under pressure than at leisure. Thackeray spoke often in his letters of living, eating, drinking his novels to the exclusion almost of his own daily life. He relished the creative pressure induced by deadlines, though he also knew the pace would wear him out.

It has been altogether too easy to overplay Thackeray in the role of procrastinator, the would-be gentleman of leisure, and to lose sight of the facts concerning Thackeray the businessman and professional writer, This part of the picture can be filled out from two other sources: his comments in his fiction on the craft of writing and the facts of his relations with his publishers revealed in letters, contracts and publishers' account books.

A key episode in establishing the image of Thackeray's view of his profession, its rank, rights, and responsibilities, took place in 1850. Thackeray brought the wrath of John Forster upon his head when, in Pendennis, he had George Warrington remark to Pen on their way home from a dreary publisher's party, "And now that you have seen the men of letters, tell me, was I far wrong in saying there are thousands of people in this town, who don't write books, who are, to the full, as clever and intellectual as people who do?"

Thackeray went on in the voice of his narrator, "And it may be whispered to those uninitiated people who are anxious to know the habits and make the acquaintance of men of letters, that there are no race of people who talk about books, or perhaps, who read books, so little as literary men".

Forster's objection, printed in the Examiner for 5 January 1850, was directed against Thackeray for disparaging literary men as a whole by presenting the Shandons, Waggs, and Bunions of the party as representative of all literary men and women. Forster attributed Thackeray's "attack" to a desire to curry favor with the nonliterary classes.

In defending himself, Thackeray gave one view of the professional writer. He claimed never to have "been ashamed of his profession, or (except for its dulness) of any single line from his pen." He considered the charge that he was currying favor among the nonliterary classes absurd, since in his experience people honored writers, and he would gain nothing through the supposed stratagem of which he was accused.

Finally, he defended his portrait of the literary world on the grounds that it was true. Why, he asked, "are these things not to be described... it such exist, or have existed, they are as good subjects for comedy as men of other callings". Forster would not let the subject alone, showing himself totally unmoved by Thackeray's explanations,

He distinguished between identifying humbug in a profession and identifying humbug with a profession. Here the public debate lapsed into silence without a winner. It is quite likely that Forster was predisposed to pick a fight with Thackeray over this issue because of a long-standing and fundamental difference between them, friends though they had been, concerning the status of professional writers and their role and in society. Forster and Dickens, as has been suggested by Craig Howes, represented the author in a romantic light, as a dignified, inspired artist.

The author's role, according to this view, was that of inspirer and castigator - as social conscience for the betterment of society [Howes]. Michael Lund has cited various nineteenth-century versions of this view suggesting that authorship is not work like other trades or professions but rather a gift or inspired avocation.

Thackeray, on the other hand, had long been speaking and writing from a different perspective, emphasizing the trade relations, admitting the work involved, and making fun of pretentious writing and pretentious writers. Thus, the controversy over the dignity of literature boils down to one side trying to uphold an ideal and a social responsibility (which they see as doing good) and the other side trying to be honest and unpretentious (which they see as being true). The object of fiction for the one is to change society; for the other, to understand it. There is no resolution for such a controversy.

Privately, in a letter to his friend Abraham Heyward, Thackeray admitted, however: "The words in Pendennis are untenable be hanged to them: but they were meant to apply to a particular class of literary men, my class who are the most ignorant men under the Sun, myself included I mean. But I wrote so carelessly that it appears as if I would speak of all, and even if it were true I ought never to have written what I did". Yet this apology expresses regret for having written carelessly, not for having thought the thought. Thackeray did not change his mind about writers; rather, he was sorry to have stirred up this particularly fruitless controversy.

In the novel Pendennis goes on to become a successful novelist, serving first a sort of apprenticeship writing reviews. He later becomes the author of Thackeray's The Newcomes, in which he gives the following description of the profession of authorship:

The drawbacks and penalties attendant upon our profession are taken into full account, as we well know, by literary men, and their friends. Our poverty, hardships, and disappointments are set forth with great emphasis, and often with too great truth by those who speak of us; but there are advantages belonging to our trade which are passed over, I think by some of those who exercise it, and for which, in striking the balance of our accounts, we are not always duly thankful.

We have no patron, so to speak - we sit in ante-chamber no more, waiting the present of a few guineas from my lord; in return for a fulsome dedication. We sell our wares to the book purveyor, between whom and us there is no greater obligation than between him and his paper-maker or printer. In the great towns in our country, immense stores of books are provided for us, with librarians to class them, kind attendants to wait upon us, and comfortable appliances to study. We require scarce any capital wherewith to exercise our trade. "at other so called learned profession is equally fortunate? A doctor, for example, after carefully and expensively educating himself, must invest in house and furniture, horses, carriage, and men-servants, before the public patient will think of calling him in.

I am told that such gentlemen have to coax and wheedle dowagers, to humour hypochondriacs, to practise a score of little subsidiary arts in order to make that of healing profitable. How many many hundreds of pounds has a barrister to sink upon his stock in trade before his returns are available?

There are the costly charges of university education - the costly chambers in the Inn of court -certain expenses all to be defrayed before the possible client makes his appearance, and the chance of fame or competency arrives. The prizes are great, to be sure, in the law, but what a prodigious sum the lottery ticket costs! If a man of letters cannot win, neither does he risk so much. Let us speak of our trade as we find it, and not be too eager in calling out for public compassion.

This description of the author's life and work emphasizes one aspect at the expense of others. Pendennis, as the narrator of The Newcomes, has constantly to remind himself not to think in inflated terms about authorship. This litany of the trade relations and modest requirements reveals that authorship is open to one and all who care to risk the chance of publication. Elsewhere, Thackeray emphasized other requirements, most notably the need to develop, through extensive reading, a sense of history. The comparison with the professions of medicine and law both elevate and deflate the picture being presented.

It is not so difficult nor so lucrative as those relatively bourgeois professions; but if it is like a trade involving paper sellers, printers, and booksellers, it yet also has freedoms and responsibilities unlike those trades which made it nonetheless a profession. Among those responsibilities Thackeray included the moral one of avoiding inflated language and slipshod moral implications - the two main butts of his humorous attacks in Novels by Eminent Hands.

Like Thackeray's celebrated redefinitions of snob and gentleman, his view of the professional writer as tradesman is a double one reconciling in itself traditionally opposing views. just as a middle-class or poor gentleman seemed a contradiction in Regency terms, so too the poet as tradesman seemed contradictory in romantic terms. Both Dickens and Forster remonstrated with Thackeray for his failure to hold high enough the dignity of the profession - their arguments smacking of conventional notions of the smudge of trade.

There is a tawdry irony in the notion of Dickens and Forster, both with tradesman connections in their backgrounds, and particularly Forster, who besides writing was a paid employee of a publisher, objecting to Thackeray's portraits of writers as tradesmen.

But Thackeray's view cuts through the pomposity and cant about the dignity of literature to the heart of the ideals of his profession - to love and truth, upholding the ideals without losing sight of the mundane business facts of authors writing for money, relying on and being relied upon in turn by publishers in much the same way that the printers and the paper sellers rely on one another in the business transactions that make books and periodicals.

To admit that the author is one in a line of necessary manufacturers and purveyors of literature that includes the publisher, printer, stationer, and bookstall vendor is to pursue truth where there seems to be nothing to gain except the miserable satisfaction of knowing it. In fact, however, that view is subversive to establishment conventions - a fact that goes a long way toward explaining the disagreement between Forster and Thackeray. Of course, this truth is not the whole truth any more than is that other much better known image Thackeray created of the novelist as the preacher in cap and bells That is to say, Thackeray was not just an exposer of sham, nor was he just a satirist.

Thackeray's double view of the word trade as it applied, without shame, to his own profession, is reminiscent of his similar treatment of trade in Vanity Fair where poor Dobbin in school is the butt of all the jokes because his father, a grocer, pays his bill in goods. Dobbin gains respect by beating Cuff in a fight, but the narrator notes that the lordly little George Osborne's grandfather was a tradesman too.

Dobbin's father becomes a respected alderman albeit none too refined a man, and Dobbin is unquestionably the real gentleman of the book. If authorship and publishing have the taint of trade, they also can have the honour of trade. And where there is honour, there is the risk of dishonor. The ideals of the profession could be traduced not only by inflated rhetoric but by dishonest shows of learning or of sentiment.

In an early review Thackeray complained of writers who sugared their instructions in manners and morals and academic subjects by putting them into fiction, but at the same time he firmly believed in the novelist's responsibility, even in the guise of a clown's cap and bells, to instruct - not with moral platitudes, of course, but with the lessons inherent in what he thought was unvarnished truth.

To the editor of Punch, Mark Lemon, he wrote on concluding the "Snobs of England": "A few years ago I should have sneered at the idea of setting up as a teacher at all, and perhaps at this pompous and pious way of talking about a few papers of jokes in Punch - but I have got to believe in the business, and in many other things since then. And our Profession seems to me to be as serious as the Parson's own".

One need not agree with Trollope that the vagueness or ambivalence in Thackeray's work reveals lack of commitment or conviction or strength. What some of his contemporaries thought of as a feigned "want of earnestness," an "undervaluing of his art," a carelessness about details, plain ineptitude, or tired repetitions in narrative structures may better be understood as the deliberate manifestations of a cast of mind that rejected, or at least suspected, the values represented by earnestness and narrative order. Thackeray's narrative technique undermines surface realism and the sense of certitude and stable values implied by authorial omniscience.

I think it likely that Thackeray deliberately undermined such values because he did not believe in them, because he thought the danger lay in overvaluing art. Thackeray saw more clearly than most of his contemporaries the problems of trying to create or capture "reality" in "fiction," and he knew more clearly than many a historian of his day that the coherence created by the orderly arrangement of historical data, commonly taken for "truth" in "history," is an illusion.

Jack Rawlins has recognized and described in some detail Thackeray's habit of undercutting the fictional realities he had created, but Rawlins seems not to have understood the implication of the narrative strategy, deploring Thackeray's refusal to adopt the novelist's responsibility to impose a moral order beneficial to society." In this regard Rawlins agreed with Forster.

From time to time scholars, noting the "lapses" in Thackeray's "artistic values," explain them as carelessness or as the inevitable, though lamentable, results of a hectic mode of production - John Sutherland, in Victorian Authors and Publishers, and N. N. Feltes, in Modes of Production of Victorian Novels, have turned this argument on its head as a means of praising Henry Esmond, which was produced under circumstances different from those attending any other Thackeray work; it is the only novel Thackeray finished before it was published. However, the very same kinds of disruptions of realism occur throughout that book, as a multitude of readers have noted, particularly Elaine Scarry.

John Sutherland has remarked that "the mode of production confirmed in Thackeray a kind of narrative opportunism. One always feels that he has reserved the right to switch the course of his narrative whenever and however it suits him. He alludes jokingly to the arbitrariness of his power over plot in the preface: 'Perhaps the lovers of "excitement" may care to know that this book began with a very precise plan, which was entirely put aside.

Ladies and gentlemen, you were to have been treated and the writer's and publisher's pocket benefited, by the recital of the most active horrors.... Nay, up to nine o'clock this very morning, my poor friend, Colonel Altamont, was doomed to execution, and the author only relented when his victim was actually at the window." Sutherland opined that this was "high-spirited nonsense" and the "element of truth" about Thackeray's work was the lamentable one of "narrative opportunism." That particular interpretation is apparent only to persons committed to the tradition of English fiction adhering to Jamesian inevitability, to Trollope's insistence on the novelist's right (and need?)

To be able to adjust the beginning to the end, to a Joycean refining of the author out of existence. But it is not "nonsense," high-spirited or otherwise, to anyone willing to face the possibility that these "lapses" (they seem rather too frequent and to come in too strategic locations to be lapses) are, if not deliberate, at least characteristic gestures reflecting a point of view about history, fiction, and reality that is controlled by a value system rejecting the Jamesian striving for realism precisely because realism is a contrived illusion.

The particular example of "opportunism" in question is from Pendennis. It illustrates the carefully planned contrivance of this illusion, for the "communicating leads" and window box that make Altamont's escape possible were first planted, so to speak, 330 pages earlier (2: 38) and had already been used by Colonel Strong to escape a bailiff.

No reader finding Altamont cornered in the same apartments could be surprised by the escape. To accuse Thackeray of opportunism - that is, to take seriously his remark about relenting at the last moment - is both to underestimate the control he had over his materials and to misunderstand his deliberate exposure of the illusion of reality in order to make his point.

For Thackeray, fiction was fun, and the illusion of reality was fascinating. All his sympathies were on Dobbin's side, for example, when on a school half-holiday the boy sits under a tree, carried away by a book into the world of the Arabian Nights. But he continually insisted that that world was not real; reality obtrudes for the reader of Thackeray's fiction in the form of his "lapses" just as surely as it did for Dobbin when the altercation between Cuff and George Osborne broke in on his fictive Arabian world.

Thackeray addresses the reader, laughs in his sleeve, imagines Jones yawning over the number, and "reserves the right to switch the course of his narrative whenever and however it suits him" because, much as he likes creating the illusion of reality, he likes more reminding his readers that in actuality he, Thackeray, is telling the reader, sitting in a chair, a story.

That is realism with a significant philosophical point: that the author, like the reader, is subject to human limitations of knowledge and judgment. Authors may have a keen view of human foibles but are no better at prescribing for the world than any other reader, Thackeray refused to set himself up to be the hero as man of letters. And for all that, paradoxically, there is more of truth in his sheets than in the pages of many a self-proclaimed regenerator of the age.

Thackeray's realism is one that his contemporaries and, it seems, many later generations of Thackeray's readers have been unprepared to see or accept. Thackeray must have known that, for he introduced his disruptions of fictive realism gently; they can be dismissed as "lapses" or the eccentricities of genius. Perhaps it has been too easy for readers to miss the implications.

Thackeray's sardonic view of aristocratic airs, his tracing of meanness and snobbery from top to bottom of the social scale, his "failure" to produce a moral framework within which the indeterminacies can come to moral closure have variously been explained as gentlemanly detachment, as declining to be the moral enthusiast, or as a weakness of spirit or lack of moral fibre.

Among Thackeray's most enthusiastic fans, these matters have been, at worst, irritations to be ignored. Thackeray was, to my mind, deliberate and committed in this fundamental point from his early writings throughout his life. But he was not prepared to make the point at the expense of his livelihood or the fortune he intended to make and leave for his daughters. He was very much aware of the commercial exigencies of novel writing, and it was not his aim to disrupt profits by focusing attention on his private beliefs and values. But there was good and ample reason for him to introduce into his fiction those elements that so irritated John Forster and Charles Dickens and that apparently disappointed Trollope and John Sutherland.

In such passages as the one in Philip where Thackeray discussed the amount of money the paragraph he was writing would earn him or the closing of Vanity Fair where the emphasis falls so heavily on the show and contrivance that his puppets "really are," he reminded his readers that the illusion of realism is created in the reality of storytelling.

The neat wrapping up of loose ends where villains are punished and heroes vindicated and rewarded, Thackeray knew, is an illusion. Reality is ambiguous and indeterminate. The true realist does not know enough to pass out poetic justice justly. So Thackeray reminds his readers constantly and truthfully that the puppet show is not real. He forces an ultimate realism upon his readers by denying the possibility of honest satisfaction in fictive endings. To him, the truth about the world included the truth about writing fiction for a living.

Thackeray's methods expose the sham realism in which the author pretends to know not only what his characters think and do but by what moral standards characters should he measured. Thackeray's tentativeness, his apparently cynical view of good, and his supposedly infirm or sentimental stance on evil resulted, I believe, from honesty, humility, and simple acknowledgment of the true limits of authorial knowledge. Henry Dodd Worthington's description of his father in James Gould Cozzens's Morning Noon and Night suggests something of what I am trying to identify in Thackeray's character.

> Then there was that manner of his. You could not say it was shy, but you felt some lack of self-assertion, by most people associated with weakness, infirmity of purpose....What these were plain signs of I can now see. They were signs of deep and thorough skepticism, That I then didn't see it wasn't, I think, just boyish imperceptiveness, I would guess that few people saw it, that few people ever thought of him as skeptical. What people expect from a skeptic is skepticism in its

commoner loud, assertive form of scorning, challenging, contemptuously rejecting. This kind of skepticism will often be superficial, professings of men who basically are cynics, men of shallow thinking and loose feeling. My father's kind of skepticism made no show. It worked as a sort of silent patient withholding of judgment, almost as though his mild steady distrust of all appearances or supposed certainties went so far that when he felt serious doubts about anything those very doubts had to he held open to doubt.

To many of his contemporaries, Trollope and Carlyle particularly, Thackeray was a weak man, indecisive, lacking positive force. I believe they mistook his distrust of certainty.

The other extreme response to Thackeray, typified by Charlotte Brontë's remarks in the dedication of the second edition of Jane Eyre, calling Thackeray "the first regenerator of the day" who resembled Henry Fielding "as an eagle doth a vulture," is a corrective that goes too far.

Reacting to Thackeray's bold cutting through the cant and hypocrisy of the upper middle class, Brontë and other admirers tended to see in him a prophet whose attack on conventional values established art alternative foundation of values enshrining duty, loyalty, humility, and social responsibility. When upon meeting him Brontë discovered that Thackeray was no Carlyle, her disappointment arose from a misunderstanding not far removed from Trollope's. Alike, they failed to recognize and admire the profound honesty of Thackeray's aversion to overconfident assertions of values. Intense assertion of values was a common Victorian stance, but it was not Thackeray's.

Thackeray's respect for the "uncertainty principle," the humility with which he declined to be sure, is, of course, not peculiar to him, though it was a rare enough position in Victorian England. The position has had its influential manifestations, notably following periods of rigid or excessive authoritarianism. It played roles in the decline of the Spanish Inquisition and the rejection of Puritan rigidity following the excess of the Salem witch trials.

But it can be seen also in the tremendous variety of human

foibles tolerated without authorial condemnation in Shakespeare and in the attitudes revealed in Fielding's Tom Jones, Sterne's Tristram Shandy, and Keats's Odes all hesitating to judge too finely or too finally and, consequently, all creating problems for earnest moralists. In Thackeray's case it is particularly necessary to distinguish, also, between a mere dislike of rigidity or discipline (which he indeed had) and a deeply felt suspicion of certitude (which I think he also had). The former results from an irritable or sensitive personality, the latter from a philosophical position.

In his own day Thackeray's satiric view of the romantic ideals of his profession made him appear weak, ambivalent, his own worst enemy. And that view, with a hefty boost from Trollope, has carried over into the image of Thackeray as an undisciplined craftsman, leading more than one critic to characterize him as a "careless putter forth" or hasty or even lazy improviser [the phrase comes from George Saintsbury's Introduction to Pendennis, in which he also calls Thackeray a shrewd reviser]. And this unflattering view extends to the image of Thackeray the businessman or, as he implied with characteristic deflation, tradesman.

The word tradesman in Victorian England denoted, as it still to some extent does, an outlook and a rank in life that were incompatible with imagination and beauty, which were central to the concept of artist, poet, or even novelist. One equates tradesman in Victorian England with Mr. Pumblechook in Great Expectations and Mr. Polly in H. G. Wells's History of Mr. Polly or, on a higher economic though not sensibility scale,

Mr. Freeman in John Fowles's French Lieutenant's Woman, whose industrial and commercial sensibilities are impervious to art. But Thackeray was a practical man who had learned, from more than one penniless crisis, the reality of writing for money. That reality was a fact to be honestly acknowledged.

If authorship had certain high ideals, it included, on the other hand, the mundane practical details of the trade of writing. By using the loaded word trade for the artist,

Thackeray undercut both the social snobbery and the mystical trappings of artist, which some writers cultivated.

The social snobbery probably was an unconscious outgrowth, rather than a desired aim, of earlier proponents of the mystical view. The Victorian version of that view derived at least in part from the notions of poet or artist promulgated by Wordsworth in the preface to Lyrical Ballads, where the poet's sensibilities above the common run of men is claimed, and by Shelley's "Defence of Poesie," where the poet's position as an unacknowledged legislator of the world is proclaimed.

But perhaps the strongest impetus to view the writer's calling in a special light with special capabilities and privileges was Thomas Carlyle's portrayal of the "Man of Letters" in On Heroes, Hero Worship, and the Heroic in History. Thackeray's early send-ups of Dr. Lardner and Sir Edward Bulwer Lytton as pompous snobs playing off their roles as artists in social settings is an indication of his suspicion of the role. As a practicing writer, he turned to the trade rather than the calling in order to deflate the aggrandized view.

Thackeray became, in fact, an able and a reliable businessman who expected publishers and illustrators to fulfill their commitments with equal promptness. To his publishers, Bradbury and Evans, Thackeray wrote in May 1854 to complain of Richard Doyle, the illustrator Thackeray himself had chosen for The Newcomes:

"However much I may regard Doyle as a friend it is clear that as men of business we cannot allow our property to suffer by his continual procrastination. The original agreement with Doyle, made between Bradbury myself and him was that the blocks and plates for the ensuing month should always be supplied by Doyle on the 15th of the month current. I have now written to him, to say that I shall hold him to his agreement and that if by the 15 June the plates and blocks of No 10 of the Newcomes are not in your hands I shall employ another designer".

It would have been the height of arrogance and insensitivity for Trollope's Thackeray to require promptness and commitment from another man holding Doyle to standards too rigid for himself. But Trollope's Thackeray was a fiction. The real Thackeray was a reliable professional masked by a public image.

The popular concept of a harried Thackeray dashing off the last lines of the monthly number for the printer just in the nick of time is a romantic misunderstanding of serial publication. In thirty years of professional writing, Thackeray failed to meet only three deadlines that seriously affected a publisher. Only one of these commitments lay within his power to fulfill.

The October 1844 installment of Barry Lyndon was delayed one month for lack of copy, and even then there were mitigating circumstances. He mailed off the October installment on 23 September from Smyrna while on his Eastern tour, and it arrived too late in London for the October number of the magazine. He finished the book on 3 November. In September 1848 he become so ill he had to suspend the writing and publishing of the monthly numbers of Pendennis for three months, and in August 1859 he was too ill to write a complete final double number for The Virginians, providing instead a one-part number 23 and a one-part final number in September.

Thackeray's sense of the business requirements of authorship was hard won. Though he had earned his livelihood by journalism for ten years when he began Vanity Fair, he was in 1846 still very much a petitioner appealing to the largess of the proprietors of Punch and other publishers, and he was dependent on their valuation of the goods he brought for sale.

But by 1854 the author of The Newcomes saw himself as coproprietor with the publisher, The change is dramatic, and the composition, production, and financial success of Vanity Fair mark the watershed of Thackeray's career as a businessman, transforming him from the investor/ gambler, the writer waiting upon publishers with his goods, into the propertied tradesman who built himself a debt-free mansion at 2 Palace Green, Kensington.

Five chapters of Vanity Fair were written by early spring 1846. Thackeray announced to his mother that serial publication would begin on 1 May, and in March or April the first five chapters were set in type18. Production problems immediately became apparent: when the corrected galleys were paged, it was discovered that the fourth chapter reached page 28 and the fifth chapter extended to the middle of Page 35 Serial publication, however, required exactly thirty-two pages, no more and no less.

The first of May passed with no publication. The type for chapters 1-5 was knocked down and redistributed to the typecases, while Thackeray eked out his living with "The Snobs of England" and "Novels by Eminent Hands" contributions to Punch lasting beyond the publication of the revised initial number of Vanity Fair in January 1847.

What Thackeray learned during the eight-month delay in the publication of Vanity Fair can only be surmised from the regularity of his serial numbers from 1 January 1847 to the end of his life (except in the fall of 1848 and August 1859 when illness, not lassitude, prevented the professional fulfillment of his commitments to the public). The process he worked out was fairly simple but has only recently been understood by scholars. Except when he wrote The Newcomes, a few numbers of Philip, and Denis Duval, Thackeray never completed a monthly installment before the month it was due at the print shop.

Hs contract for Vanity Fair written and signed, curiously enough, on 25 January 1847 as the second installment was being printed specifies that he was to submit copy by the fifteenth of each month. According to his letters, however, often on about the twenty-fifth of the month he would write that he had "just ended his number."

Such statements, along with his frequent self-accusations of procrastination and the picture of the sleeping printer's devil waiting at the door, combine to give the superficial and false impression of a writer who could not meet his contracted deadlines. In fact, the process was a smooth, if hectic, coordination of writing, typesetting, proofreading, correcting, and printing responsibilities.

The reason Thackeray "ended" his numbers on the

twenty-fifth or so is that serial publication does not lend itself to the submission of a finished manuscript on the fifteenth. The first time Thackeray tried that, his installment would have occupied either twenty-eight or thirty-five pages had it been published. Instead, he would submit about three-quarters of an installment to the printer probably by the twentieth or earlier to be set in type.

With as many as five compositors working on a single installment (their names are the manuscripts), typesetting twenty to thirty pages could be completed in a day or less. The printer's devil would then carry proofs to Thackeray, who corrected them and measured them with a string corresponding in length to a page of the printed book. Arriving at a fairly accurate estimate of the amount of text still required to fill the number, he would revise and augment or cut as necessary.

A printer's boy or the mails would then return the corrected and augmented proof to the printshop. Second proofs with page headings and page numbers embedded would be ready in another day or so, making it possible for Thackeray to read proofs and make final adjustments in length by the twenty-fifth or twenty-sixth of the month. The printers and binders then usually had about five days to get an installment ready for distribution by the last day of the month. This coordination of production effort lends itself to the concept of writing as a trade. The artist's fancy is not free; the grinding schedule of production curtailed the craftsman's time and forced his energies in ways which Thackeray is on record as both appreciating and lamenting.

The conditions of serial novel writing were not very different from newspaper journalism or the scheduled inches of letterpress Thackeray was responsible for in Punch. Novel writers of Thackeray's standing today may have a fellowship or an advance front the publisher and a full year or eighteen months to write the novel. Not so Thackeray.

Yet the pressure was invigorating; he lived, talked, ate, slept his fiction up until deadline time. Thackeray's enthusiasm for the invigorating aspect of the engines of journalism shows in George Warrington's praises of it in Pendennis: There she is the great engine - she never sleeps. She has her ambassadors in every quarter of the world - her couriers upon every road. Her officers march along with armies, and her envoys walk into statesmen's cabinets.

They are ubiquitous. Yonder journal has an agent, at this minute, giving bribes at Madrid; and another inspecting the price of potatoes in Covent Garden. Look! here comes the Foreign Express galloping ire. They will be able to give news to Downing Street tomorrow: funds will rise or fall, fortunes be made or lost; Lord B. will get up, and, holding the paper in his hand, and seeing the noble marquis in his place, will make a great speech; and - and Mr. Doolan will be called away from his supper at the Back Kitchen; for he is foreign sub-editor, and sees the mail on the newspaper sheet before he goes to his own.

The mock-heroic tone of the adjective "ubiquitous, " of the exclamation "Look!", and of the juxtaposition of bribes in Madrid with the price of potatoes in Covent Garden introduces a faint distrust of the enthusiasm but does not belie the excitement Warrington feels for the press. The positive part of the passage echoes the spirit of historic significance that prompted the 1832 pressmen's parades in London, complete with a working press carried in a cart producing ink-wet pamphlets on freedom of the press for the crowd.

But Warrington's detachment, echoing Thackeray's own balances the sentiment with the dash and the pun on Mr. Doolan's mundane diurnal oscillation between the printed sheets and his bed sheets. The double view suggests that the situation is too complex to be captured by one feeling or one attitude. That same sleepless engine is also the inexorable, insatiable engine which fed on the writer and caused the haste and the drain of energy which sapped the health of more men than just Thackeray.

Thackeray's sense of the economic realities of publishing was acute-won at the price of two failed literary magazines and years of journalistic hand-to-mouth work. His image of Pegasus drawing a wagon and his unaristocratic equation of the literary profession with the trades are of a piece with his mockery of inflated self-importance in any calling in life. These self-deprecatory remarks cannot be taken to mean more than they do - that literary men must work hard, must meet their deadlines, must accept the consequences of the responses of publishers as merchandisers and readers as the market for art: they must write what will be published and purchased.

Thackeray's remarks on his profession do not mean that he held it in low regard or that he had no sense of the dignity of literature. For Thackeray the dignity of the profession lay in the integrity of presenting the world he knew as he saw it - including the business of authorship. In a letter to John Forster he indicated what humbug he thought lay at the root of attempts to assert the dignity of literature by any other means:

"I don't believe in the Guild of Literature I dont believe to the Theatrical Scheme; I think i s against the dignity of our profession, but you are honest and clever men and free to your opinion (thank you for nothing say you) well, believe that mine's loyally entertained too. " Thackeray was saying that the artist cannot with honesty or true dignity hide behind cant about a high calling.

Thackeray's position is neither starry-eyed or simpleminded. He knew the plight of many literary men who could be said to want the dignity of a bare living; his purse was frequently open to them. With similar honesty he acknowledged the ambiguity of good and evil, a view which more positive men took to reveal weakness. Nor is his position uncomplicatedly open and without subtlety of its own. A chapter of Thackeray's life remains to be written by someone who can see beyond or beneath the surface and untangle the remark in John Chapman's diary for 14 June 1851:

"I find that his religious views are perfectly free, but he does not mean to lessen his popularity by fully avowing them, he said he had debated the question with himself whether he was called upon to martyrise himself for the sake of his views and concluded in the negative. His chief object seems to be the making of money. He will go to America for that purpose. He impresses me as much abler than the lecture I heard, but I fear his success is spoiling him." Thackeray's net worth when he died unexpectedly on 23 December1863, at age fifty-three, attests for our material age his business success. His house was sold for £10,000. His furniture and personal effects sold for £2,000; his wine for £400. His copyrights brought his daughters £5,000. A total of about £18,000 - one thousand more than his father had left him.

THE SHAPING INFLUENCE OF THE MARKETPLACE

Among the Conclusions a study like this one reveals is that books are shaped by the demands they are intended to fulfill. If one is writing for money, as Thackeray quite clearly was, one must write that which will be accepted by publishers. Likewise, this study shows that the production of a book is a multifaceted cooperative affair and that the resulting printed text is not attributable to the author solely.

One is led inevitably, then, to a number of fundamental questions concerning literary works: about competing authorities for the verbal content and visual design of the books, about the authenticity of the text in any given book, about the relative claims as "best text" that could be made for competing editions.

Fundamental to any answers is another rather metaphysical question: At what point or points in a continuum from pure, free authorial autonomy to rigid social determinism does the production of literary art take place? If one thinks art is the product of the artist exercising creative freedom to write as he or she pleases, then the answers to the questions about authority, authenticity, and "the best text" will tend to be answered differently from the way they are answered by one who thinks art is the product of social forces fulfilling external demands for a market.

These concepts are more easily adjudicated in the abstract than in specific cases; so this chapter is devoted to an effort to understand the consequences of various answers as they relate to a specific work, Thackeray's Henry Esmond. I try to demonstrate that the questions raised here are of crucial importance to any reader of the novel, not just an editor trying to determine the textual details of a new edition. A brief orientation regarding theories of textual criticism will help establish their importance. The authority of the text, or more accurately, the authority for the text, is the person, persons, or "force" that has the final responsibility for "getting the text right." Among common notions about authority are, first, that of the author, who originated the linguistic text and read proof, giving authorial approval to additions, deletions, and alterations introduced by other hands.

A second centre of authority is the production personnel, for they create the combination of verbal text and [200/201] visual book that "for the first time really" constitutes the "public work." A third idea is that regardless of romantic ideals, the final object, often referred to reverentially as "the text itself," is its own authority and, regardless of its provenance, must be treated as "the work." And a fourth is that any thinking, careful, sensitive, knowledgeable person can, through close reading and/or research into the developing text, find and correct flaws and improve the work to better represent its potential ideal artistic form. These views are basically incompatible with one another and appeal variously to different people.

Once a notion of the "properly responsible" authority has been settled, questions about the authenticity of the text in any particular copy of the work can be asked. Identifying typographical errors and unauthoritative interpolations starts the effort to authenticate the text. Locating and restoring or incorporating authoritative readings that "belong" in the text complete the authentication.

Some works, however, do not fit easily into the procrustean bed created by the concepts of authority and authenticity. Authors sometimes revise, or the works become significantly altered in other ways, so that alternate authoritative and authentic versions vie for attention.

Persons who think a literary work should be one thing usually push for one text. They would like for statements about a work of art to have a stable referent. In the case of Henry Esmond, such a goal is easier to wish for than to have. There is no one answer to these questions. What needs to be recognized is that every reader answers them, perhaps not explicitly, in the act of reading by placing some credence in the symbols for the text on the page and by formulating some concept of what kind of thing is being read and what source or sources produced it. It has been usual for readers to assume that Thackeray wrote Henry Esmond, that Thackeray wrote what is printed on the pages of the book, and that what the readers understand and experience in reading the book came from Thackeray.

Some readers, of course, do not have a very clear notion of Thackeray and may think that the text before them is its own authority. More sophisticated readers may wish to discount Thackeray's authority over meaning and choose instead to read "against the grain" for meanings revealed inadvertently by the text about the author or about his society or about the means of production that created the physical book. All of these are common and legitimate readerly acts, and all require some act of faith regarding the authenticity and authority of the text.

One of the objects of this book is to explore the foundations for such acts of faith, to see more than is normally seen about the processes, aims, and social forces that influence the particular sequence of symbols on the page. The problem with this objective is that any historical construct is just that, a construct.

Constructs are influenced not just by the evidence of history put together objectively but by the historian's answers to metaphysical questions like, Are works of art the product of individual artistic talent, or are they social acts? For that reason this chapter does not argue in behalf of one point of view, but rather explores the consequences of adopting two or three different points of view.

A working proposition here is the idea that the persuasiveness of any historical construct and of any accommodation of the questions of authority, authenticity, and authorial autonomy or social determinism depends on the context identified as relevant to the construct. Of course, everything is a context for everything else, but historians, editors, and readers usually focus narrowly on "truly relevant" contexts selected from the narrow range of material that survives as evidence.

It is necessary, therefore, to identify the various contexts in which Henry Esmond has been seen and to show the differing consequences to readers and editors. Implicit in the procedure is the idea that coherent explanations can be attempted within defined contexts.

In everyday practice: the meanings of verbal utterances are guided heavily, if not actually established, by contexts. In The History of Henry Esmond, Thackeray, writing in 1851 - 52, had a mid-nineteenth-century audience consisting of book reviewers, circulating-library readers, his mother, his publishers, his friends, and his ex-lady love Jane Octavia Brookfield.

These people can be seen as having been addressed by the novel. But Thackeray said not one word in Henry Esmond, for his narrator, the aged Esmond, and the memoir's editors and commentators, Esmond's wife and daughter, do all the writing. The writing is understood to take place in the second and third decades of the eighteenth century and records events said to have occurred between 1670 and 1720. Esmond's memoirs are addressed to his grandsons, but his audience clearly includes his wife, who is thought by most critics to resemble Jane Brookfield. The speakers in the novel, in passages of dialogue, also produce their utterances in contexts that help identify their meanings.

One can ask what the character meant, what Esmond meant by reporting the character's speech, and what Thackeray meant by having Esmond report it. One can ask what the passage may have meant to a Victorian totally ignorant of the author and what it may have meant to Jane Octavia Brookfield. And, of course, modern readers produce their own responses to these meanings by contrasting them with their own sense of acceptable beliefs and behaviors. Thus readers contextualize the text in various specific ways as a means of producing what they think are appropriate understandings of the text.

This is only the tip of an iceberg of contexts within which the novel's words can be set and understood. Each context illuminates the text in a different way. Readers know this and act upon that knowledge almost without reflection - they are that good at using and understanding language.

And when a scholar/critic points out to readers an aspect of context they had not considered, they gratefully add it to the mix of factors that influence their understanding of the text. The study of genre, the author's other works, biography, cultural history, the history of ideas, all these are understood to extend the readers' awareness of the contexts within which texts create and convey meaning. Even the physical embodiments of texts, the books themselves as paper, ink, and bindings, influence interpretations.

There is, however, a major flaw in the ordinary idea of authentic texts. If it is assumed that the text of a work is stable, that is, if we work with a text that is thought to have been established, we use the principle of contexts to produce "readings of the text" for contemplation. But if it is recognized that the text itself is not stable, we tend to use the principle of contexts to produce a "reading of the text" that will help establish what the text is by leading us to the right critical choices among variants. That is clearly circular reasoning and leads to predictable texts that best fulfill the editor's particular contextual construct. But the situation is worse than that.

It does not matter that no variant survives at a given point in the text; each word or mark of punctuation is potentially an erroneous witness to the context identified for use in interpreting the text.

That may seem good to the editor, for that is what makes emendation of errors possible. Editors tend to think that some errors, like typographical errors and scribal errors, are "demonstrable," and they emend them. But they may be too quick to [203/204] believe an error to be demonstrable because they are not sufficiently aware of the influence of the contextualization that they are using to determine the meaning which identifies the textual anomaly as a demonstrable error.

To illustrate the consequences of this approach, a useful

example is The History of Henry Esmond, which for these purposes will have to be examined in the original edition, published in London by Smith, Elder and Company in 1852 in three volumes. In what follows I speak as an editor of Henry Esmond, but I mean to imply that in order for an editor to know what is being edited and why it is being edited, he or she must first be a reader, must know how to read, and must know what effect the editing is having on reading. Consequently, everything I say about the editor is applicable also to any careful reader.

To do a contextual reading, one must try to draw together the historical details of authorship as a profession and printing and publishing as a complex of economic traditions and interests in a continuous struggle with innovation - both technical and moral - and with attitudes toward gender, family, and moral conventions, particularly as they reflected the audiences for lending libraries in order to see what Henry Esmond was. Then, perhaps, it can demonstrate more clearly what the reader's and editor's task is, or, at least, what purposes modern scholarly editions serve.

While not forgetting that authors attempt to create something original that will fulfill their own purposes (including the purpose of making money), we will have to examine bibliography, printing history, papermaking, taxes on books and newspapers, copyright law, labour relations, trade guilds relating to printing, publishing, and bookselling, marketing associations, professional societies, the apprentice system, lending libraries, the three-deckers in relationship to parts publication and magazine serials, the growth of the literate public, the development of authorship as a profession, and the developing division of labour into literary agents, publishers, printers, wholesalers, and booksellers.

Each of these can be thought of as a force field influencing what the work became, limiting what the work could say, shaping the work, and thereby influencing reactions to and understandings of the final product. (Incidentally, one of the nice things about scorning historical reconstructions is that there is less work involved.)

Now obviously all of that cannot be detailed here, but it has been done, and its salient details can be summarized The History of Henry Esmond is Thackeray's only book to appear originally as a three-decker. It was published by a firm whose head, George Smith, was an executive member of the Bookseller's Association.

It was Thackeray's second book with Smith, Elder and Company - his first major book with that publisher - and it represented the first significant step in an attempt by George Smith to make Thackeray one of his authors - an object he accomplished thoroughly mid completely in 1859. Smith descended into publishing from the banking business by way of substantial reference works and scientific publications. His literature list, his fiction, was respectable, yet he was bold and aggressive.

He published Charlotte Brontë's Jane Eyre and later went on to acquire as his authors Anthony Trollope and George Eliot. Esmond, therefore, by virtue of its publishing house belongs to a tradition of book production controlled by establishment wealth and power. To be published by Smith implied certain standards of literary and moral content that Thackeray had never been clearly subject to before, though he was subject in a general way to the Mrs. Grundy censorship affecting all Victorian publications above pulp street literature.

Thackeray rose to the Smith, Elder house from his major publisher, Bradbury and Evans, which in turn had risen into publishing from bookselling, newspaper publishing, and being proprietor of that low comic magazine, Punch, and other comic and sporting publications. In spite of the firm's industry and success, Bradbury and Evans belonged to a decidedly antiestablishment point of view, and in the 1840s Thackeray was one of its chief writers. Thackeray's sojourn in bohemia as an art student in Paris and as a writing hack in London were social and financial descents from which the economic success of books like Vanity Fair and Pendennis were raising him.

Those works and the bulk of his writings in the 1840s reflect the satirical, antisnob, antiestablishment attitudes of Punch and Fraser's Magazine, the main outlets for his writings.

Esmond was to be different. The author of Esmond was a man financially and socially restored to the level of his upbringing. He was a popular writer and successful public lecturer, having delivered his urbane lectures on the eighteenth-century English humorists to receptive and aristocratic audiences in London, Edinburgh, Oxford, Cambridge, and the larger industrial cities. Esmond was to be his calling card and proof that he could write a thoroughly good, artistically complete, and serious work of art. By and large, Esmond has been seen, both by his contemporaries and by generations of literary critics up to our own day, as a peak in Thackeray's rising career as a writer and artist.

The book belongs to the establishment in otherways, too. The three-decker was in mid-Victorian England a thoroughly establishment commodity, an expensive book made possible and necessary by circulating libraries whose large guaranteed prepublication purchases made three-decker production a book publisher's staple.

It was nearly impossible for a book publisher to lose money on a three-decker that had been adopted by Mudie's library, but the discounts Mudie demanded and the price regulations that kept most ordinary customers from purchasing their own copies instead of subscribing to Mudie's made it equally difficult for a publisher to make very much money on a three-decker.

The price-maintenance system for three-deckers worked to the benefit of publishers and the circulating libraries from the mid-1840s to the mid-1890s by providing stability; no one was making an inordinate amount of money, but the system could be counted on. This stability depended not only on control of prices but also on certain simple controls over the content and size of the books.

These constraints imposed by Mudie's are now relatively easy to document; their primary focus was on the length of the book and the moral character of the plot and characterizations. An author and publisher who could work within the library constraints and win selection could count on a sound though not spectacular financial return.

But the respectability of the publisher and the library demands are not the only determining or constraining forces observable. Esmond is a historical novel created within a tradition of historical fiction which Thackeray may be said to have modified but not to have invented. Among these constraints was the demand for historical plausibility and the historical research which that demand entailed.

Plausibility was judged by the depth and breadth and accuracy of the historical detail surrounding the fictional characters and events. It was not necessary, however, to maintain historical perspective in moral and intellectual concerns or issues; Sir Walter Scott had made the historical novel both respectable and relevant to current moral and political concerns. But the freedom offered by historical fiction within the establishment contours of the three-decker published by Smith, Elder was a narrow freedom indeed.

N. N. Feltes, in considering Esmond in its marketplace context, has noted that the Booksellers Association and the circulating libraries were fighting a losing battle against an encroaching democratizing, proletarian invasion of the world of books and literature represented by cheap books, serializations in shilling parts, and shilling magazines.

The booksellers' battle was to save the commodity which three-deckers epitomized and thereby save the economic control and stability which they enjoyed primarily through the three-decker. Feltes saw the three-decker as symbolic of the upper-class resistance to progressing economic forces and finds in the three-decker morality and traditional structures a corollary conservatism and reactionary spirit. He found in Esmond, a historical novel redolent with nostalgia for a past age, the same conservatism and establishment resistance to mass values, mass mores, and mass tastes.

He found in Esmond's literary reputation a confirmation of conservative tastes and socioeconomic politics. In the social history of the last half of the nineteenth century, on the other hand, Feltes saw the slow but irresistible subversion of the commodity book by the new cheap, democratizing commodity text. The triumph of this movement was the demise of the three-decker novel in the 1890s. For Feltes, therefore, Esmond represents a reactionary, establishment work. As such it represents a change or an anomaly in Thackeray's role, which for Vanity Fair and the early journalism was that of satirist of the establishment. Feltes posited the explanation that within the constraints of the three-decker, Thackeray was determined by cultural forces greater than himself and that an examination of these cultural contexts proves that the language and the culture speak the author, that the autonomous author is a figment of the romantic imagination; "reality" is the reality of social determinism.

If this discussion were to stop here, the weight of the social contract might seem irresistible; the social theory of texts would convincingly vest authority for the linguistic text and the meaning of the work in the social context. And the editorial solution for Esmond would be to select the first edition as the copy-text, emend nothing, and present the novel as a commodity book with large margins, heavy paper, and expensive packaging, thus perpetuating its role as representative of the establishment, [207/208] standing as an anomaly in Thackeray's literary corpus.

But the author, his text, and his meaning need not disappear behind this sociological arrangement of historical details. It is a significant shortcoming in Feltes's work that he did not apply his critical apparatus to a reading of the text.

Careful rereading of Esmond suggests a conclusion opposite to the one Feltes reached. He skated over the elements in the book that do not confirm his social deterministic theory of book production. The flaw of his approach is the rigidity with which his view of the social contract theory of texts controlled and limited his reading of the work by paralyzing his belief in authorial intentionality. Social determinism apparently obviates autonomy in Feltes's way of looking. Although all that Feltes pointed out about the cultural milieu surrounding Esmond is true, it is hardly as comprehensive or constraining a view as he suggested.

Though the novel was hailed by many of its original readers (particularly its better-educated and better-heeled readers) as a critical triumph, and though it for many years has been held in high regard even by readers who do not generally admires Thackeray's works, it was and is a profoundly troubling book to many others.

Many of its first readers and reviewers were shaken and angered by the ending, in which Esmond marries the woman he has long treated as his mother. That that denouement was Thackeray's intent from the beginning is perfectly clear on rereading with close attention to Rachel's character - she knew her heart's true relation to Henry well before her husband died and years before naive Esmond himself recognized it.

It shows in her nearly hysterical reaction to the news that Henry has exposed himself to smallpox by visiting Nancy Sievewright, the blacksmith's daughter, although a superficial reading allows one to think that she is reacting merely as a social snob and doting mother (bk. 1, chap. 8). It also shows in her behaviour to Henry on his third visit home from college when young Frank reveals that she has been fussing over Henry's room for days, having worked a new counterpane for his bed and put fresh-cut roses in his window in anticipation of his arrival, though she pretends not to know if the housekeeper has prepared his room (bk. 1, chap. 11).

It shows in her reaction to the news that "Henry" has been killed in a carriage accident, though the Henry involved turned out to be Melton, not Esmond (bk. 1, chap. 13). It shows in the nearly psychopathic rejection scene in prison after Lord Castlewood has been killed in a duel (bk. 2, chap. 1). And it shows in the news that she has sneaked off to Southampton to watch from hiding as Esmond returns from the Continental wars (bk. 2, chap. 7). Rachel clearly believes that God has punished her for her disaffection to her husband and her secret affection for Henry by allowing her husband to be killed.

She tells Esmond years later when they meet again that God has forgiven her sin: "But I would love you still - yes, there is no sin in such a love as mine now; and my dear lord in heaven may see my heart; and knows the tears that have washed my sin away" (bk. 2, chap. 6). Rachel's secret love was even more disturbing to the Victorian consciousness than the apparent though not real incest at the end of the book, for it portrays a good woman - the heroine angel in the house - in the grip of a powerful and lifelong illicit passion she must and does suppress with visible effort. Morally the book's psychological realism, though delicately handled, is profoundly subversive to the establishment. It is a measure of Thackeray's artistry that he portrayed these telling scenes in ways susceptible to more conventional interpretations, though to read them as such is to believe Thackeray has overwritten them.

But the book is subversive in an even more important way, for Esmond's ostensibly weak character, his apparent vacillation and inability to cast himself passionately and unreservedly behind any cause, religious, political, economic, or amorous - though goodness knows he tries - arguably stems not from a psychological weakness but from a fundamental philosophical uncertainty and humility that is very dangerous to establishment mentality.

The elderly narrator of the book, recounting Esmond's youthful naive enthusiasm for Father Holt's Catholicism, Rachel's Anglicanism, the Dowager Castlewood's Jacobitism, Beatrix's concepts of heroism and honour, constantly reveals Esmond discovering himself in an assumed and uncomfortable role-playing.

Esmond spends his life fulfilling or trying to fulfill other people's expectations for himself and repeatedly discovering that the goals were not worth winning. He ends ashamed of himself as a soldier witnessing his fellows attack nuns, of Father Holt's tawdry lies and deceptions, of Frank Esmond's subjugation to Clotilde, of Beatrix's head-hunting selfishness as courtesan, and ultimately of his own complicity in these other shames he has participated in as a role player rather than in propia persona.

The measure of Esmond's superiority over other characters is that he recognizes his self-delusions and those of his fellow actors. Esmond's way of thinking and suiting action to thought is antiestablisliment. That is why Beatrix has no permanent use for him. Esmond is constantly giving away

[208/209] the store on the grounds of scruples; he loses ground for honour and principle without any compensating social or economic or political gain. He is ultimately anti-imperialist and antiroyalist, and he rejects the optimism of the intellectual rationality for which his age, the eighteenth century, is known. At the end of the book he retreats happily enough to the margins of the empire, where he establishes a domestic kingdom of his own.

The question about Thackeray's "intentions" with regard to Esmond and its potentially antiestablishment meanings can be pursued a bit further in two directions. They both bring to bear on the reading of Esmond other contexts than the Marxist economic contexts just examined.

The first is the biographical background and in particular the events in the year immediately preceding the writing of Esmond concerning Thackeray's love life. By 1851 Thackeray's wife had been confined under special care for insanity for seven years, In the three years before the writing of Esmond his love for Jane Octavia Brookfield, the wife of his best friend, the Reverend William Brookfield, had gotten as heated as a platonic relationship can get.

Thackeray was clearly in love, though he was fully aware of the impossibility of the situation. He imagined that Jane suffered under a sense of repression and lack of appreciation by her husband, which may have been greater in Thackeray's mind than in reality. Whatever the case, in September 1851 William Brookfield, who had tolerated Thackeray's attentions to Mrs. Brookfield with increasing wariness, put his foot down, banning Thackeray from the society of his home and wife. It is not hard to trace Thackeray's melancholy in the Henry Esmond/ Rachel Castlewood relations in the book he was then commencing.

Though he had not written any part of the book, he signed the contract for Esmond in June 1851. It was a story he claimed was boiling up within him as early as January, though his work on his lectures on eighteenth-century English humorists came first. That the rupture with the Brookfields affected the story there can be no doubt. Thackeray complained to Smith as late as December that he could not get on with the book under the effects of an ailment which time alone could mend. In the book itself there is a romanticized version of what could have been: Lord Castlewood's insensitivity to his wife may be read as William Brookfield's insensitivity to Jane writ large; Rachel's deep love for Esmond, suppressed and denied but tortured and irrepressible, may be Thackeray's portrait of what he saw or wished to see in Jane Brookfield's relation to himself.

Thackeray seems to have been much more interested, to judge also from his letters, in assuaging his own sorrow than in upholding establishment social mores. And in the character of Henry Esmond, Thackeray was able to make Rachel suffer the jealous pangs of seeing her unattainable love object throw himself at the feet of another-Beatrix, who was Rachel's daughter.

Nor is it hard to see Thackeray beating his own breast and exploring the ecstasies of rejection while describing the perpetual and nearly unstiflable but unrequited love of Esmond for Beatrix. The psychological realism of a complicated and confusing network of love and jealousy involving mothers and sons and other forbidden attractions is carefully handled, for in Victorian fiction serious and troubling life passages could be explored only in code.

And finally, to focus on the way in which interpretation bears on editing, the rhetorical context of Esmond must be considered. It is a memoir: The History of Henry Esmond, Esq., a Colonel in the Service of Her Majesty Q. Anne. Written by Himself. It has all the rhetorical characteristics of an extended dramatic monologue, addressed by Esmond to his grandsons. Thackeray, the author, said not one word in propia persona in the whole book; even the introduction is written by Esmond's daughter.

As with any first-person narration, the potential for irony and for misapprehending irony is great. Traditionally, critics have read Esmond's narrative as something like the preachments of the author's alter ego. Esmond's opening comments, on the nature of history, strike readers as honest and commonsensical. "Why shall History go on kneeling to the end of Time? I am for having her rise up off her knees, and take a natural posture: not to be for ever performing cringes and corgees like a Court-chamberlain, and shuffling backwards out of doors in the presence of the sovereign.

In a word," Esmond writes engagingly, "I would have History familiar rather than heroic." It sounds like the sort of attitude Thackeray would adopt; it is like his reviews of pictures in the Academy, knowledgeable but unimpressed. Esmond seems to reflect Thackeray's own attitude also by placing himself and his neighbors on the stage of history and comparing them with the figures normally found there:

"I have seen too much of success in life to take off my hat and huzza to it, as it passes in its gilt coach: and would do my little part with my neighbours on foot that they should not gape with too much wonder, nor applaud too loudly. Is it the Lord Mayor going in stare to mince-pies and the Mansion House? Is it poor Jack of Newgate's procession, with the sheriff and javelin-men, conducting him on this last journey to Tyburn? I look into my heart and think I am as good as my Lord Mayor, and know I am as bad as Tyburn Jack, " In short, the book abounds with reasons not to draw a sharp distinction between the narrator and the author.

Moreover, Esmond has a basic distrust of absolutes - that is, of other peoples' absolutes - he does not trust the judgment of priests, military leaders, political leaders, or kings. His love and his loyalty are always tinged with sardonic self-detachment. As one critic has noted, "Like Vanity Fair, Henry Esmond is a sustained argument against the reality of moral absolutes. Esmond himself does much of the arguing, for he is proficient at identifying illusory values and beliefs.

His sophisticated skepticism, however, is itself founded on a dedication to one surviving absolute: truth." This personal truth of Esmond's is the foundation of his appeal to the reader in his autobiography. And, as with most monologists, Henry constantly asks the reader to share in his personal recognition and judgment of the self-deception of others. Furthermore, he seldom expects the reader to take him very seriously, and he appears to be disingenuous when he does.

Feltes probably would not rejoice over this coup d'état within the camp of the dying establishment, for the book does not subvert the establishment on behalf of the rising proletariat. Instead, the subversion emanates from the principles of a small intellectual elite, the freethinkers of England's Victorian intellectual class. Some of those freethinkers were ideologues, but Thackeray's religious and philosophical ideas did not develop in a cell of like-minded philosophers or so-called freethinkers (though it was not insignificant that he was a close friend of Edward FitzGerald, the translator of Omar Khayyám's Rubáiyát).

Thackeray's philosophy is revealed in his letters and private papers as a deep and fundamental individual skepticism about causes of every sort. It got him into trouble with many proponents of causes in need of money or moral support who approached Thackeray.

If the cause was individual, to honour an admirable writer's family, to provide charity on nonsectarian bases, Thackeray was a patsy. But if it was to establish a guild for literature or to propose an evangelical school or cause, his purse and ear alike were closed. He did not trust institutionalized schemes.

Esmond is subversive to the establishment it represents, but not on behalf of emerging socioeconomic ideologies. Even the fact that both Thackeray and his publisher made a good bit of money from Esmond, which was all unusually good seller despite its price, does not indicate that its themes or its production was determined or dominated by either a vested production tradition or an emerging public taste. Both of those "ideologies" claim the book by ignoring its subversive elements.

So much for Feltes's establishment interpretation of Esmond; this "establishment" book has a strikingly antiestablishment text - it is a wolf in sheep's clothing. And this interpretation makes the social contract solution to the editorial problem unacceptable. To take the first edition as copy-text for the linguistic text of all edition would be to accept the work of the minions of the establishment. Now, it so happens that in 1852, George Smith did not own his own printing establishment, so he sent Thackeray's manuscript to Bradbury and Evans to be typeset and printed. There may be comfort to be found, then, in the fact that the compositors of Thackeray's "proletarian serial novels" also typeset his "establishment commodity book," but the principle of authorial autonomy which the antiestablishment interpretation tends to support leads one to question the whole production process. That is to say, belief in the possibility of authorial autonomy, even of a limited sort, requires the rejection of any blanket rules for editing.

Rejecting Feltes's conclusions about the meaning of Henry Esmond in three volumes and rejecting the conclusion that a social contract requires special respect from an editorial view I do not mean that the three-volume format and the production process are unimportant.

Quite the contrary. The book could not be a wolf in sheep's clothing without the sheep's clothing, and such a wolf means far different things from regular wolves or regular sheep. The novel is quite definitely a collaboration, or at least a joint venture between the author and the social institutions of book production and marketing. And that identifies serious editorial problems.

A close look at Esmond reveals an extensive network of evidence suggesting an intentional subversion of the narrator by the author. Thackeray seems not to have trusted Esmond's foundation rock of personal truth, Elaine Scarry in a 1975 article compiled an extensive list of errors in the book.

These she invariably attributed to Esmond, claiming that Thackeray put them there on purpose. Scarry was not the first to notice that Esmond occasionally contradicts himself or forgets what he has said earlier in the narrative, but she was the first to attribute these errors to Esmond instead of to Thackeray or to the publishers. John Sutherland's Penguin edition annotations, for example, point out scores of historical and plotting errors, but Sutherland encouraged the readers to ignore them as understandable though regrettable characteristics of Thackeray's fiction.

Scarry identified an astonishing array of errors and anomalies, including an undermining of the rhetorical force of Esmond's own protestations - as when, having renounced the doctrine of divine right of kings and declared himself a republican, he nevertheless couches his adoration for Beatrix in the language of subjugation to royalty - and other more direct contradictions - as when he declares that an event so impressed him that memory would never fail him, whereupon he recounts the event in such a way as to contradict or distort his own earlier account of it. I believe Scarry is right to say that Esmond, "who has taken truth for his motto," was ironically undercut by Thackeray, "who has taken the absence of truth for his theme."

J. Hillis Miller, following a different line of reasoning altogether, arrived temporarily at the same conclusion Scarry reached. Miller brilliantly revealed the older Henry's ironic stance with respect to the younger Henry and then showed the ironic self-destruction of the self that Henry Esmond the narrator has constructed. Miller saw Thackeray's presence behind the narrator undercutting his claims to memory's sovereignty and the basis upon which Esmond allows himself to become "king" of the Virginia Castlewood and to accept the "worship" of Rachel and his daughter.

Miller did not use any references to the "narrative errors" in the book to detect this irony. But his view of Thackeray undercutting the narrator was a temporary stop an Miller's deconstructive way through the novel, for he then undercut or deconstructed this third level of irony by arguing that Thackeray was trying to "understand and control his life by taking ironic authority over that assumed role and by showing the imagined person to have made a false interpretation of himself."

Miller was more interested in his theory of irony as "infinite absolute negativity" than he was in the meaning of Henry Esmond, the book being in the final analysis only an illustration for what Miller had to say about irony. Furthermore, his conclusion about the novel could not stop with resolution, for it is the nature of deconstructive criticism to deconstruct the deconstruction. Resolution would put an end to the fun and games. However, Miller's point is not without seriousness. Resolution - say, the conclusion Miller considered at one point, that Thackeray undercut the narrator through telling references to Oedipus Rex and Hamlet which the reader with the help of Freud's Interpretation of Dreams can use to see Thackeray's ironic distance from his narrator - cannot be reached with any conviction if one is fully cognizant of the slippery ground such a resolution must take for its base. Miller implied that Thackeray, like his narrator, revealed himself rather than justified himself in the endless cycle of ironic undercuttings.

This view makes Henry Esmond "one of the best texts in English fiction by means of which to explore the workings of irony in narrative." But in order to get boxed up, as Miller wanted the reader to be, one must agree that Thackeray was seeking "authority over his own life by way of a detour representing that life in ironically displaced form in a fiction." Miller's conclusion that Beatrix is a sad mirror image of Esmond, revealing unconsciously the "corrosive power" of both characters and of their author, was based on the idea that Thackeray was seriously trying to present a "Pretense of mastery."

It would be possible - in fact, preferable - to conclude that Thackeray was not trying any such thing. Instead, he was demonstrating the inability to exercise any such mastery. Beatrix, in her cold-blooded, calculating attempts, which from the cynic's point of view should succeed, fails just as truly as does Esmond, whose machinations the reader is led to believe are wholly unconscious.

The melancholy nihilism of the book can and has been seen as Thackeray's cynicism. But it is one thing to recognize the lack of control implied by nihilism and quite another to give in to it. Beatrix recognizes it and gives in to it. Henry Esmond recognizes it up to a point; that is, he recognizes it for others but not for himself, and the sensitive reader of his memoirs is bruised by Esmond's lack of self-awareness, revealed, for example, in the way he punishes Rachel for "unfaithfulness" to him in the prison while excusing his own blatant and egregious "unfaithfulness" to her during the years of his infatuation with Beatrix. It is inconceivable that Thackeray failed to see Esmond's self-deception or the dual view of nihilism implied by Beatrix's and Esmond's stories.

Thackeray did not give in to it, as the cynical view would have it, [215/216] nor did he close his eyes to it, reverting blindly to an assertion of good that would be no more than a repetition of Esmond's quest for something worth believing in at one further level of self-deception. Anyone who has read Thackeray's own story - in the Letters and Gordon Ray's two-volume biography - can see the melancholy acceptance of uncertainty, as opposed to mastery, that characterized his mature years.

But two things mitigate against Miller's reading of Esmond, which was after all based on a reading of the text alone. One is Thackeray's determination expressed in conversation to John Chapman in 1851, thirteen days before he signed the contract to write Henry Esmond, that he did not feel "called upon to martyrise himself for the sake of his views" by expressing them too clearly to his reading public (Chapman's MS diary, Beinecke).

The second is, that Thackeray's personal reaction to his nihilistic ideas was to resist the temptation to give in. His personal intense desire not to hurt anyone, not to take advantage of anyone, not to manipulate others out of a sense that his version of "the truth" was the right version of it all reveals the light in which he created in Esmond the views Miller has described.

That is to say, in view of the emptiness of institutionalized values such as royalty, inherited rank, honour, party and country loyalty, marriage, and institutional religion, Thackeray chose not to sneer and not to pontificate, but to assert a sardonic kindliness and gentleness that are as far from sentimentality as those qualities can get.

Nihilism in Thackeray bred humility about his politics, religion, and responsibilities. It did not, of course, keep him from reacting rather dangerously when his dignity was bruised by Edmund Yates's caricature of him in 1858. That episode may appear to give the lie to the portrait sketched here, but in spite of what the episode ultimately turned into, Thackeray's actions began as self-defence against what he saw as unprovoked attack. That, at least, is not antithetical to the view that Thackeray in Henry Esmond, was giving up mastery over his life rather than desperately trying to gain control of it.

THE FORCE OF CHOSEN CONTEXTS

Now the point of all that is this: The contexts we identify as relevant to the text we read determines our interpretation, and the interpretation that is adopted determines the text we establish or edit. If N. N. Feltes's interpretation is adopted, one chooses the first edition as copy-text and makes the reading text ape the result of the social contract that originally produced it.

The emendations policy will be documentary and conservative. If, however, John Sutherland's interpretation is adopted, one selects the manuscript (or possibly the first edition) and emends the text to conform as closely as possible to one's notion of Thackeray's intentions by correcting as many errors as possible and writing notes for all the rest to explain them away or de-emphasize any damage they might do to the reader's enjoyment of Thackeray's tour de force historical pastiche.

And if Elaine Scarry's interpretation is adopted, one chooses the manuscript as copy-text and emends the text so that it effectively undermines the narrator's credibility, thus emphasizing Thackeray's rejection even of Esmond's attachment to personal truth. But if J. Hillis Miller's interpretation is adopted, there is no need to edit the text since his reading is untrammeled by information of any sort from Thackeray's life, the period in which he lived, the production institutions which enabled the book to become a book, or the genesis of the text.

If our goal is to read the text as a finished product, edited according to a "better way," then we must take a stand or abide by the editor's stand on answers to the following questions:

To what extent was the author aware of and in control of the book's potential ironies? Did Thackeray intend to undermine Esmond's trust in personal truth, or did he share Esmond's view? Did Thackeray deliberately undercut Esmond's credibility by introducing obvious errors and memory lapses into Esmond's memoirs, or are the errors those of the novelist, Thackeray? To what extent did the production crew understand the author's intention and enhance or inhibit it? These questions are to be answered by critical inquiry, not by ascertaining discoverable facts. This situation illustrates well what is critical about critical editing.

But it also illustrates the way any single text edition of the book is capable of distorting it and hiding its possible meanings by privileging one context over others as the determiner of meaning. It does not take genius to see that an editorial approach to Esmond which sets about correcting errors may well be thwarting the author's intentional and meaningful introduction of those errors.

On the other hand, not to correct the errors also may thwart authorial intention. Only persons who regard their personal solutions to these imponderables as universally acceptable would say that editing can be done by anyone correctly. The economic, biographical, and rhetorical contexts in the cultural envelope where Esmond became a three-decker historical novel all influenced what that book became; but it is a gross oversimplification to conclude that the book became inevitably what it is through determining forces over which the author had no control. A concept of the editorial task is not helped by the glittering generalities that suggest "the language [217/218] speaks the artist" or "the social complex employs authors to produce books" or "the author is dead." These conclusions are half-truths.

Likewise, it does not help one to understand the business of editing if one concludes that the author is autonomous, the sole authority over text. That view tends to cast the editor in the role of rescuer and restorer. But the illustration just detailed demonstrates that it is impossible to say with any certainty what Thackeray is to be rescued from or what needs to be restored. This brief survey of the complexities of Esmond's text seems to indicate that the author's communication to the reader is not only individual and free but constrained and directed by external forces. That is not a contradiction, nor is it a tragedy. It is a fact. Nothing understandable can be said or thought without the contextual frame of language and society and genre and custom and economic realities.

But all establishments and power structures have within them the capacity to be satirized, subverted, criticized, and amended - that is to say, the author is free within the limits allowed by the medium. The power of some texts is that their subsurface purposefully subverts the surface meanings. The question about the reader's and editor's dual responsibility to authorial intention and the social contract can be answered by saying they are both operative. It follows that a critical theory that ignores either is a lopsided theory, and it also follows that an editorial practice that edits away the evidence of either is equally lopsided.

The concept of editions which emphasize the importance of process and avoid extravagant claims for the correctness of the product is gaining ground, but not without resistance - resistance stemming from editors who are reluctant to give up power over the texts, from critics who want a stable text, and from publishers who, market driven, wish to save expense. Editions such as Hans Gabler's of Ulysses, Michael Warren's of King Lear, and the Garland Thackeray edition are attempts in different ways to emphasize alternative texts, or multiple texts, or indeterminate texts, but all these editions are controversial.

Resistance to them in preference for editions with supposedly unproblematic, stabilized texts accounts for the polemics of textual theory. Any single solution requires commitment to one of several orientations toward texts which are mutually exclusive. At that level there is considerable debate among editors about the right way to edit or the right goal or end product to present as the established text.

The alternative to a single text solution represents not an extension of polemic but a resolution. It represents a more comprehensive view of textual criticism, which, though probably not stable, at least does not stagger distractedly from one polemic to another. What then is the function of a scholarly edition? In the Garland edition of Vanity Fair, the famous last paragraph of chapter 32, in which Jos takes flight and the war is brought to a close, reads: "No more firing was heard at Brussels - the pursuit rolled miles away. The darkness came down on the field and city, and Amelia was praying for George, who was lying on his face, dead, with a bullet through his heart."

The effect is both thrilling and chilling, and even first readers of this passage as it appears here can feel the tear of opposing passions as the pleasure of seeing George dead combats the sorrow for sudden death and for poor Amelia, while at the same time the reader feels she is a sap for turning on the ever-ready waterworks for what one already knows is a "selfish humbug", a "low-bred cockney-dandy," and "padded booby," though Becky does not provide these words to describe George till chapter 67.

First-time readers will also, no doubt, sense the clean, crisp, efficient, and flat (i.e., nonpejorative, nonheroic) diction which gives the account its force and gives free play to the reader's conflicting feelings.

If readers were inclined to contemplate the passage, they might note that the phrase "The darkness came down" probably means primarily that night fell, but it allows the potential reverberations of the thought that "the darkness" has ominous symbolic overtones.

There is little to encourage such a speculation, however, except the juxtaposition of Amelia's own sorrow - which one can only partially share - and perhaps a twentieth-century propensity to see symbols everywhere. Should these readers turn to the "Record of Composition and Revision" in the Garland edition, they will find that the printed text reflects the reading of the first edition (1847) and that in 1853 someone (it is not entirely definite that it was Thackeray) revised the phrase to "Darkness came down."

Now, if the revised reading had been in the text in the

first place, the sense of potential ominous symbolic overtones to the descent of "Darkness" (now fortuitously capitalized) might have struck readers more forcibly. Some might say, because this reading is "stronger," it should have been chosen for the Garland edition.

It was not chosen because such aesthetic judgments were not part of the editorial strategy. To choose readings that correspond with the historical integrity of Thackeray's text at the time of first publication is not to reject the 1853 revisions. The point is not which of these readings is the correct one. The fact is that no one knows if either is correct or if both are correct.

The point is that in a scholarly edition both are available and have their various effects on the reading of Vanity Fair. Having read "The darkness came down," readers then find that a change was made to "Darkness came down." Either reading, by itself, conveys the fall of night, or both reveal the potential for a symbolic reading, the revised reading perhaps more so. But discovering that the reading was revised is the strongest indication that something was being attempted here beyond indication that night fell. The changing itself is a stronger indication of meaning than either phrase is alone.

That is a crucial point in understanding the importance of a scholarly edition. The aim of the editorial work should not be to produce a pristine, correct, reliable text, a product. It should instead be to trace the growth and development of the work and to place the reading text in its developing context, a process. The effect is lost on readers who insist on reading the text as product, but the potential is there for serious, sensitive reading directed in part by reaction to what the author did - as opposed just to what the author said.

This paragraph from Vanity Fair reveals a flaw in the Garland edition. The edition fails to include a parallel account of George's death from a letter Thackeray wrote to his mother who had complained about Amelia s selfishness. Thackeray's response is pretty well known, but it all should have been quoted in the edition, including his anticipation of the time two months ahead when Amelia's "scoundrel of a husband is well dead with a ball in his odious bowels" (Letters 2:309).

With that highly inflammatory and emotionally laden phrase ringing in one's ears, one cannot read the printed passage in the book without trying to account for the clean, flat, efficient diction found there in terms of Thackeray's narrative strategies and, perhaps, the demands of serial publication.

Scholarly editions should encourage and make possible such intertextual readings. The richness and satisfaction of such reading complexities go up when the countertexts are understood for what they are: parallel texts in letters, revisions in manuscripts, or alternative printed texts emanating either from revision or from compositorial or editorial intervention. The sources and relative dates of countertexts have a great deal to do with a reader's assessment of their significance. It seems, then, that the duty of a scholarly edition is not arbitrarily (and stealthily) to reduce the complexity and richness of a work of art to one correct and established standard text, but rather to lay out the materials as clearly and usefully as possible.

THE FORCE OF CHOSEN CONTEXTS

The point of all that is this: The contexts we identify as relevant to the text we read determines our interpretation, and the interpretation that is adopted determines the text we establish or edit. If N. N. Feltes's interpretation is adopted, one chooses the first edition as copy-text and makes the reading text ape the result of the social contract that originally produced it. The emendations policy will be documentary and conservative.

If, however, John Sutherland's interpretation is adopted, one selects the manuscript (or possibly the first edition) and emends the text to conform as closely as possible to one's notion of Thackeray's intentions by correcting as many errors as possible and writing notes for all the rest to explain them away or de-emphasize any damage they might do to the reader's enjoyment of Thackeray's tour de force historical pastiche.

And if Elaine Scarry's interpretation is adopted, one chooses the manuscript as copy-text and emends the text so that it effectively undermines the narrator's credibility, thus emphasizing Thackeray's rejection even of Esmond's attachment to personal truth. But if J. Hillis Miller's interpretation is adopted, there is no need to edit the text since his reading is untrammeled by information of any sort from Thackeray's life, the period in which he lived, the production institutions which enabled the book to become a book, or the genesis of the text.

If our goal is to read the text as a finished product, edited according to a "better way," then we must take a stand or abide by the editor's stand on answers to the following questions: To what extent was the author aware of and in control of the book's potential ironies?

Did Thackeray intend to undermine Esmond's trust in personal truth, or did he share Esmond's view? Did Thackeray deliberately undercut Esmond's credibility by introducing obvious errors and memory lapses into Esmond's memoirs, or are the errors those of the novelist, Thackeray? To what extent did the production crew understand the author's intention and enhance or inhibit it? These questions are to be answered by critical inquiry, not by ascertaining discoverable facts.

This situation illustrates well what is critical about critical editing. But it also illustrates the way any single text edition of the book is capable of distorting it and hiding its possible meanings by privileging one context over others as the determiner of meaning. It does not take genius to see that an editorial approach to Esmond which sets about correcting errors may well be thwarting the author's intentional and meaningful introduction of those errors. On the other hand, not to correct the errors also may thwart authorial intention. Only persons who regard their personal solutions to these imponderables as universally acceptable would say that editing can be done by anyone correctly.

The economic, biographical, and rhetorical contexts in the cultural envelope where Esmond became a three-decker historical novel all influenced what that book became; but it is a gross oversimplification to conclude that the book became inevitably what it is through determining forces over which the author had no control. A concept of the editorial task is not helped by the glittering generalities that suggest "the language speaks the artist" or "the social complex employs authors to produce books" or "the author is dead." These conclusions are half-truths.

Likewise, it does not help one to understand the business of editing if one concludes that the author is autonomous, the sole authority over text. That view tends to cast the editor in the role of rescuer and restorer. But the illustration just detailed demonstrates that it is impossible to say with any certainty what Thackeray is to be rescued from or what needs to be restored.

This brief survey of the complexities of Esmond's text seems to indicate that the author's communication to the reader is not only individual and free but constrained and directed by external forces. That is not a contradiction, nor is it a tragedy. It is a fact. Nothing understandable can be said or thought without the contextual frame of language and society and genre and custom and economic realities.

But all establishments and power structures have within them the capacity to be satirized, subverted, criticized, and amended - that is to say, the author is free within the limits allowed by the medium. The power of some texts is that their subsurface purposefully subverts the surface meanings. The question about the reader's and editor's dual responsibility to authorial intention and the social contract can be answered by saying they are both operative. It follows that a critical theory that ignores either is a lopsided theory, and it also follows that an editorial practice that edits away the evidence of either is equally lopsided.

The concept of editions which emphasize the importance of process and avoid extravagant claims for the correctness of the product is gaining ground, but not without resistance - resistance stemming from editors who are reluctant to give up power over the texts, from critics who want a stable text, and from publishers who, market driven, wish to save expense. Editions such as Hans Gabler's of Ulysses, Michael Warren's of King Lear, and the Garland Thackeray edition are attempts in different ways to emphasize alternative texts, or multiple texts, or indeterminate texts, but all these editions are controversial. Resistance to them in preference for editions with supposedly unproblematic, stabilized texts accounts for the polemics of textual theory.

Any single solution requires commitment to one of several orientations toward texts which are mutually exclusive. At that level there is considerable debate among editors about the right way to edit or the right goal or end product to present as the established text.

The alternative to a single text solution represents not an extension of polemic but a resolution. It represents a more comprehensive view of textual criticism, which, though probably not stable, at least does not stagger distractedly from one polemic to another. What then is the function of a scholarly edition? In the Garland edition of Vanity Fair, the famous last paragraph of chapter 32, in which Jos takes flight and the war is brought to a close, reads: "No more firing was heard at Brussels - the pursuit rolled miles away. The darkness came down on the field and city, and Amelia was praying for George, who was lying on his face, dead, with a bullet through his heart."

The effect is both thrilling and chilling, and even first readers of this passage as it appears here can feel the tear of opposing passions as the pleasure of seeing George dead combats the sorrow for sudden death and for poor Amelia, while at the same time the reader feels she is a sap for turning on the ever-ready waterworks for what one already knows is a "selfish humbug", a "low-bred cockney-dandy," and "padded booby," though Becky does not provide these words to describe George till chapter 67.

First-time readers will also, no doubt, sense the clean, crisp, efficient, and flat (i.e., nonpejorative, nonheroic) diction which gives the account its force and gives free play to the reader's conflicting feelings.

If readers were inclined to contemplate the passage, they might note that the phrase "The darkness came down" probably means primarily that night fell, but it allows the potential reverberations of the thought that "the darkness" has ominous symbolic overtones. There is little to encourage such a speculation, however, except the juxtaposition of Amelia's own sorrow - which one can only partially share - and perhaps a twentieth-century propensity to see symbols everywhere.

Should these readers turn to the "Record of Composition and Revision" in the Garland edition, they will find that the printed text reflects the reading of the first edition (1847) and that in 1853 someone (it is not entirely definite that it was Thackeray) revised the phrase to "Darkness came down."

Now, if the revised reading had been in the text in the first place, the sense of potential ominous symbolic overtones to the descent of "Darkness" (now fortuitously capitalized) might have struck readers more forcibly. Some might say, because this reading is "stronger," it should have been chosen for the Garland edition.

It was not chosen because such aesthetic judgments were not part of the editorial strategy. To choose readings that correspond with the historical integrity of Thackeray's text at the time of first publication is not to reject the 1853 revisions. The point is not which of these readings is the correct one. The fact is that no one knows if either is correct or if both are correct.

The point is that in a scholarly edition both are available and have their various effects on the reading of Vanity Fair. Having read "The darkness came down," readers then find that a change was made to "Darkness came down." Either reading, by itself, conveys the fall of night, or both reveal the potential for a symbolic reading, the revised reading perhaps more so. But discovering that the reading was revised is the strongest indication that something was being attempted here beyond indication that night fell. The changing itself is a stronger indication of meaning than either phrase is alone.

That is a crucial point in understanding the importance of a scholarly edition. The aim of the editorial work should not be to produce a pristine, correct, reliable text, a product. It should instead be to trace the growth and development of the work and to place the reading text in its developing context, a process. The effect is lost on readers who insist on reading the text as product, but the potential is there for serious, sensitive reading directed in part by reaction to what the author did - as opposed just to what the author said.

This paragraph from Vanity Fair reveals a flaw in the Garland edition. The edition fails to include a parallel account of George's death from a letter Thackeray wrote to his mother who had complained about Amelia s selfishness.

Thackeray's response is pretty well known, but it all should have been quoted in the edition, including his anticipation of the time two months ahead when Amelia's "scoundrel of a husband is well dead with a ball in his odious bowels" (With that highly inflammatory and emotionally laden phrase ringing in one's ears, one cannot read the printed passage in the book without trying to account for the clean, flat, efficient diction found there in terms of Thackeray's narrative strategies and, perhaps, the demands of serial publication.

Scholarly editions should encourage and make possible such intertextual readings. The richness and satisfaction of such reading complexities go up when the countertexts are understood for what they are: parallel texts in letters, revisions in manuscripts, or alternative printed texts emanating either from revision or from compositorial or editorial intervention.

The sources and relative dates of countertexts have a great deal to do with a reader's assessment of their significance. It seems, then, that the duty of a scholarly edition is not arbitrarily (and stealthily) to reduce the complexity and richness of a work of art to one correct and established standard text, but rather to lay out the materials as clearly and usefully as possible.

Chapter 10

Chronology

1811	Born July 18 in Calcutta.
1815	Death of father.
1817	Sent to school in England.
1822-28	Attends Charterhouse School, London.
1829	Enters Trinity College, Cambridge.
1830-31	Leaves Cambridge and travels in Germany.
1831-32	Studies law in London.
1833	Loss of inheritance.
1834-35	Studies art in Paris.
1836	Marries Isabella Shawe in Paris; first article appears in The Constitutional.
1837	Moves to London where begins to write for Fraser's Magazine and where daughter, Anne, is born.
1837-38	The Yellowplush Correspondence in Fraser's.
1839-40	Catherine in Fraser's.
1840	First book published in England, The Paris Sketch Book; A Shabby Genteel Story appears in Fraser's. Daughter, Harriet Marian (Minny) born; Isabella Thackeray suffers the nervous collapse that leads to permanent insanity.
1841	The Great Hoggarty Diamond in Fraser's; 2-volume collection of Comic Tales and Sketches.
1842	First contribution to Punch.
1843	The Irish Sketch Book.
1844	The Luck of Barry Lyndon in Fraser's. Tour of Mediterranean and Mideast.
1846	Notes of a Journey from Cornhill to Grand

Cairo. Daughters join Thackeray in London.

1846-47 The Snobs of England (Punch), retitled The Book of Snobs in book form (1848).

1847 Punch's Prize Novelists (retitled Novels by Eminent Hands in book form, 1856).

1847-48 Vanity Fair (January 1847 July 1848).

1848 Friendship with Jane Brookfield, wife of the Reverend William Brookfield, deepens.

1848-50 The History of Pendennis (November 1848 December 1850).

1850 Rebecca and Rowena.

1851 Lectures on humorists of eighteenth century in London (published as The English Humourists of the Eighteenth Century in 1853). Break with Jane Brookfield.

1852 The History of Henry Esmond.

1852-53 First American tour.

1855 The Rose and the Ring.

1855-1856 Second American tour, lectures on the Hanoverian kings (published as The Four Georges in 1860).

1857 Runs unsuccessfully for the Oxford seat in Parliament.

1857-59 The Virginians (November 1857 October 1859).

1859-62 Editor of Cornhill Magazine.

1860 Lovel the Widower in Cornhill.

1860-63 Roundabout Papers in Cornhill.

1863 Begins Denis Duval (unfinished, published posthumously in Cornhill in 1864).

1863 Dies December 24 in London.

Chapter 11

Breaking into Print

How Thackeray became a writer has been the subject of many books and articles, but recounting the story (with some new material) emphasizes the connections between his experiences as writer and the point of view about the writer's trade presented in the preceding chapter. It illustrates how a romantic youth developed into a young dilettante; how, without a "useful" education,

Thackeray was thrown rather summarily upon the resources of his pen to survive and to support a young and trouble-ridden family; how years of hackwork and dogged determination won for him a combination of pride in his journalistic achievements and a humility or at least unpretentiousness about art; and how, when the laurels of fame and fortune finally became his, he found the dignity of literature in the economic and social rewards for hard labour rather than in the mantle of the hero as man of letters.

His contributions as a schoolboy at the Charterhouse to the Carthusian, as a teenager in 1828-29 to the Western Luminary (a newspaper at Ottery Saint Mary's), and as a college student in 1829-30 to the Snob and Gownsman (literary newspapers conducted by students at Cambridge) have been described in detail by Harold Strong Gulliver, an account still worth reading, though corrections as well as new material can be found in Gordon Ray's Thackeray: The Uses of Adversity. In some ways, the best account of these activities and of Thackeray's attitude toward the Muse and literary work at this time is his own fictional account of young Pendennis.

As important as these ventures were in whetting

Thackeray's appetite for literary work, they cannot be seen as the beginnings of his professional career.

These literary endeavors, on a par with his contributions in 1831 to Ottilie von Goethe's Weimar literary paper, Chaos, were works of amateur enthusiasm. They were not undertaken for pay, nor were they part of any endeavor to forge a literary career, whether "for a living" or as the work of a gentleman of the world, which Thackeray could have been but for his weakness for gambling and, more importantly, the bank failures in India in late 1833 that virtually wiped out his considerable inheritance.

On his return from Weimar in March 1831, having chosen to forgo the rest of his education at college, where he had lost 11, 500 at play, he sampled with distaste the rigors of reading for the law, turned twenty-one on 18 July 1832, dissipated in Paris for three or four months, and tried his hand for three months as a bill discounter. By May 1833 he was ready to invest his money in something more congenial to his tastes and talents.

He purchased a periodical, the National Standard, thereby making himself a publisher.

He was also the editor and chief contributor. His motive was only partially economic, as is perhaps clear from the oft-quoted self-satire he printed thirty years later in Lovel the Widower where Mr. Batchelor gave himself "airs as editor of that confounded Museum, and proposed to educate the public taste... and made a gabby of" himself.

The National Standard lasted till February 1834, by which time Thackeray had learned of the Indian bank failures and knew himself to be a poor man, the bulk of his remaining inheritance having evaporated, for though the estate may still have amounted to £7000, it was encumbered by annuities which left Thackeray financially hobbled.

Even before this misfortune, while still Paris correspondent for the National Standard, Thackeray had undertaken the formal study of art in Paris as "an independent man who is not obliged to look to his brush for his livelihood." [Ray, Adversity, p. 167] But by the end of 1833 all that changed.

Thackeray first thought to repair his condition by pursuing with serious intent the calling he had chosen from inclination at a better time; however, he knew by the summer of 1835 that he could not succeed as a painter.

From need he [34/35] sought out literary assignments, selling at least one article to Fraser's Magazine, working for Galignani's Messenger in Paris, projecting and abandoning a "Picturesque Annual" for which he would both write and draw, producing Flore et Zéphyr, a book of lithographs from which he apparently made nothing, and perhaps starting, editing, or at least working for a Paris rival to Galignani's.

Like painting, writing was a high-risk speculative venture without guaranteed returns. Flore et Zéphyr, Thackeray's first book, has no text beyond captions to the lithographs. It was published in April 1836 in London by John Mitchell while Thackeray was in France.

Thackeray's letters to Mitchell betray the confusion characterizing this effort: "I cannot understand from yr. notes what is the drawing wanted," and the next day, "I do not know whether you propose to publish any letter-press with the drawing, will you allow me to see it, before its appearance" (Letters 1: 299-300).

The publication of Flore et Zéphyr was financed by Thackeray's wealthy friend John Bowes Bowes, who held an interest in Galignani's Messenger in Paris and who later wrote Thackeray that he thought Mitchell had fudged on the accounts "and put a lot of money in his pocket." Whether Mitchell made any money is not known, but Thackeray and Bowes did not, though it may not have mattered much to the later. (Time heals all wounds, it seems, for in 1851, Mitchell reappears in Thackeray's affairs as the manager of the London lectures on eighteenth-century humorists.)

Thackeray's depression over blasted hopes as a painter was alleviated somewhat by his meeting and falling in love with Isabella Shawe, an event with financial implications requiring an even more assiduous pursuit of literary work. Thackeray found that writing for a living, which he could do with some success, was far more demanding than writing occasional pieces for fun and glory. So when in early 1836 the opportunity arose to become involved with a politically radical literary paper, the Constitutional and Public Ledger, which was supposed to have a broadly subscribed economic base, Thackeray persuaded his stepfather, Major Carmichael-Smyth, to help him by subscribing the venture and serving as chairman of the company.

Thackeray's salary was set at eight guineas a week. In the flurry of setting up the company and gathering a staff, Thackeray wrote to Isabella that he was to have £450 per year (Letters 1: 306), and serious courtship and plans for marriage became possible in spite of the obstacles provided by his future mother-in-law, Mrs. Shawe. Thackeray's writings for the Constitutional began appearing in September, one month after his marriage.

The account given by Ray of those next months suggests that Thackeray thought himself arrived at stability and contentedness, with the leisure to secure and execute additional jobs as illustrator [Ray, Adversity, pp. 188-89]. But the whole project collapsed by July of the next year, crippling Major Carmichael-Smyth financially and throwing Thackeray once again upon the resources of his free-lance pen, this time with a wife and child to support. Thackeray would not again enjoy the leisure and stability of those few months as Paris correspondent for many years to come, but he had broken into print, he knew how to do it, he had developed some confidence in his abilities, and he set about his work with vigor.

When in 1833 Thackeray had commented to his mother that the National Standard was "very rapidly improving, & will form I have no doubt a property" (Letters 1: 268), he was still the investor seeking to acquire and improve a property ready made; now he was to discover that he had "no other saleable property" than his writings.

CAPITALIZING ON APPARENT SUCCESS

Although Thackeray closed no deals with Longman until five years later, within two months he made a £385 contract with Chapman and Hall for "Titmarsh in Ireland" (eventually

The Irish Sketch-Book). His star may have been a faint one yet, but it was definitely rising. The contract, or "fine," he had begged of Macrone in 1837 was delivered into his hand in September 1840 by Chapman and Hall, complete with a due date for an illustrated two volumes by 31 December!

The silver lining, however, had a dark cloud, Though the ante this time seems to have jumped from £20 to £120 "to be paid down this day" (Letters 1:471), there lurked in the background of the contract an arrangement with Chapman and Hall revealed only in Thackeray's letters to his mother asking Miss Mary Graham, his cousin and adoptive sister, to sign a letter of surety for Chapman and Hall in case of Thackeray's default; moreover,

Thackeray left his plate-chest with the publisher who held it until 1846 (Letters 1: 468, 473). Three weeks earlier Thackeray had returned from Belgium to discover his wife in a deep depression he still hoped was temporary. On 12 September, Thackeray took his family to Ireland where he hoped to write the book and see if Cork air and a visit home would restore Isabella's wandering mind and spirits. Neither endeavor was successful.

On the trip to Ireland, Isabella's depression manifested itself as insanity. She threw herself into the sea where she was found twenty minutes later "floating on her back, paddling with her hands." The Thackerays' sojourn in the Emerald Isle lasted just a month, during which Thackeray nursed his wife, chafed heavily under the tyranny of his mother-in-law, and worked intermittently on an unidentified play. His exit from Ireland [43/44] on 11 October 1840 was something of an escape or retreat from Isabella's mother. By the end of November, Isabella was institutionalized in France at J.-E.-D. Esquirol's Maison de Santé, and Thackeray could spend more and calmer time writing.

Among his first concerns was The Shabby Genteel Story. On 3 December he wrote James Fraser from Paris: "I left purposely the Shabby Genteel Story in such a state that it might be continued in the magazine or not as you and I liked best. Would you like it to be continue? In that case I should like to write the whole story off, and of course be paid for it on delivering over the MSS. Some 4 sheets I think would complete the affair. Please let me know whether I shall proceed with it, for though I can't afford to begin my new articles at your prices this one had better be gone through with if you think fit." Then, assuming that Fraser would authorize the continuation, he added, "I shall probably publish the whole tale wh. has a very moral ending in a volume with illustrations" (Letters 1: 488). The plan reveals again Thackeray's increasing desire to see his magazine work in book form.

Fraser, however, declined; a continuation, as such, was never written, though Thackeray briefly considered it in 1856 when searching for copy for volume 2 of Miscellanies to fill a vacuum caused by a miscommunication with his publisher. The incomplete story was first published in book form by Appleton in New York in 1852. But there was plenty more to keep Thackeray busy.

On 15 December 1840 Thackeray witnessed the celebrations connected with the arrival of Napoleon's body from St. Helena for burial in Paris. He claimed to have written The Second Funeral of Napoleon in four days and the appended "Chronicle of a Drum" in a week. Published by Hugh Cunningham in London in January 1841, it made a small book of 122 pages - one of the quickest productions of his career. He wrote to friends that he was to receive 7½ pence for every copy sold and claimed by 21 January to have earned £3.2.6 from the sale of 100 copies (Letters 2: 4, 7). By March he groused that the total sold was only 140 copies.

In spite of his disastrous personal circumstances at the end of 1840, or perhaps because of them, Thackeray was intensely committed to the production of new works. The initial success of The Paris Sketch Book in mid-1840 had made The Irish Sketch-Book contract possible, but when work on that scale proved impossible under the circumstances, Thackeray produced shorter pieces (A Shabby Genteel Story and The Second Funeral) and projected more by the end of the year. Cunningham advertised two new books by Titmarsh: The Second Funeral and Dinner Reminiscences:

The Young Gormandizer's Guide at Paris. The latter work was never issued, though parts of it may survive in "Memorials of Gormandizing" in Frasers Magazine, June 1841. Cunningham may have waited to see how The Second Funeral would do, deciding not to try another book in the same format when that one failed in the marketplace, or he may have decided that Comic Tales, a new two-volume venture already planned, was as much as he dare invest at one time in the as yet little known author.

Long before the first manifestation of his wife's illness and before dealing with Chapman and Hall for The Irish Sketch-Book in September, Thackeray had already planned a collection of his earlier magazine fiction, Comic Tales, to be published with Cunningham.

The idea was first mentioned in surviving letters in December 1839, and by December 1840 he remarked to James Fraser his intention to republish A Shabby Genteel Story and added, "I have got a very decent price from Cunningham for a republication of my comic miscellanies". That decent price is not known, but by then he had signed with Chapman and Hall for a new work at £385 and had begun to appreciate the market value of his work.

Serious work and new illustrations were undertaken in February and March 1841, and Comic Tales was published in April in two volumes (Letters 2: 9). The only new text in the book was Thackeray's preface clearly indicating that the American appearance of Yellowplush and the rumored but never confirmed republication of Gahagan had spurred preparation of the collection. Both those works appeared in Comic Tales.

No evidence exists to confirm that Thackeray was instrumental in having Yellowplush published that same year by Baudry in Paris in tandem with Dickens's Master Humphrey's Clock, but the Baudry text derives from the Comic Tales edition, not the Fraser's text, and Thackeray was in Paris off and on during the year and may have collected a modest amount for the republication there. If so, he was tasting the first fruits of having a literary property out of the inkwell.

During the six months after Isabella's entry to the Maison de Santé for treatment (December 1840 to May 1841), Thackeray was very productive, as Gordon Ray has pointed out. He wrote The Second Funeral in December and The History of Samuel Titmarsh in January and February, began and abandoned eight chapters of the never completed historical novel "The Knights of Borsellen" between January and April, saw Comic Tales through press in March, and wrote "between February and May a dozen magazine articles and stories." Such a flurry of activity was made both possible and necessary by the emotional crises and the increased financial burdens of the last year's ending.

But Thackeray's almost single-minded application to writing at the same time was developing in him ideas about his profession-about the cold trade relations existing between all persons making a living out of writing, printing, publishing, and bookselling as well as about the unpredictable nature of literature's new patrons, the public.

This is the period in which he wrote the two letters to Jane Carlyle from France, the first full of desperate need, the second of cheerful but, as it turned out, misplaced hope. The Second Funeral was a failure, and Comic Tales cannot have done well; not only did Cunningham never publish anything else by Thackeray, remaindered sheets from the 1841 Comic Tales were reissued with a new title page in 1848 to take advantage of the popularity of Vanity Fair. "The Knights" was abandoned, and the publisher Bentley ignored the manuscript of The History of Samuel Titmarsh. The rising star so quickly blighted by Isabella's illness had flared once more only to die back, Thackeray eking out his living with the usual magazine work.

The manuscript of The History of Samuel Titmarsh languished with Bentley from late February to the first of June when Thackeray wrote angrily to have it turned over to Hugh Cunningham. It is a notable letter revealing both frustration and a new confidence in his status that did not mind offending a publisher: "& next time your obedient Servant sends you an article you may set him down without fail to be you understand what [sketch of a donkey] yours & whatdyecallem W M Thackeray." But Cunningham did not want Samuel Titmarsh either, and it was published at magazine rates in Fraser's from September to December 1841.

During these years of hand-to-mouth existence, Thackeray entered many tentative and aborted relations with publishers, some of several years' duration or occasional renewal. His relations with Richard Bentley seem to have begun with the publication of "The Professor," a short story in Bentley's Miscellany, September 1837. That was also the end of their business together, although they both came up with other proposals. It was probably on the strength of an interest Bentley had shown that Thackeray began writing "The Knights of Borsellen" early in 1841 and it is just as probable that his anger with Bentley and break with him in June 1841 influenced him to abandon it.

Nearly a year later, still casting about for any work he could get, Thackeray approached Bentley again, offering the translation of a French novel ("strange to say it is not at all indecent") and suggesting that it "would answer for 3 volumes or for the Miscellany" (NYU). Apparently Thackeray had already translated two volumes, but the project came to nothing. We do not even know what novel it was. Three years later, Thackeray began translating a Eugène Sue novel, for which he also failed to find a publisher after having done a good deal of the work.

Later, while writing Vanity Fair, Thackeray wrote to Bentley asking for a copy of the six-volume edition of Horace Walpole's letters edited by John Wright in 1840 and offering to pay for it by writing for Bentley's Miscellany. Bentley, according to Thackeray's recollection, declined the deal but offered to pay for any of Thackeray's contributions at the rate of £12 per sheet. Thackeray apparently did not respond at the time. After the successes of Vanity Fair, Pendennis, and Esmond, it was Bentley who wrote proposals to Thackeray and the novelist who turned them down.

In 1853 Bentley suggested, probably because of the success of Thackeray's first lecture series, that he reedit Walpole's letters. Two more volumes, edited by the Reverend J. Milford, had been added in 1851, and Bentley wanted a uniform and chronologically arranged eight-volume work.

Thackeray responded, "The task wh. you propose is one wh. I should be glad enough to undertake provided we could agree upon terms. "He reminded Bentley of his earlier offer of £12 per sheet and concluded, "I'm sure that you are going to make me better proposals than the above: and awaiting them, am, very faithfully yours, W M Thackeray." [NYU] Though this was a far more polite closing than the "Yours & whatdyecallem" of twelve years earlier, no terms were agreed upon. Bentley tried once more in 1857 when, probably because of the success of Thackeray's second lecture series, he wrote to propose a work on the eighteenth-century artist and caricaturist William Hogarth.

Aside from having "my own hands quite full at present," it happened that Thackeray had inside information on a project in progress answering Bentley's description exactly. In September 1855 George Augustus Sala had first spoken to Thackeray and then written to him of his work on Hogarth. Thackeray had recommended Sala to George Smith and apparently put it out of his mind until Bentley's proposal reminded him of it. Interestingly, Thackeray, who was in Paris at the time, sent his response first to George Smith to be forwarded to Bentley, writing Smith a note at the same time on the back of Bentley's proposal (NLS). Sala's work on Hogarth appeared first as nine installments in Smith's Cornhill Magazine (February - October 1860) and as a book under the Smith, Elder imprint in 1866.

Meanwhile, in June 1841 The Irish Sketch-Book remained unwritten, Chapman and Hall holding the plate-chest and looking very like bankers making a loan instead of publishers paying an advance. Indeed, Thackeray seemed in no hurry to redeem his plate, offering instead to write a serial fiction for Fraser that might be turned into a book:

I have in my trip to the country, found materials (rather a character) for a story, that I'm sure must be amusing. I want to write & illustrate it, and as you see how Harry Lorrequer succeeds both in the Dublin Magazine & out of it, why should not my story of BARRY-LYNN (or by what name so ever it may be called) answer in as well as out of Regina.

Suppose for instance you were to give a sheet & a half per month that sheet and a half could be stretched into two sheets for the shilling number by transposing (or whatever you call it) the type: and the book would thus make a handsome saleable volume at the end of the year. My subject I am sure is a good one, and I have made a vow to chasten and otherwise popularize my style. Thus I could have 20 guineas a month from you and a farther chance of profit from the sale of the single numbers. Were we to come to a bargain I would not of course begin until 3 numbers of the tale were in hand: with the plates &c. [Letters 2: 29-30]

Here for the first time we see Thackeray planning a work as "a property" with a view to its value beyond its first appearance. And we see him acknowledging the need to write first and close deals second, offering to have three installments done on the basis of encouragement alone from the [48/49] publisher. In the event, however, Thackeray wrote The Irish Sketch-Book first.

Thackeray had removed Isabella from the Maison de Santé in early April 1841, and she seemed so much better that he spent a considerable amount of time with her over the next few months, taking her for water treatments at a sanatorium on the Rhine in August.

While they were there, two unforeseen events altered his financial situation: his half sister died, freeing to Thackeray £500 of inheritance that had been entailed while she lived, and his cousin Mary Graham, now married to Charles, Major Carmichael-Smyth's brother, lent him another £500 (Letters 2: 34). The Thackerays continued the water treatments in Boppard until October when Isabella ceased to improve, and by February 1842 she was placed under the residential care of Dr. Puzin in Chaillot (Letters 2: 41).

Over that winter Thackeray continued producing articles for Fraser's and George Cruikshank's Omnibus, but no progress seems to have been made on Barry Lyndon or The

Irish Sketch-Book until February 1842 when Thackeray wrote of his impending return to Ireland (Letters 2: 42). As that spring progressed, references to the Irish book came more and more into Thackeray's letters, including several to Chapman and Hall for whose newly acquired Foreign Quarterly Review he was writing two major articles totaling fifty pages (perhaps as a bid to become its new editor).

Payment for these articles was separate from the advance (or loan) Chapman and Hall had made for The Irish Sketch-Book. After suggesting that the ordinary rate for his article on France was too little, considering the time for research it required ("The restoration alone cost me 6 weeks labour, &- the reading of many scores of books" [Letters 2: 51]), he concluded that the continuation on Louis Philippe would "bring no profit" and would be done "for reputation's sake" (Letters 2: 65).

Thackeray at the same time had been busy with his first serial contribution to Punch, "Mrs. Tickletoby's Lectures." By 19 September 1842 nine installments had appeared, and Thackeray awaited payment from Punch's publisher, Bradbury and Evans. You may remember that when I spoke to you regarding Punch, you were ready to promise as proprietors of the journal that any articles wh. 1wrote for it should be paid. My stipulations with the editor of the paper were that my contributions should be paid at the rate of 2 guineas a page, and the only article for wh. I have recd payment was at that rate

I have now been writing for nearly 3 months (the printers have some more of my MS in their hands) I wrote a fortnight sincc to Mr. Landells [49/50] requesting him to communicate with Mr. Lemon, and beg the latter to send me what was my due, according to the account; wh. I have not kept myself but wh. can easily be arranged by reference to Punch from wh. this year I have received nothing.

I did not receive an answer from Mr. Landells & then wrote to Mr. Lemon I have likewise no reply from that gentleman. Will you have the kindness to let me know where I am to apply, in the first place for answers to my letters, and secondly for payment for my contributions? and may I beg an answer either with or without money by return post? [Bodleian]

Thackeray's letters to Landells and Lemon have not survived. But by 27 September, Thackeray had received £25 and the bad news that the publisher was not pleased with Thackeray's contribution. Evidently two more installments had been sent off already, for it appears that Thackeray broke off immediately: "I have no wish to continue the original agreement made between us, as it is dissatisfactory to you and, possibly, injurious to your work; and shall gladly cease Mrs. Tickletoby's Lectures, hoping that you will he able to supply her place with some more amusing and lively correspondent" (Letters 2: 82).

Judging from Thackeray's letters to his mother during his Ireland tour, which lasted from July to 1 November 1842, he was also writing steadily on The Irish Sketch-Book. Even before finishing it, however, he proposed, in January 1843, a new work, "FAIRY BALLADS by W. Thackeray," to Chapman and Hall and continued to write book reviews for that publisher's Foreign Quarterly Review (Letters 2: 9f). One can only imagine Chapman's response to this new proposal, with old ones pending long overdue, for there is no further reference to it in extant letters. But two weeks later Thackeray asked Mark Lemon to submit anonymously to the actor Macready a tragedy he had worked on while in Ireland (Letters 2: 93).

Apparently nothing came of the effort. In February, Thackeray reported reading proofs for the first two sheets of The Irish Sketch-Book, noting "they've spoiled my first chapter for me though... by making me withdraw some personalities, agst. the Catholics wh. might certainly have been dangerous" (Letters 2: 94, 96) This remark should, however, be read in the context of a comment he made to his mother from Ireland:

"A man coming here as I did with a strong disposition in favor of the Catholics, priests & all can't fail to get indignant at the slavish brutal superstition of the latter, and to become rather Toryfied so far. So I shall be abused by the Catholic Press for abusing the priests, and by the Tory papers for being a liberal" (Letters 2: 78). [50/51]

Oddly, though he was reading proofs by 20 February, Thackeray waited until 11 March to complain, mildly, to Chapman and Hall about the type size and page size of the book: "I find I am done out of no less than 50 pages by the size of the type &c- I bargained for 25 lines of 40 letters, and our page is 26 lines of 43 " (Letter 2: 98). While there was no stipulation in the contract for a certain number of pages, the book was "to consist of two volumes of the size... of the Paris Sketch Book," The Paris book consisted of two volumes of 304 pages and 298 pages; the Irish work turned out to be 311 pages and 327 pages.

In spite of his hope that Chapman and Hall's "perspicacious generosity will bear this fact I'm sure in mind," apparently Thackeray found himself obliged for the extra pages, some of which may have been fleshed out with added illustrations. Perhaps because of Chapman and Hall's insistence on the full complement of pages, Thackeray recovered from a genial attitude toward what the publishers were doing to his book. Earlier, complaining mildly to his mother that "they have called it Rambles in Ireland wh. I think is a foolish name," [Letters, 2: 100] he added that he was too lazy to do anything about it, but in the end he must have balked.

On 29 April 1843 Thackeray sent unbound sheets (all but the one containing the front matter) to his friend Percival Leigh asking for a quick review in the May issue of Fraser's Magazine: "Not a puff you understand, hit as hard as you like but in a good natured way and so as not to break bones." He explained that "the book is dedicated to Mr. Lever and the preface says that it was to have been called the Cockney in Ireland but for the remonstrances of the publisher wh. were so pathetic that the author was obliged to give way. In a second edition it is to be changed" (Letters 2: 106). The facetious tone of these remarks is familiar.

The title probably was an item of discussion and perhaps contention between author and publisher, but in fact there is no preface in the book and the dedication does not mention the alternate title. On the same day that Thackeray wrote to Leigh, he sent a similar request for a review to Laman

Blanchard, saying, "It is dedicated to Mr. Lever, and the author will say in the preface that it was to have been called 'The Cockney in Ireland,' but for the pathetic remonstrances of the publishers" (Letters 2: 106).

The future tense may be telling; it is conceivable that Thackeray had not yet read the proofs or settled finally on the content of the front matter. Furthermore, the reference to a second edition, as if one were already planned, was entirely facetious. Though The Irish Sketch-Book was Thackeray's greatest success to date, the 1845 "second edition," two years later, was nothing more than leftover first-edition sheets reissued with a new title page, and not with Thackeray's jocular title. No new negotiations and no additional payment came to Thackeray from that reissue. The next true English edition of The Irish Sketch-Book was not required until 1857.

THE CLIMB TO THE TOP

With Barry Lyndon in progress, "The History of the Next French Revolution" completed, and a multitude of short magazine articles keeping him from trouble with the bankers, Thackeray was still far from any peak in his career. To his mother he wrote, "It seems to me there is no time for anything here - The day occupied with nothings that must be done - and a fresh labour for almost every day - This is not very conducive to fame, nor to money somehow though it ought to be, and there's no reason why with regular labour I shouldn't make 1200 - BUT somehow it doesn't go beyond 65 or 70 a month - and in that occasional failures" (Letters 2: 170).

Ten days later he still felt that "there's no use in writing about my professional business wh. is very incessant though paltry - I don't do above 20£ a month for the Chronicle instead of 40 - but it is my own fault - the fact is I can't write the politics and the literary part is badly paid" (Letters 2: 172).

Consequently, it should strike one with no surprise that Thackeray continued to be willing to try anything that came along. Between interviews and visits to locate a place in England to which he could bring and settle his wife, he agreed to write a biography of Talleyrand. Perhaps having forgotten the lesson of the contract for The Irish Sketch-Book in 1840, Thackeray wrote Chapman and Hall on 16 July 1844: "I will engage to write the volume 'the life of Talleyrand, and to have the MS. in your hands by the 1 December - health permitting and will sign an agreement to that effect if you will have the goodness to prepare one" (Letters 2: 174). The contract, if there was one, is lost, but two weeks later he was rushing off to London from Liège where he had been spending time with his family to find books he needed in his Talleyrand research (Letters 2: 175)

Then on 20 August he had an offer he couldn't refuse - free passage to the Middle East, "I thought the chance so great that Ive accepted," he explained to his mother; "I'm to write a book for 200£ for C&H. [Chapman and Hall] on the East first, or that Cockney part wh. I shall see - then to do Talleyrand" (Letters 2: 176-77). The next day he boarded ship in Southampton, devoting himself to continuing Barry Lyndon for Fraser's, sending periodic travel accounts to Punch from "Our Fat Contributor," and writing the Cockney's Eastern book for Chapman and Hall.

Over two months later, his tour ended at Matta on 28 October, but his return to England was delayed by quarantine and a sojourn in Rome where a mix-up at "the dd dd-dd-ddd-ddd post office" kept him from his mail and his money for, he claimed, thirty-five days (Letters 2: 185-86). By 10 January 1845 he wrote Chapman and Hall to say the book "is all but done," and he promised to "go tooth and nail at Talleyrand directly I reach England" (Letters 2: 185). However, by the end of March, "Talleyrand is put off sine die" - never to be heard of again - and the "Eastern book just going into hand" (Letters 2: 190)-

At the same time he hinted at a project, possibly Vanity Fair, "wh. is projected and of prodigious importance, This is a scheme by wh I expect to make a great deal of money it is to be called - but never mind what until it is ready" (Letters 2: 190). A month later he wrote George William Nickisson, at Fraser's, "between ourselves I believe I am in a career of most wonderful money getting" (Letters 2: 191). It is generally supposed that "the commencement of a novel" which

Thackeray had earlier sent to Henry Colburn at the New Monthly Magazine and then retrieved from William Harrison Ainsworth who replaced Colburn as editor was an early draft of Vanity Fair. But it would be eight more months before the beginning of that novel was first set in type and eight more after that before it began publication.

In the meantime, A Legend of the Rhine, written as "The Childe of Godesburg" in early 1844, finally saw the light in George Cruikshank's Table Book (June - December 1845). Mrs. Perkins's Ball, begun at least as early as November 1844, projected for Christmas 1845 and nearly [60/61] finished, was eventually delayed till December 1846 (though its imprint says 1847).

And in July 1845 the Eastern book still needed work ("I want to fill two blanks in my chapter" [Letters 2: 199]). The delays may account in part for Thackeray's request to Bradbury and Evans on 9 July: "May I ask you for 100? - my funds are getting very low, and I should be very glad of a supply" (Bodleian).

It is probable that Bradbury and Evans owed him some of that already and soon would owe the rest, judging from the number of Thackeray's contributions to Punch in that year: eighty-four of which eleven appeared in July. That compares with fifty-four contributions in 1844 and seventy-two in 1846 [cf. Spielman].

However, on the very same day he sent Chapman and Hall £55 they had lent him previously, at the same time trying to sort out the terms of agreement for publishing what he still referred to as "the Eastern Book": "I have been thinking over the bargain regarding the Eastern Book, and think you are rather hard upon me.

The trip was a very expensive one. I was offered my own terms elsewhere and I assure you undertook the book for you with the full conviction that it would be paid at the price of the other volume on wh. I am engaged for you - viz two hundred guineas. I shall rely on your justice confidently however" (Letters 2: 201). It is understandable that there was no firm agreement to turn to, since whatever passed between author and publisher on 19 August 1844, when Thackeray decided to go to Egypt, must have taken place hastily. It is worth digressing to follow the fortunes of Notes of a Journey from Cornhill to Grand Cairo and the continued negotiations between Thackeray and Chapman and Hall; for in the next surviving reference to it, Thackeray equated the original agreement for the book with the agreement for The Irish Sketch-Book: "I... am glad to hear that at last I am to have the fortune of a second edition.

Our bargain for the first edition was made upon the notion that it was a half guinea book on the same terms as the Irish book - I certainly ought to have my share of the 1400 odd shillings wh. the book has brought in and suggest accordingly that division."

But a look back through surviving letters shows that Thackeray skipped over the intervening negotiations for the biography of Talleyrand and that that was the book agreed upon with reference to the Irish book. Thackeray, in the rush of embarking for the Orient, had understood that Chapman and Hall would take the Eastern book on the same terms as Talleyrand.

Now, in the latter half of 1846, operating on that understanding, he couched his demand for fair treatment in the self-deprecatory language so characteristic of his relations with publishers. "But I was always a bad hand at accounts," he continued, "and put myself honestly into your hands as men of business to deal fairly with me." He did not stop there: "We will ask Forster tomorrow whether or no I am right in my claim to the 1400 sixpences" (Letters 2: 258-59). The Talleyrand book was not finished, and there is no record of Thackeray's income from the Eastern book.

In August 1845, because of remonstrances by his mother, he "cancelled" the chapter on Jerusalem, which he found very difficult to replace, partly for lack of time, partly for trying to tread lightly between a heterodoxy that might offend the public and a hypocrisy that would offend himself.

Work on it dragged through the autumn and into December - mostly neglected while he wrote for Punch

(Jeames's Diary began appearing in November), but on 22 December he sent in the dedication and preface, and Notes on a Journey from Cornhill to Grand Cairo finally appeared in February 1846. Another small episode, beginning a new stage in Thackeray's relations with his publishers, occurred at this time.

Thomas Fraser, foreign correspondent in Paris for the Morning Chronicle, wrote asking him to act as go-between for another author and the firm of Chapman and Hall. From this time on, such letters became frequent. In those days before literary agents, well-known authors were constantly being asked by unknown authors to act as agents. In the same letter in which Thackeray fulfilled this task to Hall, he submitted an article on behalf of Mrs. Colmache, which he seems finally to have succeeded in placing with Ainsworth's New Monthly Magazine (Letters 2: 219, 230, 232).

Like other informal agents he was frequently unsuccessful; he explained to one friend that not only could he not help with the Morning Chronicle but was himself not helped there by a letter of reference from Arthur Buller (Letters 2: 252). Over the years Thackeray did what he could as literary agent, though he sometimes refused for lack of time or for lack of belief in the marketability of the writings sent to him. He expressed himself perhaps most frankly to his mother, who sometime in 1847 sent him one of her own compositions to place:

I will send your wonderful story to Chapman & to Smith & Elder who will send it back again. It may be from an angels pen and I doubt if you will get a publisher to bring it out except at the author's charges. As for getting money by it it is a vain hope - and to suppose it will succeed because it will do people good - is as green almost as my horse-dealings.

The publishers don't care a straw for a friend of mine, but for what will put money in their pockets - and consider, will your tale cover an outlay of 60 or 70£ and give them a return for their risk and trouble? say 100£ of a half crown book sold at 1/6d to the trade, costing 6d let us say to produce they would require to sell 2000 to pay £100 - & how many books do you think sell 2000 not one in as many 100. [Letters 2: 330]

American interest in Thackeray's work continued to grow. In addition to its London appearance in two genuine editions in 1846, the Eastern book was pirated by Wiley and Putman in Philadelphia. The same year saw another of his books issued in America with no economic benefit to the author: Jeames's Diary was lifted from Punch by William Taylor and Company of New York, Philadelphia, and Baltimore.

At home Mrs. Perkins's Ball, dated 1847, actually appeared in time for the 1846 Christmas trade, published by Chapman and Hall. Unlike the other books, however, Mrs. Perkins's was "a great success - the greatest I have had."

On 23 December he reported that it was selling "very fast near 1500 are gone out of 2000 already - and this is a great success for the likes of me" (Letters 2: 258). At the end of May the next year, finding himself pressed for money to pay for railway shares gone sour, he wrote Chapman a plea for cash he hoped was resulting front the second edition of Mrs. Perkins's Ball.

In 1846 Thackeray was quite busy contributing on a regular basis to Punch (seventy-two articles) and to the Morning Chronicle (eighteen articles). He had time for only five Fraser's pieces that year. The most memorable work of the year was "The Snobs of England" in Punch, a series which "hit the public," not only as a social satire but as a popular success.

His projections for 1846 had been "so good, that I calculate on laying by at least 500 next year. I am engaged to write a monthly story at 60£ a number [Vanity Fair] - I have besides 70£ between Punch & the Chronicle: though I don't calculate on the latter beyond the year as I am a very weak & poor politician only good for outside articles and occasional jeux-d'esprit - The 400 may subside possibly into 2 or 300 but you see there will be enough and to spare." [Letter to his stepfather, Letters 2: 225].

His resignation from the Morning Chronicle in February, before anything he may have written for it that year was [63/64] published, was short-lived and may have been, like his striking for wages against Fraser's in 1837, part of a negotiation. From March through October his work appeared in the Morning Chronicle regularly.

Or his brief resignation may have been connected with the proposed commencement of Vanity Fair on the first of May. However, work on that great book could not have occupied much of his time since he clearly had not progressed beyond the five chapters that Bradbury and Evans set in type in April. And, in any case, the serial publication of the novel was delayed until January 1847.

Chapter 12

Moonlighting

From January 1847 through June 1848 Thackeray's major work and single largest source of income was Vanity Fair. From October 1848 through November 1850 his major work was Pendennis.

Such work would be a full-time occupation for many an author, but in the same four-year period Thackeray produced chapters 44-52 of "The Snobs of England," twenty-one installments of Punch's Prize Novelists, fifteen installments of "Travels in London," six installments of A Little Dinner at Timmins's, a Christmas book called Our Street (December 1847, dated 1848), eighteen installments of Mr.

Browns Letters to a Young Man about Town, another Christmas book called Dr. Birch and His Young Friends (December 1848, dated 1849), seven installments of "The Proser," and over one hundred other magazine contributions, primarily to Punch.

His primary "employers" were William Bradbury and F. M. Evans, partners in a large printing firm that had begun publishing in the early 1840s and proprietors of Punch, who were for a short time the primary publisher for both Thackeray and Charles Dickens. Bradbury and Evans, riding a rising tide out of the recession of the mid- 1840s, seemed content to let Thackeray write and publish elsewhere as much as he liked, so long as the monthly installment novels continued on schedule and his Punch contributions stayed up.

Thackeray's ship had finally come in. Evidence is seen in the bookform issue in 1848 of Vanity Fair, Dr. Birch, and The Book of Snobs. Plans began in June 1848 for the reissue of The

History of Samuel Titmarsh, though a pirated American edition in November or December (by Harper and Brothers) preceded the English edition, which did not come out until January 1849. Cunningham also took advantage of the rising popularity of Vanity Fair to reissue Comic Tales with a new title page.

In 1849 the English edition of Samuel Titmarsh made its appearance, sold out, and a second edition was produced; the first volume of Pendennis appeared in England [64/65] and Germany (by Tauchnitz), Vanity Fair appeared in America (pirated by Harper and Brothers) and in Germany (paid for by Tauchnitz); a first volume of Miscellanies appeared in Germany (Tauchnitz); and Rebecca and Rowena (dated 1850) appeared in England and France.

In 1850 the second volume of Pendennis was published in England as well as in Germany; The Kickleburys on the Rhine appeared in December (and required a second printing in January); and Stubbs's Calendar was reprinted without authority in New York (by Stringer and Townsend). Throughout these three years Thackeray also contributed occasional drawings and illustrations to works other than his own.

Thackeray said he was "at the top of the tree," and it may appear that that was the case, but somehow he yet felt keenly his precarious economic condition. It took a while for Vanity Fair to catch on with the public. Though Thackeray remarked in a letter in July 1847 that "the publishers are quite contented" (Letters 2: 311), he noted in October that "it does everything but sell, and appears really immensely to increase my reputation if not my income" (Letters 2: 318).

In December he reluctantly wrote a dunning letter to Edward Chapman: "Will you send me the remaining 60£ by the bearer if you please. Indeed I'm sorry for everyone's delays and misfortunes" (Letters 2: 326). One month later he lamented to his mother that "on going to the publishers to draw my money tother day I was met with a smiling reference to some old books by wh. it appears I had overdrawn them 120£ 2 years ago - about wh. fatal circumstance I was quite ignorant" (Letters 2: 333).

Although his own finances occasionally caught him by surprise, Thackeray seemed well aware of the risk and venture that publishing involved.

He wrote in May 1848 that "the publishers are at this minute several hundred pounds out of pocket by me, that I know for certain - and I try to keep down any elation wh. my friends praises may cause me, by keeping this fact steadily before my eyes" (Letters 2: 378) It was not until August 1848, two months after the appearance of the last installment, that Thackeray could write with real confidence, "Vanity Fair is doing very well commercially I'm happy to say at last. They have sold 1500 volumes wh. is very well in these times of revolution and dismay" (Letters 2: 420).

Thackeray's increasing income seemed, however, insufficient to meet his needs. In 1847 he took a house big enough to accommodate his daughters and parents, and during 1848 he was keenly bent on clearing away his stepfather's debts, thereby enabling his mother to move to England and be with the children. In addition, he had invested and lost over £500 in the railroad mania that year. His efforts to get his parents back to England reached a peak in the summer of 1848, when in June he negotiated with Bradbury and Evans for the book publication of The History of Samuel Titmarsh.

Before a final agreement was reached, he wrote his mother, "I am to have 100£ for the reprint of The Hoggarty Diamond, perhaps today, (but I don't like to dun)... I am to have another 1000 a year for my next story [Pendennis] and with Punch & what not can do very like 700 or 750 more it is good income," and at the end of the same letter he added optimistically, "I have just seen Evans he call not give me all answer about the H. D. for 2 or 3 days but will tell me - indeed you may consider the matter as done and come as soon as you like to us all" (Letters 2: 382-83).

At about this same time in an undated letter to Evans, Thackeray pressed his proposal, with particular attention to the money: "If money is scarce could not a bill at 6 weeks be made out bearing your venerated signature? My bankers I believe would let me pay it in as cash and in that time I should have discharged my part of the obligation to you regarding the great Hoggarty Diamond by completing the 10 blocks for that work. How much are you to give me? 100 or 150? You said you would see - Let me have the just sum: and I'm sure you'll see that I ought to have 100 a month for the Pendennis" (Bodleian).

And on 18 July he wrote to Chapman asking for "50£ in advance of the Kickleburys abroad" in order to pay a bill for his stepfather (Letters 2: 399). The same day he paid the bill, which came to £30, the last outstanding debt preventing his parents' return to England. The other £20 probably went, at least in part, for the expenses of his birthday party the same day. Although his parents visited London in October and then again on several occasions, including one trying four-month stay in 1857, they did not move to England until 1859, when they set up an establishment of their own.

The rising success of Vanity Fair and the continued popularity of Punch led to two celebrations by publishers and authors. On 20 June 1848 the staff of Punch signed a sort of declaration to William Bradbury calling for the celebration of the seventh year of publication of Punch (Morgan).

The celebration itself may have been the dinner given at Greenwich for William Bradbury to which Thackeray referred in all undated letter to one of the Punch illustrators (Letters 2: 396). Apparently there was also a dinner to celebrate the completion of Vanity Fair, and it may have been to it that Thackeray referred in another undated letter to F. M. Evans in the summer of 1848, saying: "Please to send me per bearer the little ready money we spoke about yesterday. The bill for 120 Gnas at 6 weeks. and 1 dozen small knives for the dinner today. I shall look for you at 7+ " (Bodleian).

As is apparent from a variety of letters already cited, Thackeray left the daily accounting of financial obligations between himself and his major publishers entirely to the publishers. He did negotiate occasionally for the sale price or profit-sharing percentage, but when it came to second editions and the slow accumulation of profit-sharing dividends, be was, as most authors are, at the mercy of the publisher's accounting. Thus he applied to publishers for money according to his needs rather than according to the goods he had for sale. That is because his back list was beginning quietly to produce small but long-term profits which he had no other way to monitor than by asking for the money.

Thackeray's years of struggle, or "adversity" as Gordon Ray denominated them, would soon end. He had had two golden years of gentlemanly, leisurely pursuit of the Muse, followed by fifteen years of steadily beating the flanks of harnessed art in order to reach a plateau of economic security and restored financial competence. In 1847 Thackeray finally could see real prospects of restoring a fortune for his daughters equal to that he had received and lost.

The annals of nineteenth-century English literature do not sport many comparable tales. Instead, authors like Byron, Irving, Scott, Edward Bulwer Lytton, Edward Fitzgerald, and even Robert Smith Surtees cultivated the role of gentlemen amateurs, hiding their disciplined application to the work behind anonymous publication or romantic tales of tossing off the fruits of inspiration in their spare time. Every one of these men had income from other sources, either inherited estates or government posts or pensions.

Thackeray may have aspired to a similar image in his early days, though while still independently wealthy he openly entered the editorship of the National Standard as an investor and educator of public taste. All that was brushed aside by ill fate and necessity; the amateur genius or dilettante became the literary tradesman, proud of his professional accomplishments and disdainful of the pretensions of inspiration. Thackeray did not mind showing that he had to earn his living by the sweat of his brow.

On the other hand, the largely unsung history of nineteenth-century English writing is full of instances of persons with less initial luck and worse continued bad luck, folks with little but their brains and determination to carry them on - men like Douglas Jerrold, Gilbert à Beckett, John Leech, Richard Doyle, and George Augustus Sala (to name a few of Thackeray's colleagues of the Punch staff), or like George Henry Lewes, Leigh Hunt, and William Carleton who died in poverty and left no estate.

Thackeray's story is more akin to that of Charles Dickens and Thomas Carlyle whose economic competences were also wrong from their writings, though neither of them could look back upon lost patrimonies nor aspire to a restored level of social acceptance. Matthew Arnold, John Henry Newman, Anthony Trollope, and T. H. Huxley all had income from other work to keep the wolf from the door. It made a difference in one's assessment of the Muse and Pegasus if literature was an add-on rather than the mainstay of livelihood. Yet, Thackeray's view was diametrically opposed to those of Dickens and Carlyle.

Dickens's insistence on the dignity of literature seems to me based in part on a romantic view of the artist as aesthete, in greater part of Carlyle's view of the hero as man of letters, and finally but unprovably in part on a realization that the dignity of literature was the only prop he had to lean on for a place in the English social structure.

Carlyle, likewise a social outsider, disdained all standards of value outside the morally useful heroic or prophetic, perhaps because he too had no other toehold for approval by a Victorian audience. But Thackeray, equally dependent with Dickens and Carlyle on the proceeds of his writing for economic survival, had other resources for his place in society. Little as Dickens or Carlyle would have envied Thackeray's social graces or manners, the self-confidence these provided Thackeray enabled him to view with less charity or self-interest the romantic and heroic visions of the artist in society.

Though his view of writing as a trade was susceptible to the charges laid at his door by John Forster of denigrating his profession to gain status with the "non-literary classes," I choose to think, instead, that his view of the profession was more realistic and less histrionic, as his writing is also more realistic and less histrionic, than that of Dickens or Carlyle.

Chapter 13

The Final Move to Cornhill

Thackeray must have entered an early, though tentative, agreement with Smith to publish The Four Georges at some future date, for he apparently received an offer from another publisher in February 1857. Thackeray sent this no longer extant offer to Smith on 16 February, commenting: "Meditate the astounding offer contained in the enclosed not with the idea that I am going to think of accepting it. Having sold my horse to a good friend & for a good price how can I sell it to another dealer?

But the question with me is, Is the delusion about those Lectures sufficiently great to enable us to sell them as they actually stand at a good profit. And having read them (all) through the country for a few months more Shall we kill the wretched goose & have done with it. Or shall we bring out not 2 but haply 6 great volumes in future ages about the Georges with a success that might be something like Stricklands.?" (NLS).

Neither man was, however, in a hurry to kill the goose. Thackeray continued to deliver the lectures as late as June after which the parliamentary election campaign in Oxford, a holiday, and then, perhaps, the pressure of deadlines for The Virginians, which he was eking out monthly as he had Vanity Fair and Pendennis, kept him from following through with the plan to publish. Whatever the case, no action was taken on that issue until 1859.

To Charles Lever, Thackeray commented in June 1859: "I leave them [Bradbury and Evans] (we remain perfect good friends) and go over to Smith & Elder.... [I]ndeed I have had every reason to be satisfied with both firms" [Letters 4: 144). But Thackeray's profitable dealings with George Smith (Kickleburys on the Rhine, 1850, and Henry Esmond, 1852) and the fabulous offers made him by the firm of Smith, Elder to edit the Cornhill Magazine doubtless made him eager to part company with a publisher who claimed to be losing money on his latest book.

The give-and-take between the apparently easygoing author and the shrewd businessman publisher can be seen best in the history of the founding of the Cornhill Magazine. As early as 1854 Thackeray had proposed to Smith a periodical called Fair Play, which he would edit. Smith took to the idea and started making plans. Then in February 1855 Thackeray cried off after his Quarterly Review remark that Punch Magazine was nothing without the illustrator John Leech drew the anger of his former writing cronies. The incident made Thackeray doubt his abilities to be an editor without inadvertently making enemies.

Smith's final assault and successful siege to capture complete control of Thackeray's writing may have grown out of that aborted project. On 19 February 1859 Smith approached Thackeray with a memorandum announcing his intention to "commence the publication of a Monthly Magazine on January 1st, 1860," and offering a contract specifying " 1 or 2 novels of the ordinary size" to be delivered one-twelfth at a time for monthly publication in the magazine.

Thackeray would give up all rights in the novels for the magazine and one book-form publication but would share in the profits from any second or subsequent book form. He would be paid £350 each month [Letters 4: 130). Two outstanding elements of this offier are the length of the novels and the rate of pay. Smith wanted a novel in twelve parts, each "estimated to be about equal to one number of a serial," and he was willing to pay £100 per month more than the firm of Bradbury and Evans was paying for The Virginians, on which it claimed to be losing money. Smith's insurance was to be all the income from foreign editions (Harper and Tauchnitz) and one separate book edition.

Two months later, 9 April 1859, an agreement was drawn up, but the stipulations had been changed. In this agreement both men honed the clauses to suit what they thought was important.

Smith now insisted on submission of manuscript exactly one month before publication date; he insisted that the scenes "are to be descriptive of contemporary English life society and manners" (i.e., not a historical narrative); he increased his leeway in book publishing by claiming all the profits from two separate book issues (though the agreement is written in such a way as to preclude either of those from being a "cheap" edition, for which Thackeray reserved the right to share half profits); and he insisted that Thackeray write for no one else for the duration of magazine serialization.

Thackeray seems also to have worked over the contract. He is probably the one who insisted that the serial length be increased to sixteen numbers and the one who suggested "not less than twenty four original drawings for etchings on steel". By this contract Smith secured Thackeray's services for thirty-six months and Thackeray secured the highest monthly income of his life (£350) for thirty-two of those months.

One stipulation did rankle Thackeray. On the afternoon of 14 February Thackeray signed the agreement and sent it to Smith with the following note: "I have written at the side of one paragraph a remark of which you'll see the bearing. You'll see I am hankering still to write a ballad or two without my name in Punch - or do something to show my old friends that I've not quite separated from them."

And the next morning he wrote a second note to Smith: "I found your note when I came home last night having meanwhile sent you from the Club the signed agreement: by which I propose to abide. The objections written on the other leaf may be torn off if you like; but I think I ought to write a Punch paper or ballad or so, to show that there is no disagreement between me & my old employers.

This is a matter of minor importance however, <and> I consider our agreement as made" (NLS). The copy of the 9 April agreement that Thackeray signed has brackets marking the paragraph stipulating he not publish elsewhere, and the facing page has been torn away. Four months later, 20 August, Smith and Thackeray signed a substitute agreement beginning: "Some of the conditions of the agreement made on 9th. of April 1859 between Mr. Thackeray and Smith Elder & Co. are to be varied as follows-". The changes were substantial; again both men were negotiating. There is still no mention of editing the magazine.

The first part of the new agreement must represent Thackeray's new demands. The starting date for beginning the first novel was postponed six months to 1 June 1860; the length of each novel was to be expandable to twenty numbers at Thackeray's option; illustrated initials would be furnished in addition to the steel engraved plates; the novels would be separate serials rather than parts of the proposed magazine; and Smith would have the full rights to only one book form in addition to the serial. No reference is made to money; so one assumes the £350 per month specified in the April contract held good.

Furthermore, the new agreement makes no mention of foreign rights, a fact Thackeray picked up on in a letter that indicates he may have taken the agreement away with him to consider: "I have forgot the Agreement at Fkstone. but its all right.

The American reprints are mine in this case?" (NLS). Exhausted by The Virginians and unwell, Thackeray was giving himself room to breath. Four days earlier he had written to F. M. Evans concerning the last number of The Virginians: "I have been ill again, and am very much afraid I cant do the double number this month. The single number I can do - it is + done already. I hope the delay wont inconvenience you" (Bodleian).

Smith, however, was not losing his man. Thackeray agreed to supply a very short novel in six parts for the magazine, each only sixteen pages long, half the size of a normal serial monthly. In addition, The Four Georges would be serialized. Each work would belong to Smith for one book issue. The price for this magazine work was £1,500, to be paid in three installments. No date was stipulated for submission of the lectures manuscript, and in fact it began its appearance in the magazine in June after the short novel, Lovel the Widower, had run its course.

Gordon Ray has suggested that the reduced writing load was a result of Smith's decision to ask Thackeray to become the magazine's new editor, but this seems unlikely in view of the lack of any mention of editorial duties in the 20 August contract and the possible interpretation of the contract that would have put both Lovel the Widower and The Four Georges in the first issues. George Smith's own account of his decision is undated: "We were then living at Wimbledon, and I used to ride on the Common before breakfast.

One morning, just as I had pulled up my horse after a smart gallop, that good genius which has so often helped me whispered into my ear, 'Why should not Mr Thackeray himself edit the magazine, and you yourself do what is necessary to supplement any deficiencies on his part: as a man of business?...'

After breakfast I drove straight to Thackeray's house in Onslow Square, talked to him of my difficulty, and induced him to accept the editorship, for which I was to pay him a salary of £1000 a year. " The first clear indication in Thackeray's letters that he was the editor comes on 7 September when he reported to Smith on recruiting articles and remarked: "As I think of the editing business I like it. But the Magazine must bear my cachet you see and be a man of the world Magazine, a little cut of Temple Bar, or Charles I on the outside?" [Letters 4: 149-50).

The changes in the August contract reveal some important things about the hard-nosed Smith and the easygoing Thackeray. Smith was careful in the details of each contract but apparently easily induced to change or abandon provisions at the author's request; Thackeray was fairly eager to please the man with the money but insisting on changes both for health's and for art's sake. As far as money is concerned, there is a change from £350 per month to an average of £214 per month for the first six months.

What Thackeray bought with these contractual changes was time - time that the tiring author felt he needed - but simultaneously he assured himself a continuing income, since the two substantial novels were merely postponed. On his side, George Smith obtained the services of one of the day's two foremost writers of fiction for his magazine and the prospect of a continuing relationship that amounted almost to ownership of the talent, for Thackeray was not allowed to publish anything with other publishers during the life of the contract.

With the addition of the editorial salary, Thackeray's monthly income came to just over £297 per month. And then in another undated contract, Smith and Thackeray agreed to include twenty-four five-page essays, The Roundabout Papers, for another £1,000, or about £42 per month. Then because Cornhill Magazine did so well, Smith doubled Thackeray's salary, bringing the total at least briefly to £422 per month.

In the actual event, the first of Thackeray's larger novels was postponed until January 1861; so in effect, his income for the second half of 1860 consisted of his editorial salary and payments for Roundabout Papers - about £209 per month. Thackeray had never been so thoroughly controlled by contracts, nor had he ever been so well and regularly paid. Smith had his literary giant, he had the grace and flexibility to change agreements, and he had the financial wherewithal to keep his giant happy.

Thackeray took to his new duties with enthusiasm and vigor. His letters to Smith in November and December 1859 are full of accounts of meetings with contributors and comments on their articles and poems. George Augustus Sala's work on Hogarth, about which Sala, Thackeray, and Smith had corresponded in September 1855, turned up as a contribution that needed extensive reworking.

Thackeray wrote of operating, amputating, cutting, and correcting material for the first number, and early on he suggested that "a boy ought to be set on to call at my house at 2 o'clock every day" (NLS). Commentators on the editing of the Cornhill have frequently noted the powerful hand Smith maintained in editorial matters, and it is true that he exercised his right of veto to an extent only a coeditor would.

But Thackeray insisted on his own decisions as well, persuading Smith to back down on his objections to articles by Robert Bell and General John Fox Burgoyne and poems by Thomas Hood for the first two numbers. But the pressure of editorial decisions and continuous correspondence with Smith soon reached a climax. "In the name of Allah let go!" Thackeray exclaimed in December.

"I can't pretend to correct the other contributors proofs - and wouldnt, no not for 10000 a year. What a man that Reader is! but there must be a reason for him, as I never should have seen the notable blunder of the Naids until you pointed it out" (NLS).

Apparently Smith was trying to get as much for his money as he could. Friction there was, from time to time, and Thackeray finally resigned in March 1862 in terms that suggest it was not only the exigencies of the job that became too much but the difficulty of working with Smith himself. But their disagreements were kept strictly it control, and their personal and business relations continued to their mutual financial benefit [cf. Eddy for a more general account of Thackeray's role as the magazine's first editor].

By the time Lovel and the Four Georges were completed in the Cornhill, both men must have considered the contracts signed in 1859 to be ancient history, for instead of reverting to them for terms on Thackeray's next major novel, The Adventures of Philip, they drew up a new contract in December 186o, stipulating 250 guineas as the monthly rate with Smith getting all the profits from magazine and two book forms. This represents nearly £100 per month less than the earlier contract specified, but with Thackeray now also receiving £166a month as editor and £42 for each Roundabout, the total of over £450 must have struck the amazed author as adequate.

This contract stipulates the name of the novel, which suggests that its historical character was known to both parties. Earlier contracts had stipulated an unnamed novel with scenes from contemporary English life. Although the contract also specifies "sixteen consecutive numbers" as the length, Thackeray's previously negotiated option to increase the total to twenty numbers probably was omitted by oversight rather than conscious agreement, for an undated postscript on the contract, written in Thackeray's hand, adds:

"The terms of this agreement apply to 'Philip' as about to be extended to twenty numbers of the Magazine" (NLS). Other changes are also significant; the length of each installment was to be twenty-four rather than thirty-two pages, and instead of two steel engraved plates and one initial vignette, there would be one full-page illustration and two vignettes.

Publication of Philip concluded in the August 1862 issue of the magazine, four months after Thackeray's resignation as editor. On 4 March Thackeray wrote Smith:

I have been thinking over our conversation of yesterday, and it has not improved the gaiety of the work on wh. I am presently busy.

To day I have taken my friend Sir Charles Taylor into my confidence; and his opinion coincides with mine that I should withdraw from the Magazine. To go into bygones now is needless. Before ever the Magazine appeared, I was, as I have told you, on the point of writing such a letter as this: And whether connected with the CornHill Magazine or not, I hope I shall always be Sincerely your friend W M Thackeray And two days later he continued in the same vein.

I daresay your night, like mine, has been a little disturbed: but Philip presses and until this matter is over, I can't make that story so amusing as I would wish.

I had this pocket pistol in my breast yesterday but hesitated to pull the trigger at an old friend. My daughters are for a compromise. They say "It is all very fine Sir Charles Taylor telling you to do so and so Mr. Smith has proved himself your friend always." Bien. It is because I wish him to remain so, that I and the Magazine had better part company.

What the specific row was about, we do not know, but it concerned editorial policy, for Thackeray obviously continued both as Smith's friend and as main contributor to the magazine with Roundabout Papers and Philip. A new contract for The

Roundabout Papers was drafted in the month Philip concluded, for the twenty-four essays called for in the original contract had appeared. The new agreement reiterates the provisions of the contract signed in December 1859, but it spells out more specifically the essays covered. Some of Thackeray's occasional pieces had been published without the rubric "Roundabout Papers," and these were now included in the agreement by name; in all twenty-six essays are assumed to have been covered by the original contract.

Furthermore, the rate of remuneration for any new essays is specified at £12.12, or one guinea, a page; and a seven-page limit is imposed. Far from rigorous, this contract is of a piece with the previous ones and includes an escape clause whereby "either Mr Thackeray or Smith Elder & co are to be at liberty to terminate this Agreement as far as it relates to the publication of further 'Round-about Papers' in the 'Cornhill Magazine' at my period after the end of the present year". Thackeray provided four more monthly Roundahouts in T862 (skipping October), but in 1863 he wrote only five essays for the magazine.

The final contract between Smith and Thackeray concerns Denis Duval. Whether the terms of the August 1859 contract were still lingering in the consciousness of author and publisher can only be guessed. It had specified two novels for the magazine at £350 per month, and Philip represented the first of these. In his farewell letter as editor to the readers of the Cornhill on 25 March 1862.,

Thackeray anticipated his next novel: "Whilst the present tale of Philip is passing through the press, I am preparing another, on which I have worked at intervals for many years past, and which I hope to introduce in the ensuing year" [Letters 4: 260). Ray suggested that the work Thackeray had in mind was "The Knights of Borsellen," a fifteenth-century romance which in fact he never completed. Having finished Philip in August, Thackeray did not turn his attention for some time to any new work except the Roundabouts.

On 14 January he wrote to Smith, "I have been thinking over a story wh. might do but it had much better be in 8 numbers than in 4. No moral reflections and plenty of adventures." He then lapsed into the voice of what was to become Denis Duval and gave a 750-word sketch of the life of that hero, concluding with "and lived happy ever after but I could hardly do all this in one volume[.]

Couldn't we make two of it? Of course not in Old English-" [NLS] The name Denis Duval does not appear in this letter, nor does it appear in the contract signed nearly one month later on 11 February, where the work is referred to merely as "a story of eight parts of twenty four pages each".

Smith's usual stipulation that it contain scenes from contemporary life is also conspicuously absent. Submission date for the first part was "on or before the 1st of March," but that deadline came and went without any apparent anxiety on the part of either author or publisher. In May, Thackeray wrote a partly facetious letter to a Mrs. James claiming, "I have done nothing for a WHOLE YEAR and I MUST go to my horrible pens & paper" (Letters 4:287).

Thackeray frequently referred, in his 1863 correspondence, to the time he spent writing for the printers, but five essays for Cornhill and Denis Duval appear to have been his only work that year. When he died on 23 December, he had completed about half of the projected eight-number or two-volume work, which appeared in four monthly installments in the Cornhill commencing in March 1864.

Chapter 14

On Charity and Humor

Besides contributing to our stock of happiness, to our harmless laughter and amusement, to our scorn for falsehood and pretension, to our righteous hatred of hypocrisy, to our education in the perception of truth, our love of honesty, our knowledge of life, and shrewd guidance through the world, have not our humorous writers, our gay and kind week-day preachers, done much in support of that holy cause which has assembled you in this place, and which you are all abetting,— the cause of love and charity, the cause of the poor, the weak, and the unhappy; the sweet mission of love and tenderness, and peace and good will toward men?

That same theme which is urged upon you by the eloquence and example of good men to whom you are delighted listeners on Sabbath days is taught in his way and according to his power by the humorous writer, the commentator on every-day life and manners.

And as you are here assembled for a charitable purpose, giving your contributions at the door to benefit deserving people who need them, I like to hope and think that the men of our calling have done something in aid of the cause of charity, and have helped, with kind words and kind thoughts at least, to confer happiness and to do good. If the humorous writers claim to be week-day preachers, have they conferred any benefit by their sermons?

Are people happier, better, better disposed to their neighbors, more inclined to do works of kindness, to love, forbear, forgive, pity, after reading in Addison, in Steele, in Fielding, in Goldsmith, in Hood, in Dickens? I hope and believe so, and fancy that in writing they are also acting charitably, contributing with the means which Heaven supplies them to forward the end which brings you, too, together.

A love of the human species is a very vague and indefinite kind of virtue, sitting very easily on a man, not confining his actions at all, shining in print, or exploding in paragraphs, after which efforts of benevolence the philanthropist is sometimes said to go home and be no better than his neighbors.

Tartuffe and Joseph Surface, Stiggins and Chadband, who are always preaching fine sentiments and are no more virtuous than hundreds of those whom they denounce and whom they cheat, are fair objects of mistrust and satire; but their hypocrisy, the homage, according to the old saying, which vice pays to virtue, has this of good in it, that its fruits are good: a man may preach good morals tho he may be himself but a lax practitioner; a Pharisee may put pieces of gold into the charity-plate out of mere hypocrisy and ostentation, but the bad man's gold feeds the widow and the fatherless as well as the good man's. The butcher and baker must needs look, not to motives, but to money, in return for their wares.

A literary man of the humoristic turn is pretty sure to be of a philanthropic nature, to have a great sensibility, to be easily moved to pain or pleasure, keenly to appreciate the varieties of temper of people round about him, and sympathize in their laughter, love, amusement, tears. Such a man is philanthropic, man-loving by nature, as another is irascible, or red-haired, or six feet high.

And so I would arrogate no particular merit to literary men for the possession of this faculty of doing good which some of them enjoy. It costs a gentleman no sacrifice to be benevolent on paper; and the luxury of indulging in the most beautiful and brilliant sentiments never make any man a penny poorer. A literary man is no better than another, as far as my experience goes; and a man writing a book no better or no worse than one who keeps accounts in a ledger or follows any other occupation.

Let us, however, give him credit for the good, at least, which he is the means of doing, as we give credit to a man with a million for the hundred which he puts into the plate at a charity-sermon. He never misses them. He has made them in a moment by a lucky speculation, and parts with them knowing that he has an almost endless balance at his bank, whence he can call for more.

But in esteeming the benefaction we are grateful to the benefactor, too, somewhat; and so of men of genius, richly endowed, and lavish in parting with their mind's wealth, we may view them at least kindly and favorably, and be thankful for the bounty of which providence has made them the dispensers.

I have said myself somewhere, I do not know with what correctness (for definitions never are complete), that humor is wit and love; I am sure, at any rate, that the best humor is that which contains most humanity, that which is flavored throughout with tenderness and kindness. This love does not demand constant utterance or actual expression, as a good father, in conversation with his children or wife, is not perpetually embracing them or making protestations of his love; as a lover in the society of his mistress is not, at least as far as I am led to believe, for ever squeezing her hand or sighing in her ear, "My soul's darling, I adore you!"

He shows his love by his conduct, by his fidelity, by his watchful desire to make the beloved person happy; it lightens from his eyes when she appears, tho he may not speak it; it fills his heart when she is present or absent; influences all his words and actions; suffuses his whole being; it sets the father cheerily to work through the long day, supports him through the tedious labour of the weary absence or journey, and sends him happy home again, yearning toward the wife and children.

This kind of love is not a spasm, but a life. It fondles and caresses at due seasons, no doubt; but the fond heart is always beating fondly and truly, tho the wife is not sitting hand-in-hand with him or the children hugging at his knee. And so with a loving humor: I think, it is a genial writer's habit of being; it is the kind, gentle spirit's way of looking out on the world—that sweet friendliness which fills his heart and his style. You recognize it, even tho there may not be a single point of wit, or a single pathetic touch in the page; tho you may not be called upon to salute his genius by a laugh or a tear. That collision of ideas, which provokes the one or the other, must be occasional.

They must be like papa's embraces, which I spoke of anon, who only delivers them now and again, and can not be expected to go on kissing the children all night. And so the writer's jokes and sentiment, his ebullitions of feeling, his outbreaks of high spirits, must not be too frequent.

One tires of a page of which every sentence sparkles with points, of a sentimentalist who is always pumping the tears from his eyes or your own. One suspects the genuineness of the tear, the naturalness of the humor; these ought to be true and manly in a man, as everything else in his life should be manly and true; and he loses his dignity by laughing or weeping out of place, or too often.

If I do not love Swift, as, thank God, I do not, however immensely I may admire him, it is because I revolt from the man who placards himself as a professional hater of his own kind; because he chisels his savage indignation on his tombstone, as if to perpetuate his protest against being born of our race—the suffering, the weak, the erring, the wicked, if you will, but still the friendly, the loving children of God our Father; it is because, as I read through Swift's dark volumes, I never find the aspect of nature seems to delight him, the smiles of children to please him, the sight of wedded love to soothe him. I do not remember in any line of his writing a passing allusion to a natural scene of beauty.

When he speaks about the families of his comrades and brother clergymen, it is to assail them with gibes and scorn, and to laugh at them brutally for being fathers and for being poor. He does mention, in the Journal to Stella, a sick child, to be sure—a child of Lady Masham, that was ill of the smallpox—but then it is to confound the brat for being ill and the mother for attending to it when she should have been busy about a court intrigue, in which the Dean was deeply engaged.

And he alludes to a suitor of Stella's, and a match she might have made, and would have made, very likely, with an honorable and faithful and attached man, Tisdall, who loved her, and of whom Swift speaks, in a letter to his lady, in language so foul that you would not bear to hear it.

In treating of the good the humorists have done, of the love and kindness they have taught and left behind them, it is not of this one I dare speak. Heaven help the lonely misanthrope! be kind to that multitude of sins, with so little charity to cover them!

Of Addison's contributions to the charity of the world I have spoken before, in trying to depict that noble figure; and say now, as then, that we should thank him as one of the greatest benefactors of that vast and immeasurably spreading family which speaks our common tongue. Wherever it is spoken, there is no man that does not feel, and understand, and use the noble English word "gentleman." And there is no man that teaches us to be gentlemen better than Joseph Addison.

Gentle in our bearing through life; gentle and courteous to our neighbour; gentle in dealing with his follies and weaknesses; gentle in treating his opposition; deferential to the old; kindly to the poor, and those below us in degree—for people above us and below us we must find, in whatever hemisphere we dwell, whether kings or presidents govern us, and in no republic or monarchy that I know of, is a citizen exempt from the tax of befriending poverty and weakness, of respecting age, and of honoring his father and mother. It has just been whispered to me—I have not been three months in the country, and, of course, can not venture to express an opinion of my own—that, in regard to paying this later tax of respect and honour to age, some very few of the Republican youths are occasionally a little remiss.

I have heard of young Sons of Freedom publishing their Declaration of Independence before they could well spell it; and cutting the connection with father and mother before they had learned to shave. My own time of life having been stated by various enlightened organs of public opinion, at almost any figure from forty-five to sixty, I cheerfully own that I belong to the fogy interest, and ask leave to rank in, and plead for that respectable class. Now a gentleman can but be a gentleman, in Broadway or the backwoods, in Pall Mall or California; and where and whenever he lives, thousands of miles away in the wilderness, or hundreds of years hence, I am sure that reading the writings of this true gentleman, this true Christian, this noble Joseph Addison, must do him good.

Steele, as a literary benefactor to the world's charity, must rank very high, indeed, not merely from his givings, which were abundant, but because his endowments are prodigiously increased in value since he bequeathed them, as the revenues of the lands, bequeathed to our Foundling Hospital at London, by honest Captain Coram, its founder, are immensely enhanced by the houses since built upon them. Steele was the founder of sentimental writing in English, and how the land has been since occupied, and what hundreds of us have laid out gardens and built up tenements on Steele's ground!

Before his time, readers or hearers were never called upon to cry except at a tragedy, and compassion was not expected to express itself otherwise than in blank verse, of for personages much lower in rank than a dethroned monarch, or a widowed or a jilted empress.

He stepped off the high-heeled cothurnus, and came down into common life; he held out his great hearty arms, and embraced us all; he had a bow for all women; a kiss for all children; a shake of the hand for all men, high or low; he showed us Heaven's sun shining every day on quiet homes; not gilded palace roofs only, or court processions, or heroic warriors fighting for princesses and pitched battles.

He took away comedy from behind the fine lady's alcove, or the screen where the libertine was watching her. He ended all that wretched business of wives jeering at their husbands, of rakes laughing wives, and husbands, too, to scorn. That miserable, rouged, tawdry, sparkling, hollow-hearted comedy of the Restoration fled before him, and, like the wicked spirit in the fairy-books, shrank, as Steele let the daylight in, and shrieked, and shuddered, and vanished.

The stage of humorists has been common life ever since Steele's and Addison's time; the joys and griefs, the aversions and sympathies, the laughter and tears of nature. As for Goldsmith, if the youngest and most unlettered person here has not been happy with the family at Wakefield; has not rejoiced when Olivia returned, and been thankful for her forgiveness and restoration; has not laughed with delighted good humor over Moses's gross of green spectacles; has not loved with all his heart the good vicar,

And that kind spirit which created these charming figures, and devised the beneficent fiction which speaks to us so tenderly—what call is there for me to speak? In this place, and on this occasion, remembering these men, I claim from you your sympathy for the good they have done, and for the sweet charity which they have bestowed on the world.

In our days, in England, the importance of the humorous preacher has prodigiously increased; his audiences are enormous; every week or month his happy congregations flock to him; they never tire of such sermons. I believe my friend Mr. "Punch" is as popular to-day as he has been any day since his birth; I believe that Mr. Dickens's readers are even more numerous than they have ever been since his unrivaled pen commenced to delight the world with its humor.

We have among us other literary parties; we have "Punch," as I have said, preaching from his booth; we have a Jerrold party very numerous, and faithful to that acute thinker and distinguished wit; and we have also—it must be said, and it is still to be hoped—a "Vanity Fair" party, the author of which work has lately been described by the London *Times* newspaper as a writer of considerable parts, but a dreary misanthrope, who sees no good anywhere, who sees the sky above him green, I think, instead of blue, and only miserable sinners round about him.

So we are; so is every writer and every reader I ever heard of; so was every being who ever trod this earth, save One. I can not help telling the truth as I view it, and describing what I see. To describe it otherwise than it seems to me would be falsehood in that calling in which it has pleased heaven to place me; treason to that conscience which says that men are weak, that truth must be told, that fault must be owned, that pardon must be prayed for, and that love reigns supreme over all. I look back at the good which of late years the kind English humorists have done; and if you are pleased to rank the present speaker among that class, I own to an honest pride at thinking what benefits society has derived from men of our calling.

That "Song of the Shirt" which "Punch" first published, and the noble, the suffering, the melancholy, the tender Hood sang, may surely rank as a great act of charity to the world, and call from it its thanks and regard for its teacher and benefactor. That astonishing poem, which you all of you know, of the "Bridge of Sighs,"—who can read it without tenderness, without reverence to heaven, charity to man, and thanks to the beneficent genius which sang for us nobly?

I never saw the writer but once; but shall always be glad to think that some words of mine, printed in a periodical of that day, and in praise of those amazing verses (which, strange to say, appeared almost unnoticed at first in the magazine in which Mr. Hood published them)—I am proud, I say, to think that some words of appreciation of mine reached him on his death-bed and pleased and soothed him in that hour of manful resignation and pain.

As for the charities of Mr. Dickens, multiplied kindnesses which he has conferred upon us all—upon our children, upon people educated and uneducated, upon the myriads here and at home who speak our common tongue—have not you, have not I, all of us reason to be thankful to this kind friend, who soothed and charmed so many hours, brought pleasure and sweet laughter to so many homes, made such multitudes of children happy, endowed us with such a sweet store of gracious thoughts, fair fancies, soft sympathies, hearty enjoyments?

There are creations of Mr. Dickens which seem to me to rank as personal benefits; figures so delightful, that one feels happier and better for knowing them, as one does for being brought into the society of very good men and women. The atmosphere in which these people live is wholesome to breathe in; you feel that to be allowed to speak to them is a personal kindness; you come away better for your contact with them;

your hands seem cleaner from having the privilege of shaking theirs. Was there ever a better charity sermon preached in the world than Dickens's "Christmas Carol"? I believe it occasioned immense hospitality throughout England; was the means of lighting up hundreds of kind fires at Christmas time; caused a wonderful outpouring of Christmas good feeling, of Christmas punch-brewing; an awful slaughter of Christmas turkeys, and roasting and basting of Christmas beef.

As for this man's love of children, that amiable organ at the back of his honest head must be perfectly monstrous. All children ought to love him. I know two that do, and read his books ten times for once that they peruse the dismal preachments of their father.

I know one who, when she is happy, reads "Nicholas Nickleby"; when she is unhappy, reads "Nicholas Nickleby"; when she is tired, reads "Nicholas Nickleby"; when she is in bed, reads "Nicholas Nickleby"; when she has nothing to do, reads "Nicholas Nickleby"; and when she has finished the book, reads "Nicholas Nickleby" over again.

This candid young critic, at ten years of age, said, "I like Mr. Dickens's books much better than your books, papa"; and frequently expressed her desire that the latter author should write a book like one of Mr. Dickens's books. Who can? Every man must say his own thoughts in his own voice, in his own way; lucky is he who has such a charming gift of nature as this, which brings all the children in the world trooping to him, and being fond of him.

I remember, when that famous "Nicholas Nickleby" came out, seeing a letter from a pedagog in the north of England, which, dismal as it was, was immensely comical. "Mr. Dickens's ill-advised publication," wrote the poor schoolmaster, "has passed like a whirlwind over the schools of the North." He was a proprietor of a cheap school; Dotheboys Hall was a cheap school. There were many such establishments in the northern counties.

Parents were ashamed that never were ashamed before until the kind satirist laughed at them; relatives were frightened; scores of little scholars were taken away; poor schoolmasters had to shut their shops up; every pedagog was voted a Squeers, and many suffered, no doubt unjustly; but afterward, schoolboys' backs were not so much caned; schoolboys' meat was less tough and more plentiful; and schoolboys' milk was not so sky-blue.

What a kind light of benevolence it is that plays round Crummles and the Phenomenon, and all those poor theater people in that charming book! What a humor and what a good humor!

One might go on, tho the task would be endless and needless, chronicling the names of kind folks with whom this kind genius has made us familiar. Who does not love the Marchioness and Mr. Richard Swiveller?

Who does not sympathize, not only with Oliver Twist, but his admirable young friend, the Artful Dodger? Who has not the inestimable advantage of possessing a Mrs. Nickleby in his own family? Who does not bless Sairey Gamp and wonder at Mrs. Harris? Who does not venerate the chief of that illustrious family who, being stricken by misfortune, wisely and greatly turned his attention to "coals," the accomplished, the Epicurean, the dirty, the delightful Micawber?

I may quarrel with Mr. Dickens's art a thousand and a thousand times—I delight and wonder at his genius; I recognize in it—I speak with awe and reverence—a commission from that Divine Beneficence whose blessed task we know it will one day be to wipe every tear from every eye. Thankfully I take my share of the feast of love and kindness which this gentle, and generous, and charitable soul has contributed to the happiness of the world. I take and enjoy my share, and say a Benediction for the meal.

Chapter 15

Chapman and Hall

During the years of struggle to establish himself as a writer, Thackeray can hardly be said to have "had a publisher." Each new book had to find a home, often with a new publisher because his last book had failed to make money. By 1847 Thackeray's works had been published in book form by ten different publishers, of which four (Chapman and Hall, Macrone, Cunningham, and Hooper) are known to have paid him money.

Another (Mitchell) published by agreement with him but claimed that returns did not even cover production costs, so there was no payment to the author. The other five (Taylor, Baudry, Berford, Cary and Hart, and Winchester), publishing unauthorized reprints, definitely did not pay. (Baudry is a possible exception, but there is no evidence one way or the other.)

Of the four who did pay, Chapman and Hall alone stuck with the author over a significant period of time. Indeed, the firm acted as Thackeray's bankers as well as publishers in the early 1840s. Then, for four years running (1846-49), Thackeray was able to count on them to publish his Christmas books.

Thackeray's relations with the Chapman firm in the second half of the 1840s were carried on as between equals in a business venture. In the turbulent revolutionary year 1848, Thackeray wrote Chapman suggesting the projected Christmas book, Kicklebury s on the Rhine, be dropped in favor of a purely domestic and politically safe story [Letters 2: 444-45). Dr. Birch and His Young Friends became the season's offering that year. On the other hand, when Charles Lever parodied

Thackeray as Elias Howle in the next month's installment of Roland Cashel, Thackeray's protest to Chapman that his publisher should not be "the office for this dreary personality" apparently made no difference. Yet Thackeray's business relations with Chapman and Hall proceeded on a professional level; subsequent letters deal with the production problems and illustrations for Dr. Birch [Letters 2: 466).

Rebecca and Rowena was Thackeray's last book published by Chapman and Hall. On 17 September 1849, while he concerned himself primarily with producing Pendennis, Thackeray twisted his ankle badly enough to put him in bed for a few days. As luck would have it, he came down at the same time with a case of what may have been cholera, the worst of the illness coming on the night of 3 October. Obviously, he failed to prepare the next number of Pendennis for October; and though he pulled through and was declared out of danger by 15 October, he did not resume publication of Pendennis until 1 January 1850.

He spent the end of October in Brighton to convalesce with "Dr. Sea Breeze," and on 7 November he began work, with Eyre Crowe's help, on the texts for Louis Marvy's Sketches after English Landscape Painters to be published by David Bogue in 1850. Bogue had very recently taken over the business of Charles Tilt, who had published Thackeray's Stubbs's Calendar in The Comic Almanac for 1839. Bogue wished both to build on Tilt's past interest and to take advantage of Thackeray's new popularity, so he wrote to Thackeray proposing republication of Stubbs's. On 21 November Thackeray replied:

The story of Stubb's Calendar has been already reprinted by me, in the "Comic Tales & Sketches" published by Cunningham in 1840 - It is my copyright, as all my works have been by verbal agreements with the publishers for whom I wrote, with the exception of certain contributions to the "Heads of the People" about wh. I forgot to make a stipulation: though I am advised that I can with perfect safety republish these latter in case I shd. think fit so to do.

I regret that I cannot consent to the republication of the

Stubbs story, under the present circumstances. I am working at the text for M. Marvy's engravings, & hope very shortly to deliver it to you. Nothing but illness wd. have prevented me from executing this task before now.

By 3 December Thackeray was well enough to accept a dinner invitation from George Smith, publisher of Charlotte Brontë Jane Eyre. The two men had not met, but Brontë had asked Smith for a meeting with Thackeray. There is nothing in George Smith's recollections [quoted from Huxley in Letters 2: 611n] or Thackeray's own to suggest any lingering effects of his illness.

Yet in December, Thackeray had to write Joseph Cundall to explain the delay in completing the text for Marvy's book. Cundall, remembered primarily as a writer and publisher of children's books in the 1840s and 1850s, had previously been employed by Charles Tilt and had copublished several books with David [70/71] Bogue.

He had just suffered bankruptcy and was continuing his publishing activities only in conjunction with other publishers when he apparently inquired on Bogue's behalf concerning the text Thackeray was preparing [McLean, pp. 1, 18, 22]. Thackeray wrote:

The gentleman whom I had engaged to get some biographical notices for Mr. Marvy's sketches is gone to France, hence my delay during the last month - but this month at any rate I promise you that the work shall be done, and always keep my promises.

I hope Mr. Bogue will settle with Mr. Marvy - what is it that I our to be paid for my contributions? It is a very difficult task to perform. [Letters 2: 612-13]

It may be that in November, while Eyre Crowe was in France, Thackeray worked on Rebecca and Rowena, the 102-page continuation of the romance of Ivanhoe. Whatever the case, it was already December when he sent the manuscript to Chapman, at the same time asking to be paid £50 and saying, "The book has cost me more time than all the rest" [Letters 2: 613]. That left little time for publication, and it is perhaps understandable that mistakes should have been made, particularly with the title and preface, which are always the last to be prepared. Thackeray sent the preface together with copy for an advertisement to the publisher, who mistakenly assumed the preface was part of the ad.

The whole apparently appeared together, for Thackeray wrote the publisher correcting the subtitle from "A Romance on Romance" to "or Romance on Romance" and adding: "What the devil have you gone & done? Why the devil didnt you send me proof You have gone & printed the preface with the advertisement - spoiled my point: offended Dr. Elliotson & annoyed me beyond measure." [Letters 2: 613-14]

A partially corrected advertisement appeared in the Examiner on 1 December, without the preface but still sporting the erroneous subtitle, prompting Thackeray to write again: "The title as I wrote, and rewrote and recorrected is R & R or Romance on Romance not A [Romance on Romance]" [Letters 2: 614]. On 22 December the Examiner had miscorrected the subtitle to "Or A Romance on Romance," but the book itself never was corrected. Since the title page is a wood engraving, one wonders if perhaps the illustrator, Richard Doyle, might have initiated the problem.

Such irritations may seem minor, but there is an evident coolness on both sides that attends the almost gentlemanly duty Thackeray fulfilled when he offered Chapman and Hall his next Christmas book, the one that had been scheduled for two years earlier when Dr. Birch was substituted,

It is likely, too, that Thackeray's new stature as author of two successful major works made him less tolerant of Chapman and Hall's decidedly genteel, informal, and occasionally sloppy business practices. On the other hand, Thackeray himself tended to be informal about business agreements, as is suggested by his reference to the "verbal agreements" about copyrights in his letter to Bogue.

In August 1840 Thackeray dutifully broached the subject of The Kicklemburys on the Rhine, his fifth Christmas book, offering Chapman and Hall an edition of 3,000 copies for £150. "I think," he wrote, "I have a right to a shilling per copy of a 5/ & often 7/ book: and intend to stipulate for that sum with my publisher" [Letters 2: 687). Chapman's reply on the back of Thackeray's letter was:

I find that there are about 350 copies of Rebecca [the 1849 Christmas book] now on hand out of the 3000 printed and I know that there are also a great many [illegible word] with the country booksellers. I don't think that a sale of more than 2500 could be depended on for the new book.

Under these circumstances, I could not, I am sorry to say agree to your proposal with any chance of profit to myself. I am obliged to you for mentioning your intention to me before applying elsewhere & shall be sorry to lose the advantage value of your name, but it would be useless for me to undertake a speculation by which I feel assured I should lose.

How wrong Chapman was and how right Thackeray was to hold out became evident soon enough. Chapman and Hall lost whatever hold the firm may have had on Thackeray. The relationship, however, had been a long and generally friendly one; and, although Thackeray's written correspondence with Chapman and Hall seems virtually to have ceased in 1850, his letters to others contain references to his having met and conversed with one or another of the partners from time to time for the rest of his life.

If Chapman and Hall was Thackeray's publisher in any proprietary way - Thackeray had assured the firm when offering it The Kickleburys in 1850 that he had spoken to no other publishers - it did not try very hard to hold him. Chapman obviously made his decision without reading any of the manuscript, and his change in wording from "advantage," which has a positive meaning, to the ambiguous "value," suggests Chapman may not have been as sorry as he said about losing Thackeray.

In any case, two other publishers were ready to take Thackeray away. The first was Bradbury and Evans. Vanity Fair became that company's publication almost by default. Thackeray had thought, when he first became a Punch writer for Bradbury and Evans, that he was associating himself with a less respectable magazine, but by 1846 this connection was not only economically important but one Thackeray had come to take seriously as a means of satire and ridicule against political and social evil.

Yet to have his first major book published from "THE Punch office," after being rejected by at least one and possibly four other publishers, is an indication that he was settling for a familiar, somewhat lower class publisher. (Dickens, publishing his first work,

Dombey and Son, with Bradbury and Evans at the same time, had no reference to Punch in the imprint of his numbered parts.) And once Bradbury and Evans had carried Vanity Fair through the risky part of its production to success and had offered Thackeray increased pay for his next novel before a word of it was written, he became a Bradbury and Evans author.

That was not, however, an exclusive arrangement. The other publisher wooing Thackeray from Chapman and Hall did so far more deliberately and intentionally. With Chapman and Hall's release of its courtesy claim to his next Christmas book, by declining to pay £150 for it, Thackeray was free to offer it to George Smith of Smith, Elder, and Company, who immediately sent him a check for the full amount.

Thackeray replied in August 1850, "I went out of town early on the mg. of the 25th or I should sooner have acknowledged your letter, & the enclosed cheque for £150: the price of the Copyright of 3000 copies of my Xmas book for 1851 [i.e., December 1850]" (NLS).

The first edition of 3,000 copies sold out immediately. On the day Smith wrote Thackeray with this news (and, by the way, enclosing a £50 bonus check), the Times printed an unfavorable review (later attributed to Charles Lamb Kenny). Thackeray's response, "An Essay on Thunder and Small Beer," appeared in the second printing of The Kickleburys, announcing itself as a "Second Edition," dated 1850. Two more reprints, the second called a "Third Edition," were issued in 1851.

The printer's records for Smith, Elder no longer exist for the years preceding 1853, but it is clear that Chapman and Hall turned down a chance to make a tidy profit and thereby also lost any chance of enlarging its share in an increasingly valuable literary property. Chapman and Hall's dealings with Thackeray had begun with caution, the formalities of contracts, and the proffer of advances in exchange for a security, the deposit of the family plate.

These formalities later were dropped, and there were no written contracts for the Christmas books and no formal registration of titles with the Stationers' Register, facts discovered by George Smith in 1865 when he was trying to gain control of all Thackeray's copyrights [MS correspondence between Smith and Chapman, used by permission of John Murray, Publishers, the present owners]. Nevertheless, the Chapman and Hall firm seems to have paid its small profit-sharing dividends regularly, relying on gentlemen's agreements.

Bradbury and Evans exhibited a similar tendency toward informal agreements, and the company's hold on Thackeray was never a very firm one. It never stipulated for anything except the work it was about to publish. Anything else Thackeray undertook at the same time was none of its business or concern.

With Smith, Elder, for example, Thackeray published The Kickleburys in 1850, The History of Henry Esmond in 1852, and Lectures on Eighteenth Century English Humourists in 1853, but in fact he was primarily a Bradbury and Evans author from 1847 to 1859.

Chapter 16

Bradbury and Evans

William Bradbury and Frederick Mullet Evans had gone into partnership as a printing firm in 1830. The company became the primary printer for the publisher and bookseller Moxon and later for Chapman and Hall. In the late 1840s and 50s appears to have done much of Smith, Elder's printing until that firm acquired its own printing works in 1857. Bradbury and Evans began, then, as a printer, not bookseller and publisher.

When the partners purchased Punch in 1841, they launched a publishing career that seems to have been extraordinarily lucky rather than expert or self-assured. Charles Dickens considered a long while and turned down several offers from Bradbury and Evans because he was not convinced the firm knew enough about advertising and book distribution to make the most of his works. Thackeray's connection with Bradbury and Evans had begun, of course, with his contributions to Punch in 1842 and included occasional pieces in such Punch Office publications as George Cruikshank's Table-Book (1845) and Punch's Pocket Book for 1847.

Perhaps like Dickens, Thackeray distrusted his Punch employers as book publisher, for he tried other publishers with his first truly ambitious book before settling with their firm. The first number of Vanity Fair, issued on 1 January 1847, was the first Thackeray title published separately by Bradbury and Evans, and it marked the beginning of eleven years during which the firm was Thackeray's primary publisher.

This relationship ended in 1859 with the purported failure of The Virginians and the successful wooing of Thackeray by

George Smith, which bore fruit in the Cornhill Magazine. By then Bradbury and Evans had published Thackeray's four longest novels and three of the four volumes of Miscellanies collecting many of his better early productions. Thus, Bradbury and Evans continued to exercise publication rights in the majority of Thackeray's work until July 1865, when Smith, Elder and Company purchased the unsold stock, stereotyped plates, and copyrights from all other interested parties.

Thackeray's business association with Bradbury and Evans can be detailed rather fully because the firm's account books are still extant, and while the various records seem incomplete and do not always agree on amounts, especially in accounting for the distribution of copies printed, the archive provides what is in the main a faithful picture of the financial relationship between author and publisher.

Sales figures provide a clue to the circulation of Thackeray's works; the size and number of printings suggest the development and decline in the popularity of individual titles; a clearer view is gained of the financial "failure" of The Virginians; and a previously unknown edition of one of his books is revealed.

Although Vanity Fair (1847-48) earned Thackeray less money than any of his other parts-issued novels (£3,006.3.3, compared with £3,207.18.1 for Pendennis and £4,561.3.9 for The Newcomes), it was his most widely circulated book. Of the two editions published by Bradbury and Evans, 32,500 copies were printed, and only 931 of these remained in stock in June 1865. Most of the sales were of the cheap edition, which was printed eleven times between 1853 and 1865 to produce 22,0000 copies.

Aside from the fact that Thackeray received only £60 per number as initial payments for Vanity Fair, production costs kept it from earning much on the profit-sharing system, and although the total number of copies of the first edition (10,500) exceeded that for Pendennis (9,500), it required twice as many printings to reach that figure. The obvious reason for this was that Vanity Fair was written by a relatively unknown author for whom no [75/76] publisher would be likely to risk large printings, whereas Pendennis (1848-50) was written by the author of Vanity Fair - a fact which had a considerable bearing on the size of the initial printings (9,000 per number for Pendennis compared to an average of 4,500 per number for Vanity Fair).

After Vanity Fair Thackeray's most purchased books were Pendennis and The Newcomes (20,000 copies printed of each with only 500 copies of The Newcomes and 423 of Pendennis left in stock in 1865). For both publisher and author The Newcomes (1854-55) was a bigger money-maker than Pendennis because it sold more copies in the more expensive first edition and because production costs were slightly lower (fewer and larger reprints); for Thackeray himself The Newcomes had the additional advantage of initial payments £50 per number higher than those for Pendennis.

The Book of Snobs, riding the rising wave of popularity developed by Vanity Fair, also had a large circulation. In two separate editions (1848 and as an "off-print" of Miscellanies, vol. 1, in 1855) Snobs circulated 11,750 copies, When this figure is added to the 10,000-copy printing of the first volume of Miscellanies, which contained it, it appears that Snobs may have reached a higher circulation figure than Pendennis. However, the records do not indicate clearly how many copies of each volume of the four-volume Miscellanies were included in the total of 1,600 copies left in stock or unaccounted for in 1865.

Although the The Virginians (1857-59) was recorded by Bradbury and Evans as a financial failure, it was Thackeray's greatest financial success while with that firm. No contract survives to tell us the details of Thackeray's agreement with Bradbury and Evans, but on 10 September 1856 he wrote to his friends Mrs. Elliot and Kate Perry that he was to receive £6,000 for the novel [Letter 3: 60).

He repeated that information to his mother in December [Letters 3: 655). Since The Virginians is a twenty-four-part novel, like Pendennis and The Newcomes, this figure averages out at £250 per month. As late as February 1857, however, Thackeray referred to it as "that novel expanded into 20 or 4 numbers wh. was to have been the continuation of Esmond — embracing the American War" (NLS). Thackeray seriously contemplated making it a twenty-part novel, like Vanity Fair, for he mentioned to William Bradford Reed in May 1857 that he was to receive twice as much for The Virginians as he had gotten for any other publication [Letters 4: 44).

His highest previous payment was for The Newcomes, for which he had received £150 per month. Thackeray used the same phrase to Baron Tauchnitz on 12 November 1857: "my publishers here pay me twice as much as for the Newcomes." [Verlag Bernhard Tauchnitz, p. 123]. The first installment appeared on 1 November, but sales were not as high as expected.

Thackeray wrote to his American friends the Baxters in that month, "I tremble for the poor publishers who give me 300£ a number - I don't think they can afford it and shall have the melancholy duty of disgorging" [Letters 4: 56). And sure enough, on 21 December he wrote to John Blackwood: "We don't sell 20000 of the Virginians as we hoped, but more than 16000 and should have done better but for the confounded times.

I have thought proper to knock 50£ a month off my pay from Bradbury & Evans till we get tip to a higher number - For you see Sir my publishers have always acted honestly and kindly by me and I don't want any man to lose by me" (Morgan). It is tempting to speculate that the novel was extended from twenty to twenty-four numbers, as Pendennis had been, so that while Thackeray's pay dropped from £300 to £250 per month, the total initial payment remained at £6,000, but that might just be an ingenious way to reconcile the varying figures in the surviving correspondence.

It had been Bradbury and Evans's practice with Pendennis and The Newcomes to record the firm's own share of income as one of the costs of production. The split on Pendennis was £100 to Thackeray and £75 to the publisher, and the split on The Newcomes was £150 to Thackeray and it £112.10 to the publisher. Both of those books began showing a profit over and above these initial payments to author and publisher within a year of publication. But in accounting for The Virginians, the publisher did not figure in its share as a cost of production. According to the records, then, the author received his £6,000 while the publisher was still showing a deficit of £3,257.2.3 in 1865. There never were any profits to share from the first edition of The Virginians.

Two reasons for the publisher's alleged predicament emerge from the records. First, it grossly overestimated the sale of the book: of the first number, 20,000 copies were printed; the print order was immediately reduced to 16,000 each for numbers 2 and 3, and reductions continued until, finally, only 13,000 copies each were printed of numbers 18-24; even this was too many, for in 1865 there were still 16,000 parts (equivalent to 690 copies of the book) left in stock. Second, the publisher agreed to pay more for this novel than Thackeray ever earned from a single title during the entire period of the company's connection with him.

Every commentator on the financial fortunes of The Virginians, Thackeray included, has believed that Bradbury and Evans lost money on the book. They point to the fact that Thackeray agreed to a £50 per month reduction in pay and to the fact that Bradbury and Evans let Thackeray go to Smith without protest.

In fact, however, Thackeray never stood to earn more than £6,000 in initial payments for the book, all of which he received, and a look at the records shows that the publisher's loss was a loss of expected profits, not a loss of capital outlay. By December 1857, after three numbers of The Virginians, there was a £66 deficit after paying production costs and after paying Thackeray but before paying Bradbury and Evans. By December 1958, after fifteen numbers, there was a surplus of £546 after paying production costs and author.

The surplus continued to grow, Bradbury and Evans enjoying the fruits of it but not recording the firm's share until January 1863, when the surplus recorded was £1,199. At this point Bradbury and Evans credited the company with £4,500, which would have been its share in profits if the book had made enough to pay that share.

By December 1863 the account showed a loss of £3,291, which really means that Bradbury and Evans made a little over £1,200 on the book. The firm recovered, through sales, all the costs of production, including all the money it had paid to Thackeray, and paid itself just over £1,200 in real money from profits. The deficit reported represents the amount required to pay the company its share of the proceeds from the book before the bookkeeper would declare the account balanced and proceed to ring up profits for sharing with the author.

Since Bradbury and Evans apportioned to the company only £4,500 to Thackeray's £6,000, it appears, in the absence of any surviving contract, that, the profit-sharing arrangement for The Virginians was to have been three to four, very slightly less for Thackeray than the two-to-three agreement in effect for the Miscellanies. Since Bradbury and Evans earned only a fourth of its three-sevenths share on the first edition of The Virginians, the deal was the worst it had made with Thackeray, earning it a profit of just over one half what it had made from the first edition of Vanity Fair.

The Newcomes (1853-54), the second highest money-maker for Thackeray, had netted him only £4,561.3.9 by 1865, but it was a far more satisfactory bargain for the publisher, showing a profit within a year of the novel's completion in July 1855. To show a profit in that case meant the publisher had been able to pay itself as much as it had paid Thackeray.

The History of Samuel Titmarsh and the Great Hoggarty Diamond (circulation about 15,000) almost equaled the sales of The Virginians (about 15,500), but both lagged behind the Ballads, a sleeper of which 18,000 [78/79] copies were printed (8,000 in a separate edition requiring nine printings and 10,000 as part of the first volume of Miscellanies).

The relationship between Thackeray and the firm of Bradbury and Evans was for the most part a pleasant and fruitful one. The records show the publisher always increasing remunerations to the successful author: initial payments for parts-issued novels climbed rapidly from £60 per number for Vanity Fair to £100 for Pendennis, £150 for The Newcomes, and finally to the supposedly disastrous £250 for The

Virginians. Likewise, in profits Thackeray's share, usually a half, became three-fifths for the Miscellanies (1855-57) and four-sevenths for The Virginians (1857-59).

Thackeray's relations with Bradbury and Evans were personal as well as professional, The weekly Saturday Punch dinners for the magazine staff promoted both camaraderie and business, as is apparent from Henry Silver's diary recording the conversation at the table.

Bradbury and Evans gave Thackeray a punch bowl, engraved as from the publisher of Vanity Fair and Pendennis, in May 1849 [Letters 2: 530); in May 1852, in a letter to Evans asking if the agreement for Pendennis had not specified his share to be four sevenths rather than one-half, Thackeray also asked both cheekily and deferentially for a couple of commemorative cups "that my children might have after me — the Dobbin cup and the'Warrington' say. 20 might buy them; and they would slave who knows at what sideboards when you and I are passed away — "(Bradbury Album).

It would seem that there was no contract for Pendennis to which Thackeray could appeal for support of his memory of the agreement, and the profit sharing for that book proceeded at half for the author, half for the publisher.

What Thackeray seems not to have known when he wrote his complaint, but which might have been told to him in person, is that Bradbury and Evans had undertaken a sacrifice on his behalf, which the firm probably felt was sufficient to satisfy the author. The publisher routinely charged 10 per cent of gross income as a commission. This overhead cost was assessed as a cost along with production and in the case of Vanity Fair meant that Bradbury and Evans earned nearly £700 more than Thackeray did from the first edition of that book, which was published on a half-share contract.

In December 1851, after having charged the Pendennis account £787.13.10 for the publisher's commission, Bradbury and Evans seems to have had a change of heart, for it restored the full amount to the credit side of the ledger, pushing the Pendennis account from a deficit to a profit and enabling the first profit-sharing check to be drawn. It was that check which prompted Thackeray's letter of complaint about his portion. Bradbury and Evans never charged a publisher's commission again on Pendennis or on Thackeray's two other serial novels.

It was inevitable, of course, that the relationship would have its low points. One instance, more a case of panic than crossness, interrupted the otherwise smooth production of The Newcomes. Thackeray had a hard time getting Bradbury and Evans to deal expeditiously with Sampson Low for the sale of advance sheets to Harper and Brothers.

In the end he lost about £150 by the company's failure to press the matter. Perhaps more important was the sharp tone used by Thackeray concerning Richard Doyle's tardy work in illustrating The Newcomes, but here Thackeray's irritation was shared with Bradbury and Evans, not directed against it.

Serious problems and a near rupture in the relationship occurred, however, early in 1855. In December 1851 Thackeray had resigned from Punch because of political disagreements, primarily with Douglas Jerrold. His last contribution to Punch as a regular staff member appeared in that month. The break was not without its tense feelings, but it seems not to have been personal between Thackeray and the publisher.

In 1853 and 1854 Thackeray again contributed a few occasional pieces to Punch, apparently taking little heed to the rate of payment until, having dunned the editor, Mark Lemon, for back pay, he noticed in October 1854 that his rate of pay had been reduced.

In a humorous but restrained letter to Lemon, Thackeray calculated the relative rates of pay for Punch, The Newcomes, and Blackwood's by adding up letters per line, lines per page, and pages per sheet, demonstrating in that way that he could no longer afford to work for Punch. It is clear also, however, that he was miffed [undated letters to Mark Lemon, privately owned, photocopies supplied by William Baker].

These money matters, just the current irritation, were easily exacerbated by a series of events beginning in December 1854. Thackeray wrote an article about Punch in the Quarterly Review which he said was intended to be good-natured but in which he praised John Leech, the illustrator, at the expense of all other contributors. Other staff members were understandably upset, though Douglas Jerrold in particular was predisposed to resent any remark Thackeray might make. The first result of the ensuing tempest was that Thackeray, who had been proposing to George Smith that he start a periodical called Fair Play with Thackeray as editor, decided he could not undertake such a task. To Smith he wrote: another incident has occurred to put a spoke in Fair Play's wheel; and I must give up all idea of the paper.

I wrote an unlucky half-line in the Quarterly about the Punch men saying that Leech was Punch, and that without him the learned gentlemen who wrote might leave the thing alone — an opinion wh. true or nor, certainly should not have been uttered by me, and has caused the saddest annoyance and pain amongst my old comrades[.] I had quite forgotten the phrase until it stared me in the face on my return home. Jerrold had attacked me about it, and with perfect reason calling me a Snob & flunkey - and on the face of the matter I think I was a Snob - but thats not the question.

I wrote to confess my fault to my old friends the Publishers & Editor and passed ½ the night awake thinking of the pain I had given my kind old companions. This is for ½ line written in an article intended to be entirely good-natured - Don't you see the moral?

If in writing, once in 5 years or so, a literary criticism intended to be good natured, I manage to anger a body of old friends, to cause myself pain and regret, to put my foot into a nest of hornets wh. sting and have their annoyance too, to lose rest and quiet, hadn't I better give up that game of Fair Play wh. I thought of, stick to my old pursuits, and keep my health and temper?

[Letters reprints this letter from Centenary Biographical Edition; my text is from the original, NLS] To Bradbury and Evans, Thackeray explained: "you know how carelessly I read my proofs over that is all I can say. Phrases pass under my eye, and I don't see them. And I am obliged to go back constantly to my own back numbers; and find new blunders every time I take them up" (Bradbury Album).

But that was not the end. Rumors and allegations (no longer, if ever, existing in writing) began circulating concerning the original reasons for Thackeray's resignation from Punch in 1851. Clearly the remarks on Leech opened festering wounds, and Thackeray found to his surprise that his old friends Bradbury and Evans were not willing to back him in a dispute with [81/82] their Magazine's continuing staff. In March 1855 Thackeray wrote Evans one of his rather frequent dunning letters for payments on The Newcomes, then added:

I met Murray the Publisher the other day, and cannot help fancying from his manner to me that there is some screw loose with him too about that unlucky Leech article. Lemon answering one of my letters said that he previously complained that my account of my leaving Punch was not correct.

There was such a row at the time and I was so annoyed at the wrong that I had done, that I thought I had best leave Lemon's remonstrance for a while and right it on some future occasion.

I recal now to you and beg you to show to him and to any other person who may have recd. a different version of the story - what the facts were. I had had some serious public differences with the conduct of Punch - about the abuse of Prince Albert & the Crystal Palace on wh. I very nearly resigned, about the abuse of Lord Palmerston, about the abuse finally of L. Napoleon — in all wh. Punch followed the Times, wh. I think and thought was writing unjustly at the time, and dangerously for the welfare and peace of the Country.

Coming from Edinburgh I bought a Punch containing the picture of a Beggar on Horseback in wh. the Emperor was represented galloping to Hell with a sword reeking with blood. As soon as ever I could, after my return, (a day or 2 days after) I went to Bouverie St. saw you and gave my resignation.

I mention this because I know the cause of my resignation has been questioned at Punch - because this was the cause of it. I talked it over with you and Leech saw me coming out of your room and I told him of my retirement.

No engagement afterwards took place between us; nor have I ever been since a member of Punch's Cabinet so to speak. Wishing you all heartily well I wrote a few occasional papers last year - and not liking the rate of remuneration wh. was less than that to wh. I had been accustomed in my time - I wrote no more.

And you can say for me as a reason why I should feel hurt at your changing the old rates of payment made to me - that I am not a man who quarrels about a guinea or two except as a point of honour; and that when I could have had a much larger sum than that wh. You give me for my last novel [The Newcomes]- I preferred to remain with old friends, who had acted honorably and kindly by me.

I reproach myself with leaving written a ½ line regarding my old Punch Companions, wh. was perfectly true, wh. I have often said — but wh. I ought not to have written. No other wrong that I know of leave I done. And I think it now about time that my old friends and publishers should now set me right. But Evans declined, it seems, to arbitrate or to support Thackeray, who on April 3 wrote Evans again:

I have copied out from my letter to you of 24th. March the statement I then made respecting my retirement from Punch and have forwarded it to Lemon. As my Punch arrangements were always made with you and not with him, I am sorry you cannot help me in confirming a fact to which you and I alone were privy — but for which I luckily have an out-door witness in Leech. -

I am at a loss to think how you should imagine that my contributions to Punch continued up to my departure for America. My successor Mr Shirley Brooks came on, if I remember aright, very soon after I went off. I remember to have contributed nothing but a Ballad for which I never asked or received any payment, and that point must be set at rest by the certainty that if I had sent any contributions wh. were paid to me at a less rate than that for which I had been accustomed to write I should assuredly have "struck work", as I did when we came to our last unlucky little settlement of Punch Accounts.

Will you have the kindness to pay into my bankers the sum due to me for the current number? According to my Banker's Account there is still a month of last year owing to me.

The crisp concluding reminder lacks any of the humor usually attending such requests; it is clear that the friendship had been strained. And yet Thackeray's business relations with Bradbury and Evans survived four and a half years longer. Much of the interaction between the author and publisher, of course, is not represented in surviving letters, for the next letter, undated but obviously not much later, is in a much kinder tone and regretfully declines a dinner meeting with the Punch staff because of a prior engagement. Thackeray concluded, "Commend me to all my friends & believe me yours always" (Bodleian).

One might have thought that Thackeray's 1851 resignation from Punch or his 1855 controversy with the Punch staff in which Evans betrayed his trust would have led to a clear rupture, particularly since George Smith was perpetually in the wings offering to be Thackeray's publisher.

But the facts, as Thackeray saw them, were that Bradbury and Evans had launched him when he was unknown and that the firm's dealings with him were always honest and ever improving. By August 1855 the relationship was back to normal: Thackeray dunned Bradbury and Evans for back pay and raised the question of a cheap edition of Pendennis - an idea that saw the light in October of the same year (Bodleian).

From the completion of Pendennis on 1 December 1850 to the commencement of The Newcomes on 1 October 1854, Thackeray published no new works with Bradbury and Evans outside Punch. Three new works written during this period went to Smith, Elder (Kickleburys, Henry Esmond, and English Humourists) and a fourth (Rose and the Ring) would be published by that firm in December 1854, and yet Thackeray considered Bradbury and Evans to be his primary publisher.

Why this should be so is open to question, for in fact Thackeray published as many titles with Chapman and Hall and with Smith, Elder as he did with Bradbury and Evans. But it is evident from his letters and the amount of his magazinery published in Punch, as well as from the coterie of Punch writers to which he belonged, that in the late 1840s Thackeray's most substantial financial and personal connection with publishers was with William Bradbury and F. M. ("Pater") Evans.

Further, though Vanity Fair and Pendennis may have represented only one working contract each and can be listed in a bibliography in just two entries, they were the major continuing writing obligation of Thackeray's life from January 1847 to December 1850 - four continuous years of service, producing the two works which made the difference for Thackeray between "odious magazinery" and the "fight at the top of the tree."

And yet, as well as Thackeray seems to have gotten on with Bradbury and Evans and as loyal to the company as he felt with regard to his next serial fiction, Bradbury and Evans had not been his first choice as publisher for Vanity Fair; he did not turn to the firm with his Christmas books when Chapman and Hall declined to meet his price; and he turned easily to George Smith with Henry Esmond and the lectures.

What George Smith had that Bradbury and Evans did not was a certain air of substance, perhaps even elegance, attached to the publisher's imprint, which was associated with works of scholarship in zoology, astronomy, art history, and geography and with elegant illustrated works.

These matters may have weighed as much with Thackeray as Smith's purported generosity with money, for which he became known as the "Prince of Publishers." A third factor, however, must have been the personal attraction between the two men.

If Smith was, after all, a "mere tradesman," he was also intelligent. Smith had been asked to leave his boarding school at age fourteen not because he was a poor scholar (he was academically one of the top three students in his class) but because he was, to put it politely, too energetic.

He immediately was apprenticed to his father's new partner, Patrick Stewart, where he learned all aspects of bookselling, stationery, trade with India, and banking. He continued his reading in history, science, religion, and fiction and could read French and Latin well. Furthermore, Smith, like Thackeray, was an avid theatergoer. He was over six feet tall, of slender, not athletic, build.

Thackeray might well have found these abilities and characteristics congenial in a businessman publisher who was not only energetic but was cultivated enough to be a successful host for literate people in social settings.

The personal relationship is attested by the fact that Thackeray seconded Smith's bid in 1861 to become a member of the Reform Club (NLS). Though Thackeray had been on friendly terms with his previous publishers, he was not on such a footing with them as he developed with George Smith.

Bibliography

Catherine, a Story, by Ikey Solomons, Esq., junior. Ptd. in Fraser (7 nos.), May, 1839–Feb., 1840. Not rptd. until 1869 (Library edn., vol. XXII).

Stubbs's Calendar; or, the Fatal Boots. 1839. (Cruikshank's Comic Annual, ill. by Cruikshank, George.) Rptd. in Comic Tales and Sketches, vol. II, 1841. New York, 1850. Also, as The Fatal Boots, in Miscellanies, vol. I, and with Cox's Diary, 1855.

The Bedford Row Conspiracy. Ptd. in The New Monthly (3 nos.), Jan.-April, 1840. Rptd. with A Shabby Genteel Story, New York, 1852, 1853, in Comic Tales and Sketches, vol. I, 1841, in Miscellanies, vol. III, 1856, and with A Little Dinner at Timmins's, 1856.

A Shabby Genteel Story. Ptd. in Fraser (4 nos.), June-Oct., 1840. With The Professor, etc., New York, 1852, 1853. Rptd. in Miscellanies, vol. IV, and separately, 1857.

The Paris Sketch Book, by Mr. Titmarsh. 2 vols. 1840. The contents included some miscellaneous sketches, already ptd., with new matter.

An Essay on the Genius of George Cruikshank. 1840. Rptd. from The Westminster Review, June, 1840.

Barber Cox and the Cutting of his Comb. 1840. (Cruikshank's Comic Annual, ill. by Cruikshank, George.) Rptd. as Cox's Diary, in Miscellanies, vol. I, and with The Fatal Boots, 1855.

The History of Samuel Titmarsh and the Great Hoggarty Diamond. Ptd. in Fraser (4 nos.), Sept.-Dec., 1841. As The Great Hoggarty Diamond. New York, 1848. Under original title. 1849. Rptd. in Miscellanies, vol. IV, 1857.

The Second Funeral of Napoleon and The Chronicle of the Drum. 1841. The Chronicle of the Drum rptd. with the Ballads in Miscellanies, vol. I, 1855.

Sultan Stork; being the One Thousand and Second Night, translated from the Persian by Major G. O'G. Gahagan, H.E.I.C.S. Ptd. in Ainsworth's Magazine (2 nos.), Feb. and May, 1842. Rptd. in Sultan Stork, and other Stories and Sketches ... now first collected [ed. Shepherd, R. H.], 1887, and in vol. XX of the American collected edn., Boston, 1889.

The Fitz-Boodle Papers. Ptd. in Fraser (5 nos.), June, 1842–Feb., 1843 (viz. Fitz-Boodle's Confession, June, 1842; Professions, by George Fitz-Boodle, on July, 1842; Fitz-Boodle's Confessions: Miss Löwe, Dorothea, Ottilia, August, 1842, Jan., Feb., 1843).

The Confessions of Fitz-Boodle; and Some Passages in the Life of Major Gahagan. New York, 1852. Rptd. as The Fitz-Boodle Papers, without Miss Löwe, Dorothea and Ottilia, in Miscellanies, vol. IV, and with Men's Wives, 1857. Dorothea and Ottilia were rptd. with the rest in the Library edn., 1869, vol. XXII. Miss Löwe was rptd. separately in vol. XXIII, 1885, and collected with the rest in the pocket edn., 1887.

Men's Wives. Ptd. in Fraser (8 nos.), March—Nov., 1843, under the general title Confessions of George Fitz-Boodle; Men's Wives (viz. I Mr. and Mrs. Frank Berry, March; II The Ravenswing, April—June, Aug., Sept.; III Dennis Haggarty's Wife, Oct.; IV The——'s Wife, Nov.). New York, 1852. Rptd. (without IV) in Miscellanies, vol. IV, and with The Fitz-Boodle Papers, 1857.

Bluebeard's Ghost, by M. A. Titmarsh. Ptd. in Fraser, October, 1843. Rptd. in Early and Late Papers, Boston, 1867, and collected in the Library edn., vol. XXIII, 1885.

The Irish Sketch-Book, by Mr. M. A. Titmarsh. 2 vols. 1843.

The Luck of Barry Lyndon, a Romance of the Last Century, by Fitz-Boodle. Ptd. in Fraser (12 nos.), Jan.—Dec., 1844. 2 vols. New York, 1852. Rptd. as Memoirs, etc., 1856.